Contents

KT-443-762

148

ABOUT THE GUIDE

The *Time Out New York Shortlist* is one of a series of pocket guides to cities around the globe. Drawing on the expertise of local authors, it distils their knowledge into a handy, easy-to-use format that ensures you get the most from your trip, whether you're a first-time or a return visitor.

Time Out New York Shortlist is divided into four sections:

Welcome to New York introduces the city and provides inspiration for your visit.

New York Day by Day helps you plan your trip with an events calendar and customised itineraries.

New York by Area is the main visitor section of the guide. It includes detailed listings and reviews for the very best sights and museums; restaurants and cafés ❿; bars ❿; shops and services ❿, and entertainment venues ❿, all organised by area with a corresponding street map. To help navigation, each area of New York has been assigned its own colour.

New York Essentials provides practical visitor information, including accommodation options and details of public transport.

Shortlists & highlights

We have selected a Shortlist of stand-out venues in each area, which are marked with a heart ♥ in the text. The very best of these appear in the Highlights feature (*see p10*) and receive extended coverage in the guide.

Maps

There's an overview map on *p8* and individual street maps for each area of the city. Venues featured in the guide have been given a grid reference so that you can find them easily on the maps and on the ground.

Prices

All our **restaurant listings** are marked with a dollar symbol category from budget to blowout (**\$-\$\$\$\$**), indicating the price you should expect to pay for an average main course: **\$** = under \$15; **\$\$** = \$15-\$30; **\$\$\$** = \$30-\$45; **\$\$\$\$** = over \$45.

A similar system is used in our **Accommodation** chapter based on the hotel's standard prices for one night in a double room: **\$** = under \$150; **\$\$** = \$150-\$300; **\$\$\$** = \$300-\$500; **\$\$\$\$** = over \$500.

Introduction

Celebrated in countless films, books and songs, New York is the quintessential American big city, yet its compact core, Manhattan, is surprisingly small: a mere 13.4 miles long and 2.3 miles across at its widest point. At street level, however, it seems larger than life, from the iconic skyscrapers looming above broad avenues to vast landmarks like the National September 11 Memorial. The island is a densely packed deli sandwich of diverse, characterful neighbourhoods. And as the cutting-edge arts, food and nightlife scenes shift to areas of Brooklyn and Queens, the metropolis feels more expansive than ever.

A trip to NYC can be overwhelming as well as exhilarating. Must-visit museums vie for attention, and even plugged-in locals struggle to keep up with the packed calendar of world-class culture. Relax: much of the pleasure lies in simply being here. Take time to wander the film-set-perfect, townhouse-lined streets of the West Village; get a ringside view of Central Park promenaders from a well-positioned bench, or linger over a boozy brunch. The Big Apple is best savoured one bite at a time.

Welcome to New York

Oculus at the World Trade Center p72

7

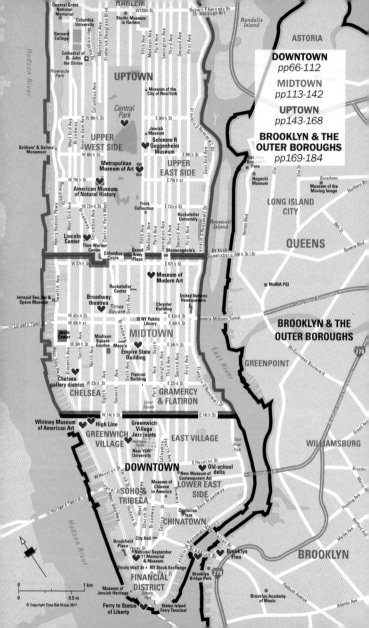

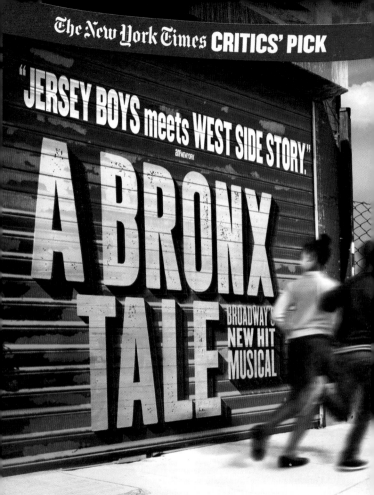

Highlights

Whether you're a foodie or a shopping fiend, an architecture aficionado or a culture junkie, the metropolis offers endless options for every niche interest. But where to start your NYC odyssey? We count down the city's essential sights and experiences, from iconic skyscrapers, cult markets and dazzling nightspots to world-class museums and massive sandwiches.

01

Empire State Building *p135*

King Kong recognised the Empire State's skyscraper supremacy when he commandeered the iconic tower. It may no longer be the city's tallest building, but it has more than 80 years of movie cameos over 1 World Trade Center. Brave the crowds to escape the urban jungle and get a pigeon's-eye panorama of the metropolis and beyond.

02

Statue of Liberty *p70*

Symbolic and surreal (a monumental statue-cum-lighthouse?), Lady Liberty was a beacon to millions of immigrants who subsequently shaped the city, and America. Impressive viewed from land, up close she is an immense marvel. A climb to the crown affords an exhilarating view of New York Harbor and the chance to see the literal nuts and bolts of Frédéric Auguste Bartholdi's creation.

03

Metropolitan Museum of Art *p160*

Not only does this massive institution – comprising 17 curatorial collections and more than two million objects – preserve such treasures as an Egyptian temple from c15 BC, but it is also in a state of constant self-improvement. The American Wing, the European Paintings Galleries and the Costume Institute have all received impressive revamps, and in 2016 the museum opened Met Breuer, showcasing contemporary art and performances in the old Whitney space. A ticket grants you entry to both Upper East Side locations, plus the Cloisters, the Met's exquisite uptown medieval outpost.

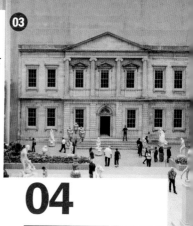

04

Museum of Modern Art *p137*

You could spend a day getting lost in the permanent collection, which showcases some of the best-known works by Picasso, Van Gogh and other modern masters. But equally essential are the museum's other elements, including an attached cinema that combines arthouse fare and more accessible offerings, a sculpture garden with works by Rodin and Moore, and fine-dining destination, the Modern.

05

Central Park *p148*

Urban visionaries Frederick Law Olmsted and Calvert Vaux sought a harmonious balance of scenic elements: pastoral (the open lawn of the Sheep Meadow), formal (the linear, tree-lined Mall) and picturesque (the densely wooded paths of the Ramble). Today, the 843-acre plot draws millions of visitors to its skyscraper-bordered vistas in all seasons: sunbathers and picnickers in summer, ice-skaters in winter, and bird-watchers in spring and autumn. It's also an idyllic venue for beloved cultural events like Shakespeare in the Park and the New York Philharmonic's annual open-air performances.

06

Broadway shows *p130*

The epicentre of American theatre for more than a century, the Great White Way offers new musical spectacles, big-budget revivals and explosive straight plays. Today's blockbuster shows can be ground-breaking or deal with serious issues and still have plenty of populist appeal (*Hamilton, Dear Evan Hansen*), and there are usually ample opportunities to see movie stars strutting their stuff on stage. But no small part of the pleasure of seeing a show on Broadway comes from experiencing the elegance of one of the opulent houses, many of which date from the early 20th century.

07

High Line *p105*

There's something uniquely New York about this eyrie. Built on an abandoned railway track, the space is ingenious in its use of reclaimed industrial detritus, a necessity in footage-starved Manhattan. The pathway takes you above the city while keeping you rooted in urban life – where else can you walk through a field of wildflowers or sprawl on a lush lawn as taxis zoom along the street beneath you? Keep an eye out for iconic sights (from the Statue of Liberty to the Empire State Building) and intriguing art installations. And it has one of the city's most important art hubs, the Whitney Museum of American Art, at its foot.

08

Old-school delis *p91*

New York may be known for its delis, but these kosher canteens are a dying breed, and some celebrated purveyors of pastrami sandwiches and lox and bagels don't live up to their overstuffed reputations. Seek out the stellar survivors, and worthy nostalgic newcomers, on the Lower East Side and beyond. The granddaddy of them all is Katz's Delicatessen. Plastered with shots of famous noshers, the cavernous cafeteria delivers on its history, with hand-carved, tender smoked meat, bookended with rye bread, and served with just a slick of mustard.

09

Brooklyn Bridge *p172*

No mere river crossing, this span is an elegant reminder of New York's history of architectural innovation. When it opened in 1883, the Brooklyn Bridge was the longest suspension bridge in the world. Stride along its wide wood-planked promenade from lower Manhattan and discover the pleasure of arriving at a completely different and very pleasant destination (Dumbo) on foot – with an expansive vista of New York Harbor, the Statue of Liberty and downtown's skyscrapers along the way.

09

10

Solomon R Guggenheim Museum *p157*

When it was completed in 1959, Frank Lloyd Wright's curved concrete edifice ruffled a few feathers. Not just among its conservative Upper East Side neighbours, but also some artists, who felt their works weren't best viewed from the museum's winding interior ramps. Today, the iconic spiral – Wright's only building in Manhattan – is considered as much a work of art as are the paintings it houses (which include masterpieces by Picasso, Chagall and Kandinsky).

11

Lincoln Center *p152*

The largest campus of its kind in the world, this Upper West Side institution is home to a staggering array of theatre, music, dance and film. Construction began in 1959 with the help of John D Rockefeller III, largely in an effort to provide new stomping grounds for the Metropolitan Opera, the New York Philharmonic and the Juilliard School. Today the complex encompasses 11 world-class resident organisations that mount thousands of events each year. After a campus-wide renovation, it's looking better than ever. Standing in Josie Robertson Plaza at twilight, with the fountain spouting white-lit jets of water and the lobby of the Met glowing golden behind it, is one of Manhattan's more transporting experiences.

11

HIGHLIGHTS

12

Chelsea gallery district *p119*

We're not suggesting you skip the essential museums on our list, but in west Chelsea's contemporary art mecca you can often catch museum-calibre shows without spending a dime. The former industrial buildings have been converted into around 300 galleries, from sleek blue-chip salons to densely packed warrens of smaller art spaces.

13

Greenwich Village jazz joints *p111*

The Village may no longer be the low-rent bohemian bastion of the 1950s and '60s, but you can recapture some of the old vibe in the retro jazz bars dotted around the neighbourhood. At the iconic Village Vanguard, catch such improvisational maestros as trumpeter Tom Harrell or bassist Dave Holland in a room that once hosted Miles Davis and John Coltrane, or settle into one of several smaller, newer spaces to discover emerging innovators.

14

Brooklyn Flea *p39*

New Yorkers aren't content with merely shopping at the weekend, they want a complete cultural experience that involves local artisans, people-watching and cult eats. Since its debut in 2008, the Brooklyn Flea has elevated the vintage-and-craft market concept, spawning several offshoots as well as imitators. The food-only spin-off Smorgasburg – a glutton's paradise packed with up to 100 vendors – gives you the opportunity to taste your way across the city in one convenient spot. Other markets scattered across the city feature beer gardens, gigs and themed events.

15

Whitney Museum of American Art *p107*

A visit to the Whitney extends beyond viewing outstanding American paintings, sculptures and installations, though its holdings include many iconic and cutting-edge works of the 20th and 21st centuries. The dramatic contemporary building at the foot of the High Line, overlooking the Hudson River, incorporates spacious terraces that double as outdoor galleries. Not only do they provide stunning views, but also an interplay between the art on display and the surrounding cityscape. The institution embraces all forms of artistic expression, bringing film and performance under its roof.

16

American Museum of Natural History *p150*

An essential destination for families, AMNH inspires awe and fascination regardless of age or interests, from the towering Tyrannosaurus rex in the peerless dinosaur halls to glittering displays of gems and minerals. The exquisitely restored vintage dioramas depicting North American mammals, such as bison and brown bears, in their native habitats are the next best thing to trips to the Wyoming prairie or the Alaska Peninsula coast. In the stunning Rose Center for Earth and Space, the state-of-the-art Hayden Planetarium projects a spectacular and scientifically accurate representation of the universe.

17

National September 11 Memorial & Museum *p72*

It was a decade in the making, but New York finally got a suitably awe-inspiring memorial of the terrible event that shook the city to its core. It's impossible not to feel moved as you gaze at the monumental waterfalls cascading down the sides of the vast chasms where the Twin Towers once stood. Above you, the soaring 1 World Trade Center serves as a reminder that this town never stays down for long. Santiago Calatrava's striking, bird-like Oculus, perched above a sprawling transport and shopping complex, is pure selfie gold. Below ground, in the fallen towers' foundations, the 9/11 Memorial Museum brings home the immense scale and far-reaching repercussions of the tragedy.

18

House of Yes *p45*

For a truly spectacular night out, this cavernous Brooklyn warehouse delivers time and again with variety shows featuring circus acts and burlesque, and arty, frequently risqué extravaganzas complete with aerialists, DJs and immersive performances. Be sure to check the website for the theme of each party and come appropriately costumed, since the organisers want attendees to take part fully in the creative experience.

BROADWAY'S GOLDEN TICKET

ROALD DAHL's CHARLIE AND THE CHOCOLATE FACTORY
THE NEW MUSICAL

CharlieOnBroadway.com

Lunt-Fontanne Theatre, 205 West 46th Street
(Between Broadway and 8th Avenue)
TICKETMASTER.COM or +1 877-250-2929

Sightseeing

New York City is made up of five boroughs: the island of Manhattan, which contains most of the city's iconic sights, plus Brooklyn, Queens, the Bronx and Staten Island. The sheer volume of world-class museums, attractions and cultural institutions add up to tough choices on a short visit to the metropolis. To avoid frustration, try to accept you can never see it all. Prioritise, pace yourself and take time to enjoy aimless wandering, which is part of the pleasure of exploring the city. If you've only a couple of days at your disposal, consider following one of our itineraries (see pp50-56).

Best views
Brooklyn Bridge *p172*
Empire State Building *p135*
Statue of Liberty *p70*

Best art
Chelsea gallery district *p119*
Metropolitan Museum of Art *p160*
Museum of Modern Art
(MoMA) *p137*
Whitney Museum of American
Art *p107*

Best parks
Central Park *p148*
High Line *p105*

Best architecture
Solomon R Guggenheim
Museum *p157*
Chrysler Building *p22*
Flatiron Building *p121*

Best for NYC history
National September 11 Memorial &
Museum *p72*
New-York Historical Society *p145*

Best for kids
Bronx Zoo *p181*
Gulliver's Gate *p129*
American Museum of Natural
History *p150*

Slicing up the Apple

Manhattan grew upwards from its historic tip, and
happening bars, restaurants and nightlife are still
most densely concentrated downtown. The **Financial
District** contains the seat of local government, **City Hall**
(*see p68*), and the country's epicentre of capitalism,
Wall Street. It's also the site of the rebuilt **World Trade
Center**, with the **National September 11 Memorial &
Museum** (*see p72*). The **Statue of Liberty** (*see p70*)
stands in New York Harbor.

To the north, the former industrial districts
of **Soho** and **Tribeca** are now prime shopping and
dining destinations. **Little Italy** has shrunk in recent
years, crowded out by ever-expanding **Chinatown**,
with its myriad inexpensive Asian eateries, and
boutique-riddled **Nolita**.

Nearby, the erstwhile immigrant neighbourhood
the **Lower East Side** is now bursting with trendy
bars, boutiques and galleries, but you can still see
how the other half lived at the **Lower East Side
Tenement Museum** (*see p88*).

With **Washington Square Park** at its heart, former bohemian stomping ground **Greenwich Village** still resounds with cultural associations. The leafy, winding streets of the **West Village** give way to the **Meatpacking District**'s warehouses, now colonised by shops, eateries and nightspots. Here, the southern foot of the **High Line** elevated promenade (*see p105*) and the **Whitney Museum of American Art** (*see p107*) draw large crowds. The once-radical **East Village** brims with bars and restaurants.

Just north of the Meatpacking District, **Chelsea** contains New York's main contemporary-gallery enclave (*see p119*) while its eastern neighbours the **Flatiron District**, named after the distinctive building of the same name, and **Gramercy Park** offer some of the city's best upscale restaurants.

Midtown is home to dazzling **Times Square** and the historic theatres of **Broadway** (*see p130*). To the west, **Hell's Kitchen** is the site of Hudson Yards, the city's largest development since Rockefeller Center.

Several major attractions, such as the **Empire State Building** (*see p135*) and the **Museum of Modern Art** (*see p137*), are in the vicinity of Midtown's **Fifth Avenue**. The busy commercial stretch is also home to some of the city's poshest stores.

Times Square

Race to the Top

How NYC's architects egged each other onwards and upwards

For nearly half a century after its 1846 completion, the 281-foot steeple of Richard Upjohn's Gothic Revival **Trinity Church** (see *p73*) reigned in lonely serenity at the foot of Wall Street as the tallest structure in Manhattan. The church was finally topped in 1890 by the since-demolished, 348-foot **New York World Building**. But it wasn't until the turn of the century that New York's architects started to reach for the skies. So began a mad rush to the top, with building after building capturing the title of the world's tallest.

When it was completed in 1899, the 30-storey, 391-foot **Park Row Building** (15 Park Row, between Ann and Beekman Streets) enjoyed that lofty distinction. However, its record was shattered by the 612-foot **Singer Building** in 1908 (which, in 1968, became the tallest building ever to be demolished); the 52-storey, 700-foot **Metropolitan Life Tower** of 1909; and the 793-foot **Woolworth Building**, Cass Gilbert's Gothic 1913 masterpiece.

The Woolworth stood in solitary splendour until skyscraper construction reached a crescendo in the late 1920s, with a famed three-way race. The now largely forgotten former **Bank of Manhattan Building** at 40 Wall Street was briefly the record-holder, at 71 storeys and 927 feet in 1930. Soon after, William Van Alen, the architect of the **Chrysler Building**, unveiled his secret weapon: a 'vertex', a spire of chrome nickel steel put together inside the dome and raised from within, which brought the building's height to 1,046 feet. But then, 13 months later, Van Alen's homage to the Automobile

Age was itself outstripped by Shreve, Lamb & Harmon's 1,250-foot **Empire State Building** (see *p135*). With its broad base, narrow shaft and needled crown, it remains the quintessential skyscraper, and one of the most famous buildings in the world. (The ESB's lightning rod/broadcasting antenna, which officially brings the structure's height up to 1,454 feet, was added in 1950.)

Incredibly, there were no challengers for the distinction of New York's – and the world's – tallest building for more than 40 years, until the 110-storey, 1,362- and 1,368-foot **Twin Towers** of Minoru Yamasaki's World Trade Center were completed in 1973. They were trumped by Chicago's **Sears Tower** a year later, but the **World Trade Center** (see *p72*) has since regained the title. With the 1,776-foot 1 World Trade Center, NYC has beaten the Windy City as home to America's tallest skyscraper.

1 World Trade Center

Central Park

Uptown, bucolic **Central Park** (*see p148*), with its picturesque lakes, expansive lawns and famous zoo, is the green divider between the affluent **Upper West Side** and the equally well-heeled **Upper East Side**. Between them, they contain a wealth of cultural institutions: the UWS has the Metropolitan Opera, the New York Philharmonic and the New York City Ballet at **Lincoln Center** (*see p152*), while the UES claims a world-class collection of museums, including the massive **Metropolitan Museum of Art** (*see p160*) and the architecturally striking **Guggenheim** (*see p157*), on Fifth Avenue's Museum Mile. Further north, **Harlem** offers a vibrant restaurant scene and plenty of cultural history.

These days, a trip to NYC isn't complete without crossing the East River to **Brooklyn**, which is at the centre of the city's more adventurous food and arts scenes with major cultural institutions including the excellent **Brooklyn Museum** (*see p171*). The other outer boroughs have worthwhile draws, such as progressive art centre **MoMA PS1** (*see p182*) in **Long Island City**, **Queens** and **Yankee Stadium** (*see p183*) in **the Bronx**.

Grand Central Terminal

Making the most of it

The best way to see the city is on the ground, and you'll be able to tackle clusters of sights on foot. Once you've mastered the grid, it's easy to find your way (although it gets a little trickier in downtown neighbourhoods that pre-date the grid system). To get from one area of the metropolis to the next, it's hard to beat the subway, which is highly efficient and runs 24 hours a day. It's fairly easy to navigate, but bear in mind that on most lines some numbered or lettered trains go local (stopping at every stop) while others are express and skip stops. Adding to potential confusion, on some lines this changes at weekends and late at night – for example the local W service is replaced by the usually express N. We've provided weekday transport information in our listings and on the maps, so be sure to check www.mta.info for weekend updates. The subway system is almost comprehensive, but one drawback is the lack of crosstown options uptown. This is where buses come in handy. The extensive bus system can be a pleasant way to travel, especially outside of rush hours, but routes through traffic-heavy parts of town are often slow. Taxis are usually plentiful, apart from during bad weather, but can also get stuck in traffic, bumping up prices. In 2017, the city expanded its ferry service, offering affordable, convenient and picturesque routes to parts of Brooklyn and Queens. For more information, *see p193* Getting Around.

Because the city's museums are privately funded, admission prices can be steep. However, they usually include entry to temporary shows as well as the permanent collections, and many institutions offer one day or evening a week when admission fees are either waived or switched to a voluntary donation (and remember, 'suggested donation' prices are just that). Be warned that some museums are closed on Mondays, except on certain holidays, such as Columbus Day and Presidents' Day. Many top attractions and museums offer cheaper admission if you purchase tickets in advance on their website.

If you're planning to visit a number of attractions during your stay, it's worth considering one of a trio of package-deal cards. The following details are correct for current deals, but check the websites as they're subject to change. The **New York CityPASS** (www.citypass.com) gives pre-paid queue-jumping access to six big-ticket attractions, among them the Empire State Building and the Met. The pass is valid for nine consecutive days and costs $122 ($98 reductions). A three-sight option is also available ($76; $56 reductions). If you're determined to pack in as much as possible during a trip, the **New York Pass** (www.newyorkpass.com) can save you a lot of money. It grants admission to more than 90 museums, sights and tours. The card is time-tied: it costs from $109 ($89 reductions) for a one-day pass up to $399 ($249 reductions) for ten days. The **New York Explorer** Pass (www.smartdestinations.com) lets you spread out your sightseeing over 30 days, with the option of bundling from three to ten attractions (from $84; $65 reductions).

RIGHT NEAR.
RIGHT NOW.

You're only seconds away from a great bar, an amazing new restaurant or the latest things to do in London.

DOWNLOAD
THE APP TODAY

TimeOut

DISCOVER | BOOK | SHARE

Eating & Drinking

New York offers a delicious blend of high-minded and no-frills food. The city's haute French restaurants, three-figure sushi counters and tasting-menu temples gleam with enough Michelin sparklers and James Beard awards to light up its famous skyline, but its busy streets are also lovingly populated by crowd-pleasing bagel shops, halal carts, burger and pizza joints, taco stands and dumpling dens. It's a dining scene that's dizzying and dazzling in scope and, like the city it's in, constantly changing.

Best classics (and neo-classics)
Carbone *p104*
Grand Central Oyster Bar &
Restaurant *p141*
Katz's Delicatessen *p91*
Peter Luger *p175*

Best Locavore eats
High Street on Hudson *p106*
Olmsted *p175*
Roberta's *p175*

Best for beer and wine
The Four Horsemen *p176*
Tørst *p34*

Best for a blowout
Aska *p173*
Le Coucou *p79*
Eleven Madison Park *p123*

Best global flavours
Cosme *p122*
Lilia *p174*
Red Rooster Harlem *p167*

Best cocktails
Attaboy *p92*
Bar Goto *p92*
Blacktail *p74*

Toques of the town

Every year, a freshman class of toques – think Greg
Baxtrom at **Olmsted** or Jeremiah Stone of **Wildair**
(*see p90*) – joins the city's varsity-level chefs and
restaurateurs like Eataly boss Mario Batali and
Momofuku kingpin David Chang. Other empire builders
include **Andrew Carmellini**, who with partners Josh
Pickard and Luke Ostrom, is behind some of Manhattan's
best restaurants, including **The Dutch** (*see p80*) and
Lafayette (*see p98*).

British-born burger queen April Bloomfield – already
famous for her patty prowess at Michelin-starred eateries
including the **Spotted Pig** (*see p108*) – has branched
out with longtime partner Ken Friedman and star
butchers Erika Nakamura and Jocelyn Guest with the
Upper West Side meat market/all-day restaurant **White
Gold Butchers** (*see p154*).

Major Food Group – the restaurant group overseen
by chefs Rich Torrisi and Mario Carbone, and business
partner Jeff Zalaznick – has a portfolio that includes
red-sauce clubhouse **Carbone** and the **Parm** (*see
p85*) sandwich chain.

Where to eat & drink

New York is a complex patchwork of distinctive neighbourhoods, each with its own food and drink scene. The city's two biggest **Chinatowns**, in Manhattan and Flushing, Queens, are packed with restaurants serving regional cuisines from China and other Asian countries.

On the **Lower East Side**, stellar dining and drinking options have joined iconic Jewish nosh spots. Along with Ivan Orkin's namesake noodle house **Ivan Ramen** (*see p90*) and the double punch of **Contra** and **Wildair** from innovative young guns Jeremiah Stone and Fabian von Hauske, the downtown neighbourhood is home to some of the city's finest bars. You can enjoy artful Asian tweaks to classic cocktails at Kenta Goto's **Bar Goto** and caffeinated cocktails and improved daiquiris at third-generation mixologist Giuseppe González's **Suffolk Arms** (*see p92*). Eclectic bars and a vast array of inexpensive eateries are also conveniently close together in the **East Village**.

Olmsted

In the know
Price categories

All our restaurant listings are marked with a dollar symbol category, indicating the price you should expect to pay for a standard main course. Bear in mind, however, that prices of individual dishes can vary widely on restaurant menus, and the final bill will of course depend on the number of courses and drinks consumed.

$ = under $15

$$ = $15-$30

$$$ = $30-$45

$$$$ = over $45

Soho has long been a fashionable-dining bubble, with high-profile options like **Le Coucou** (*see p79*) – the graceful, James Beard Award-winning French spot from chef Daniel Rose and prolific restaurateur Stephen Starr (Buddakan, Morimoto). But its eastern neighbour, **Nolita** has been coming into its own and has two notable spots that are sequels to already-successful restaurants: **Pasquale Jones** (*see p85*) is the pizza-loving sibling to Ryan Hardy, Grant Reynolds and Robert Bohr's jaunty, wine-charged Soho spot **Charlie Bird**, while **Mr. Donahue's** (203 Mott Street, 1-646 850 9480, www. mrdonahues.com) comes courtesy of married co-chefs Matt Danzer and Ann Redding, who follow Michelin-starred acclaim for their electric Thai cooking at **Uncle Boons** by pivoting to soft-focused American eats for the pint-size Nolita den.

Slightly north, the **Gramercy/Flatiron** area has also seen restaurant resurgence in recent years, with newcomers joining essential neighbourhood eateries such as Michelin-starred **Eleven Madison Park** (*see p123*) from Daniel Humm and Will Guidara. The chef/restaurateur duo introduced **Made Nice** (*see p123*), a counter-service concept where diners can get deconstructed versions of dishes from their more upscale restaurants. Similarly, restaurateur Danny Meyer added a fast-casual bakery-café adjunct, **Daily Provisions**, to his recently relocated flagship, **Union Square Cafe** (*see p126*). The new incarnation has retained much of its original appeal in nostalgic design touches as well as staple dishes and new menu additions by long-serving executive chef Carmen Quagliata.

In the know
Reservations

No-reservation restaurants have become increasingly common in recent years, but if you show up, most will take your name and mobile phone number and call you when a table is available, so you can spend the wait time sightseeing or in a nearby bar. Others, including most Momofuku locations and Major Food Group eateries, can only be reserved online.

You can't talk foodie neighbourhoods without delving into **Williamsburg** in Brooklyn, a name that has seen a near-meteoric rise in culinary clout in recent years. There, you'll find **Lilia** (*see p174*), the airy pasta parlour that simultaneously serves as the kitchen comeback and solo debut from acclaimed A Voce vet Missy Robbins; **Aska** (*see p173*), the Michelin-starred Scandinavian kitchen helmed by Swedish wunderkind chef Fredrik Berselius; and the **Four Horsemen** (*see p176*), the minimalist, wine-fuelled dining room co-owned by LCD Soundsystem frontman James Murphy.

Contemporary food courts

Even neighbourhoods more traditionally known for lofty skyscrapers and ubiquitous business suits are getting serious culinary cred these days. The lowly food court has seen much advancement in Midtown, an area once plagued by its dearth of quality food options. Inside Grand Central Terminal, Claus Meyer (co-founder of the world-shaking Copenhagen dining room Noma) launched **Great Northern Food Hall** (*see p141*) a 5,000-square-foot marketplace that features Nordic-inspired food pavilions peddling everything from fresh-baked pastries to *smørrebrød* topped with smoked fish or house-cured meats. The hall is part of a multi-pronged terminal takeover from Meyer, which also includes **Agern** (*see p141*), a serene Scandinavian tasting-menu restaurant incongruously set amid the commuting cacophony of the rail hub.

Nearby, **Urbanspace Vanderbilt** (*see p142*) changed the workaday lunch game near Park Avenue with snacks by grade-A Brooklyn vendors such as Roberta's, Mimi's Hummus and burger-fan favourite Hard Times Sundaes. In Hell's Kitchen, **Gotham West Market** (*see p132*) is a worthy pre- or post-theatre stop with vendors such as the El Colmado tapas bar from Seamus Mullen

(Tertulia) and Ivan Ramen Slurp Shop, where noodle guru Ivan Orkin offers his famed shio, shoyu and chilli-sesame varieties. Fast-casual food hall **Hudson Eats** (*see p73*) boosted refuelling options near the World Trade Center when it opened inside Brookfield Place.

Hooked on classics

Even in an era of quick neighbourhood turnover and flavour-of-the-week restaurant buzz, NYC has a wealth of old-school eating establishments still kicking it with the young'uns. For delicious proof, head downtown to the Lower East Side, which was a veritable Jewish Plymouth Rock in the late 19th and early 20th centuries when immigrants from Eastern Europe flooded the area. Though the neighbourhood's Yiddish accent has softened in more recent decades, you can still sample its culinary history at three long-time Houston Street stalwarts. Grab a fluffy, golden potato knish at **Yonah Schimmel Knish Bakery** (*see p92*), which has been doling out Jewish-American comfort foods since 1910; pick up some old-world pickled herring at **Russ & Daughters** (*see p91*) down the street (the 'appetising' institution has been selling the stuff since its pushcart beginnings in 1914); and cap off the tour with a sandwich stop at the iconic **Katz's Delicatessen** (*see p91*), where smoky pastrami has been hand-sliced since 1888.

Pizza is another rich NYC culinary legacy, especially in Brooklyn,

> **In the know**
> **Essentials**
>
> Restaurants are generally open for lunch between 11.30am and 3pm and in the evening from 5pm until 11pm (though some may close as early as 9 or 10pm, and other kitchens stay open as late as midnight or 1am). Bars generally close between 2am and 4am, though it varies considerably. Most restaurants, apart from some small or cheap eateries, accept credit cards. It's common to tip 15%-20%, or more if service is exceptional. NYC sales tax is 8.875%, so an easy way to calculate tip is to double the tax. Some restaurants, such as those in restaurateur Danny Meyer's stable, have done away with tipping altogether and include it in the pricing. If this is the case, it will be clearly stated on the menu.

Mother of Pearl   Suffolk Arms   Tørst

which boasts some of the borough's most acclaimed and time-honoured pie operations. Beat the lines by arriving early at Midwood's **Di Fara Pizza** (1424 Avenue J, at E 15th Street, 1-718 258 1367, www.difarany.com, closed Mon), opened by Italian immigrant Dom De Marco in 1964. You may even see the octogenarian pizza legend behind the counter, snipping fresh basil on to his world-class Neapolitan pies.

Many visitors will want to get their teeth into a traditional New York steak. At **Peter Luger** (*see p175*) in Brooklyn's Williamsburg, waistcoat-wearing waiters had been serving beautifully rosy porterhouses for decades before the hipsters moved into the area. In the equally historic Midtown chophouse **Keens** (*see p126*), you can tuck into its signature gargantuan mutton chops under a massive collection of churchwarden pipes.

What's brewing?

In the late 19th century, Brooklyn was the hub of New York's – and much of the nation's – beer industry. In recent years, the taps have started flowing again across all five boroughs. Brooklyn makes a strong showing, with such additions as Carroll Gardens' IPA-driven **Other Half Brewing** (www.otherhalfbrewing.com), **Threes Brewing** (www.threesbrewing.com) in Gowanus and brewery-distillery hybrid **Interboro Spirits and Ales** (interboro.nyc) in East Williamsburg joining local staples like **Brooklyn Brewery** (brooklynbrewery.com) and Red Hook's **Sixpoint Brewery** (sixpoint.com). Queens is loaded with hoppy options, from **SingleCut Beersmiths** (singlecutbeer.com) in Astoria to the beachside enterprise of **Rockaway Brewing Company** (rockawaybrewco.com).

Apart from tasting rooms in the breweries themselves, the most dependable spots to sample local offerings are hops-head havens such as subterranean East Village tavern **Jimmy's No. 43** (*see p100*) and Greenpoint's **Tørst** (615 Manhatten Avenue, Greenpoint, 1-718 389 603, www.torstnyc.com), a rare-beer taproom from Scandinavian brew rock star Jeppe Jarnit-Bjergsø (Evil Twin Brewing) that offers a more sophisticated pint experience.

Cocktail culture

With all due respect to everywhere else on the planet, New York is the cocktail capital of the world for breadth and quality. Audrey Saunders's second-floor Soho sanctum, **Pegu Club** (*see p80*), begat many of today's standard-bearers, including nouveau speakeasy **PDT** (*see p101*). More recently, Sean Muldoon and Jack McGarry – the world-renowned duo behind time-capsule cocktail bar the **Dead Rabbit** (*see p74*) – introduced **BlackTail** (*see p74*) to the historic Pier A Harbor House complex, which channels Prohibition-era Cuba with a meticulously researched menu of retro drinks. Across the East River, **Clover Club** (*see p176*), the standard-bearing Brooklyn cocktail parlour from mixology matriarch Julie Reiner, is known for its regal crystal bowls of punch and finely wrought drinks.

New York also has an impressive selection of niche bars devoted to a single spirit or type of cocktail. The driving force behind agave spirits-focused **Mayahuel**, Ravi DeRossi is also behind neo tiki bar **Mother of Pearl** (*see p101*).

Window display at Bergdorf Goodman

Shopping

One of the best cities in the world in which to drop your hard-earned cash, New York offers anything you could possibly want to buy, and at the best prices – as long as you're prepared to shop around or hit some sample sales. Locals may complain about the 'mallification' of certain neighbourhoods such as Soho, but for visitors (and, if they're honest, many New Yorkers), these retail-rich areas are intoxicating consumer playgrounds. As America's fashion capital, and the site of the prestigious Fashion Institute of Technology and other high-profile art colleges, the metropolis is a magnet for creative young designers from around the country. This ensures that the shops and markets are stuffed with unique finds, and it also means that the Garment District is a hotbed of open-to-the-public showroom sales.

Best fashion
Dear: Rivington *p101*
Modern Anthology *p178*
Opening Ceremony *p82*

Best department stores
Barneys New York *p163*
Bergdorf Goodman *p136*
Century 21 *p75*

Best design and gifts
ABC Carpet & Home *p125*
Magpie *p155*
Uniqulee *p88*

Best vintage and antiques
Erie Basin *p177*
Mantiques Modern *p118*
What Goes Around Comes
Around *p83*
Wooden Sleepers *p178*

Best market
Brooklyn Flea *p39*

Best books and music
Printed Matter *p118*
Rough Trade *p178*
Strand Book Store *p102*

Make it here

Many of the country's most popular designers are based
in New York, from long-established names like Diane von
Furstenberg and Marc Jacobs to contemporary stars such
as Phillip Lim, Alexander Wang and Rachel Comey. Made-
in-NYC items – jewellery by **Erica Weiner** (*see p87*)
or cards printed at **Bowne & Co** (*see p74*), for example
– are chic souvenirs. Stores that stock items by local
designers, among other merchandise, include **American
Two Shot** (*see p81*) and **Opening Ceremony** (*see
p82*). There are also opportunities to buy goods direct
from emerging designers at popular weekend markets
such as the **Brooklyn Flea** (*see p39*), and Chinatown's
Canal Street Market (*see p86*) showcases a revolving
array of design-centric local vendors. Some budding
shopkeepers test the waters by opening pop-ups, which,
if successful, put down permanent roots, such as Hell's
Kitchen men's accessories trove **Fine and Dandy** (*see
p132*). Likewise, online companies are opening brick-
and-mortar locations, such as **Tictail Market** (*see
p94*), which now showcases a rotating selection of
its website's globe-spanning indie-designer goods in
shabby-chic Lower East Side premises.

One-stop shopping

Of course, many visitors to New York will simply be looking to make the most of the incredible variety of big brands on offer in the city. For young, casual and streetwear labels, head to Lafayette Street or Broadway in **Soho**. **Fifth Avenue** heaves with a mix of designer showcases and mall-level megastores. **Madison Avenue** is more consistently posh, though contemporary designers (Helmut Lang, Maje, Iro, Alice + Olivia and more) have joined the line-up of deluxe labels like Alexander McQueen, Chloé, Lanvin and Ralph Lauren.

If you prefer to do all your shopping under one roof, famous department stores **Macy's** (*see p127*; good for mid-range brands), **Bloomingdale's** (*see p164*; a mix of mid-range and designer), **Barneys** (*see p163*; cutting-edge and high-fashion) and **Bergdorf Goodman** (*see p136*; luxury goods and international designer, plus some quirky one-off shops within a shop) are all stuffed with desirable items.

New York City was never much of a mall destination, but suddenly large mixed-use complexes stuffed with shops and restaurants, combined with offices or apartments, seem to be everywhere, from the rebuilt

Tictail Market

In the know
Essentials

In general, local shops are open from 10am or 11am to 7pm or 8pm Monday to Saturday and noon to 5pm or 6pm on Sunday, though it varies widely. Many large retailers and book and record stores stay open later. Hours may also change seasonally or during sales. Most stores accept credit cards, apart from some smaller shops, sample sales and market vendors.

Greene Street, Soho

World Trade Center, which now features a sprawling underground **Westfield** shopping centre, to nearby **Brookfield Place** (*see p75*) anchored by a branch of **Saks Fifth Avenue**.

Sniffing out sales

New York is fertile bargain-hunting territory. The traditional seasonal sales (which usually start just after, or sometimes even before, Christmas and in early to mid June) have given way to frequent markdowns throughout the year. Keep an eye out for sale racks in boutiques, chains and department stores.

Numerous designer studios and showrooms give rise to a weekly spate of sample sales. The best are listed at www.timeout.com/newyork, but a good bet is **Clothingline** (1-212 947 8748, www.clothingline.com), which holds regular sales for a variety of labels – from R13 and Milly to Helmut Lang and Derek Lam, at its Garment District showroom (Second Floor, 261 W 36th Street, between Seventh & Eighth Avenues). The most popular designers draw long queues, so it's best to skip the lunch hour and early evening. While some sample sales accept credit cards, others don't so bring plenty of cash. Fitting rooms, if provided, are likely to be communal.

🖤 Brooklyn Flea

Rummaging in the city's outdoor flea markets, often combined with brunch, has long been a favourite New York weekend pastime. Launched in 2008 by Jonathan Butler, founder of real-estate blog Brownstoner.com, and Eric Demby, former PR man for the Brooklyn borough president, the **Brooklyn Flea** (www.brooklynflea.com) was the first of a new breed of bazaar in NYC, offering high-quality crafts, locally designed fashion and gourmet snacks alongside vintage wares. Around 80 vendors operate under the Manhattan Bridge Archway and adjacent Anchorage Place in Dumbo, Brooklyn, on Sundays from April to October. Spin-offs include the nosh-only **Smorgasburg** (in Williamsburg's East River State Park on Saturday, and Prospect Park on Sunday). Now the Flea has ventured across the river to Soho with a year-round, indoor weekend market at 100 Avenue of the Americas (Sixth Avenue), at Watts Street.

The Brooklyn Flea isn't the only market in town. **Artists & Fleas** (www.artistsandfleas. com) showcases wares by a rotating selection of around 100 craftspeople, designers and artists at its weekend location in Williamsburg, Brooklyn, and operates a smaller daily outpost in Chelsea Market. You can sample everything from locally made ice-cream sandwiches to Thai fried chicken as you browse vintage fashion, hand-crafted jewellery, ceramics and more from 60 vendors at the **Hester Street Fair** (www.hesterstreetfair.com). Located on the site of a former pushcart market, the Lower East Side market is open Saturdays from late April to the end of October.

The popular **Chelsea Flea Market** (W 25th Street, between Broadway & Sixth Avenue, www. annexmarkets.com) and its Hell's Kitchen sibling (W 39th Street, between Ninth & Tenth Avenues) are traditional antiques and bric-a-brac markets open Saturday and Sunday year-round (weather permitting). Sunday-only Upper West Side old timer **Grand Bazaar** (100 W 77th Street, at Columbus Avenue, www.grandbazaarnyc. org) started as a standard outdoor flea market in the 1980s but, in line with recent trends, it now includes artists and artisans selling jewellery, photographs and food among its 100-plus vendors.

Chief among the permanent sale stores is discount department store **Century 21** (*see p75*). It's beloved of rummagers, but detested by those with little patience for sifting through less than fabulous merchandise for the prize finds. Department store cut-price offshoots **Nordstrom Rack Union Square** (60 E 14th Street, between Broadway & Fourth Avenue, 1-212 220 2080, www.nordstromrack.com) and **Saks Fifth Avenue Off Fifth** (125 E 57th Street, between Lexington & Park Avenues, 1-212 634 0730, www.saksoff5th.com) are worth checking out too.

Consumer culture

Despite the loss of some independent bookshops, others such as the **Strand Book Store** (*see p102*) have been holding their own for years. **Printed Matter** (*see p118*) in Chelsea's gallery district specialises in art books. The **Metropolitan Museum of Art** (*see p160*), the **New Museum of Contemporary Art** (*see p89*) and **MoMA** (*see p137*) all have excellent bookstores. The latter also has two standalone design stores, one across the street from the museum at 44 W 53rd Street, the other in Soho (81 Spring Street, between Broadway & Crosby Street, 1-646 613 1367, store.moma.org). At either location, you can pick up design classics such as a George Nelson wall clock, fun souvenirs like a Louise Bourgeois eye mask, as well as cool tech and kitchen gadgets. The **Museum of Arts & Design** (*see p145*) is a great source of handmade items, including a wide range of jewellery.

While some treasured record stores have closed in recent years, Brooklyn gained a huge flagship of UK indie retailer **Rough Trade** (*see p178*) in Williamsburg, and smaller shops are thriving in the borough, especially in neighbouring Greenpoint.

Entertainment

Given the impressive sweep of New York's cultural life, it's easy to be overwhelmed by the number of performances and events on offer. Venues span everything from vast modern arenas to hole-in-the-wall dives, by way of venerable Broadway theatres, avant-garde nightspots and art-house cinemas. With a little planning, however, you can take in a concert, show or club night that will make your visit more memorable. Consult *Time Out New York* magazine or www.timeout.com/newyork for the latest listings.

Best for gigs
Bowery Ballroom *p94*
Rockwood Music Hall *p95*
Village Vanguard *p111*

Best comedy
Comedy Cellar *p112*
Upright Citizens Brigade
Theatre *p120*

Best club nights
House of Yes *p45*
Output *p180*

Best performing arts venues
Bargemusic *p179*
Brooklyn Academy of Music *p180*
Lincoln Center *p152*

Best theatre
Ars Nova *p133*
Broadway shows *p130*
Public Theater *p103*

Best LGBT venues
The Eagle *p115*
Stonewall Inn *p109*

Keep on clubbing

Over the years, the nightlife scene has survived such buzz-killing trends as Mayor Giuliani, four-figure bottle service, 5am sober raves and celebrity iPod DJs. But Gotham has got its groove back. This is largely thanks to numerous nomadic shindigs, often held in out-of-the-way warehouses or other spaces, which have sent the energy of NYC nightlife where it belongs: underground. Long-running techno bash **The Bunker** (www.thebunkerny.com) blazed a trail for nights devoted to envelope-pushing electronic dance music, while the DJ duo behind the popular Mister Saturday Night and Mister Sunday parties has opened a sprawling indoor-outdoor venue, **Nowadays** (56-06 Cooper Avenue, at Irving Avenue, 1-718 386 0111, www.nowadays.nyc), near the Brooklyn border in Ridgewood, Queens. Recent years have seen a burst of new permanent spaces, especially in Brooklyn's Williamsburg and Bushwick neighbourhoods, the epicentre of the clubbing and indie-rock scenes. These include megaclub **Output** (*see p180*) and a cavernous home for **House of Yes** (*see p45*), a creative collective that stages arty nightlife extravaganzas. Comedy, meanwhile, is killing it with thriving venues such as the **Upright Citizens Brigade Theatre** (*see* *p120*), where some of the best weekly shows are free or cheap, making going out for a few laughs an inexpensive night on the town. And at many comedy clubs, you never know who might stop by for an impromptu performance.

Out and about

Today's LGBT New York offers much more than drag and piano bars (though, delightfully, they still thrive). Each June, NYC Pride brings a whirl of parties and performances. The weekend-capping event, the **NYC LGBT Pride March** (*see p60*), draws millions of spectators and participants. In spring, the Black Party Weekend and Urban Bear Weekend also draw hordes to NYC, and autumn kicks off with Bushwig (bushwig. com) showcasing alt drag. While there are good LGBT bars across the city in areas including the West Village (home of gay rights landmark **Stonewall Inn**; *see p109*), Chelsea and Williamsburg, Hell's Kitchen is Gotham's gayest gaybourhood, with a relaxed, straight-friendly scene.

NYC LGBT Pride March

Live from New York

Indie-music clubs dot the East Village and Lower East Side, but don't miss the **Mercury Lounge** (*see p94*), the no-nonsense spot that launched the career of the Strokes, among others; **Rockwood Music Hall** (*see p95*), a small storefront venue showcasing up-and-comers; and **Joe's Pub** (*see p103*), the classy cabaret room tucked inside the Public Theater that presents great acts of all genres. For larger seated shows, try the posh theatres in Midtown and further north. The palatial art deco **Radio City Music Hall** (*see p139*) gives grandeur to pop performances, while Harlem's **Apollo Theater** (*see p168*) still hosts its legendary Amateur Night competition. New York City has been a hotbed of improvisational talent since the 1920s, and you can soak up the old-school vibe at the **Village Vanguard**, the iconic jazz club that once provided a platform for the virtuoso experiments of Miles Davis, John Coltrane and Thelonious Monk. Some of music's biggest acts play at **Madison Square Garden** (*see p128*). But after 45 years, Manhattan's legendary music and sports hub got some serious competition – from Brooklyn contender the **Barclays Center** (*see p179*).

At the big classical institutions, such as the Metropolitan Opera at **Lincoln Center** (*see p152*) and **Carnegie Hall** (*see p138*), confident artistic leaders such as Peter Gelb and Clive Gillinson are embracing new productions, living composers and innovative approaches to programming. It remains to be seen whether Jaap van Zweden, the recently appointed music director of the New York Philharmonic, will continue in the progressive spirit of his predecessor Alan Gilbert.

The standard New York concert season lasts from September to June, but there are plenty of summer events and performances. Box office hours may change in summer, so phone ahead or check websites for times.

💙 House of Yes

2 Wyckoff Avenue, at Jefferson Street, Bushwick, Brooklyn (houseofyes.org). Subway L to Jefferson Street. **Admission** *Variety shows $20-$30; club nights $30 (online discounts and free entry before 11pm with RSVP usually available).*

House of Yes started life as a ramshackle Brooklyn live-in loft space for artists, musicians and circus folks, who hosted skill-sharing nights where devotees practiced juggling, aerial arts and drumming. This punky utopian idyll was destroyed by a massive fire, but that didn't stop the plucky arts collective, which raised enough money to move into a run-down former ice house that was double the size of the original. The new space became a hub for spectacular shows, creative bashes and classes. The group was made homeless a second time in 2013 – this time by rising rents – and the search for a new space began again. But since its resurrection in December 2015, House of Yes has been firing on all cylinders with a jam-packed roster. The venue's new and improved Bushwick home – a nearly 22,000-square-foot teal warehouse identifiable by a giant YES painted on the side – is spacious enough to accommodate all sorts of revelry, from indie shopping markets, variety shows and Sunday brunch to visually stunning, immersive film parties and costume-mandatory DJ raves with acrobats and stilt walkers. During one shindig that was billed as a sensual celebration of food and flesh, attendees kicked off the night by eating a meal off women's nude bodies with their hands before a programme of interactive erotic performances. Just say yes.

On (and off) pointe

New York dance includes both luminous tradition and daring experimentation. While Lincoln Center remains the hub for traditional balletic offerings, with annual seasons by American Ballet Theatre and New York City Ballet, the David H Koch Theater has opened itself up to modern dance too with Paul Taylor's company each spring. Increasingly, museums, such as **MoMA** (*see p137*) and the **Whitney** (*see p107*), are broadening their reach from the visual arts to showcasing dance and performance.

The companies of modern dance icons such as Martha Graham, Alvin Ailey, Trisha Brown, Paul Taylor and Mark Morris are still based in the city, alongside a wealth of contemporary choreographers who create works outside the traditional company structure. Multidisciplinary festivals such as **Crossing the Line** in autumn, presented by the French Institute Alliance Française (22 E 60th Street, between Madison & Park Avenues, 1-212 355 6100, www.fiaf.org) showcase the latest developments in dance and performance. Autumn also brings **Fall for Dance** at the **New York City Center** (*see p139*), which focuses on eclectic mixed bills.

Screen stars

Every corner of NYC has been immortalised in celluloid, so it's not surprising that the city has a special relationship with the movies. The calendar is packed with festivals (*see p57* Diary), including Tribeca in the spring, autumn's New York Film Festival and several others organised by the excellent **Film Society of Lincoln Center**, which has state-of-the-art cinemas at the Elinor Bunin Monroe Film Center (*see p152*). Cinephiles love **Film Forum** (*see p83*) for its wide range of revivals and new indie features, while at the Lower East Side's **Metrograph** (*see p95*), you can have dinner and a movie under one chic roof.

AFTERNOON · · · · · 5 30 M
COMRADES · · · · 1 2 30 M 5 15
CRIME · PUNISHMENT · · 1 ½
EQUINOX FLOWER · · 2 45 6 ½

Metrograph box office

Broadway and beyond

Broadway theatre is one of New York's crowning attractions. The oldest venues, such as the New Amsterdam and the Belasco, date back to the early 20th century, and unique architectural features enhance the experience. Musicals continue to be the big crowd-pullers. Straight plays tend to have shorter runs but can generate considerable excitement, especially when they include big stars. And serious theatre fans will want to visit the more intimate world of Off (and Off Off) Broadway. You don't have to leave midtown to find the Frank Gehry-designed **Pershing Square Signature Center** (*see p134*).

You can also find Off Broadway work at the **Public Theater** (*see p103*), which mounts free **Shakespeare in the Park** (see *p59*) shows each summer. The **Brooklyn Academy of Music** (*see p180*) stages first-rate productions from around the world at its **Harvey Theater**.

Nearly all Broadway and Off Broadway shows are served by big ticketing agencies, but to score seats to same-day performances that aren't sold out for as much as 50 percent off face value, your best bet is **TKTS** in Times Square (Father Duffy Square, Broadway & 47th Street, www.tdf.org). There are also TKTS booths in downtown's South Street Seaport and in Brooklyn. These branches are much less busy and also sell matinée tickets the day before a show (see website for addresses and hours).

THE RHYTHM OF NY

STOMP™

ESTABLISHED IN 1994 NYC

ticketmaster **or 800-982-2787**
ORPHEUM THEATRE, 2nd Ave. at 8th St.

StompOnline.com

New York
Day by Day

1 World Trade Center

49

Itineraries

Of course, it's impossible to take in all of NYC's sights and cultural offerings in a single trip (or even multiple visits), but these tailored travel plans will help you to make the most of every New York minute. Choose from our Essential Weekend, Budget Break, Family Day Out and Two Boroughs in One Day tour, or cherry-pick elements from each to suit your own itinerary.

▶ *Budgets include transport, meals and admission prices, but not accommodation and shopping.*

ESSENTIAL WEEKEND

New York in two days
Budget $300-$400 per person
Getting around Walking, subway, bus, taxi

DAY 1

Morning

Boost your calorie intake for some serious sightseeing with a hearty breakfast sandwich or house-baked pastry from Meatpacking District gem **High Street on Hudson** (*see p106*), before heading to the **Whitney Museum of American Art** (*see p107*), in Renzo Piano's striking asymmetrical structure overlooking the southernmost stretch of the High Line. If you've booked in advance online, you'll sail through without waiting in the ticket line. If you don't want to make the time commitment, you can check out the free lobby gallery without a ticket. The **High Line** (*see p105*), a disused freight-train track reborn as a public park-cum-promenade, is one of the most popular spots in the city for both visitors and locals. Stroll north, keeping an eye out for iconic structures like the Statue of Liberty and the Empire State Building.

Afternoon

In the warmer months, you can stop for light eats (sandwiches, salads, charcuterie and cheese plates) and a tipple on the High Line at 15th Street, at seasonal open-air vino spot **Terroir** (*see p105*). For a more substantial meal, exit at 23rd Street for one of two choices: seasonal New American restaurant **Cookshop** (*see p115*) or the restored 1940s **Empire Diner** (*see p115*).

Whitney Museum of American Art

Now you're ready for more cultural sustenance. The city's main contemporary gallery district is between Tenth and Eleventh Avenues from 18th to 29th Streets (for our picks, *see p119*). And if you want to pick up a souvenir, stop by arty bookshop **Printed Matter** (*see p118*).

Your art tour isn't over when you resume your High Line perambulation – the park has a dedicated curator of temporary site-specific installations, so keep an eye out for works along its length. You'll come to the end of the line at 34th Street and Eleventh Avenue.

Evening

Here, you can hop on the 7 train at 34th Street-Hudson Yards station and take the subway two stops to the heart of Times Square. Around 5pm or 6pm, when initial crowds have thinned out, is a good time to score cut-price Broadway tickets at **TKTS**. Tickets in hand, if you have time, walk west or jump in a cab to contemporary food court **Gotham West Market** (*see p132*), a great pre-theatre pitstop that will keep everyone happy with a choice of several cult eateries from ramen to tapas.

Times Square

DAY 2

Morning

A short break in the Big Apple involves some tough choices: the Upper East Side's Museum Mile alone is lined with more than half a dozen world-class institutions. Fortify yourself with Bavarian ham and eggs and exquisite coffee at **Café Sabarsky** (*see p159*) as you mull over your itinerary. If you opt for the **Metropolitan Museum of Art** (*see p160*), you can either take a brisk two-hour essentials tour or forget the rest of the itinerary entirely – the vast museum is home to more than two million objects. Don't miss the famed European Paintings Galleries, the Ancient Egyptian Temple of Dendur and the Costume Institute among the many highlights. The Iris & B Gerald Cantor Roof Garden has a view over Central Park, as well as a new installation each year, and is open in the warmer months. Afterwards, even if you decide you can't manage another Museum Mile institution, walk a few blocks north to the **Guggenheim** (*see p157*) to admire the curvaceous lines of its Frank Lloyd Wright-designed exterior.

Afternoon

It's time to clear your art-saturated head with a stroll in **Central Park** (*see p148*). Enter at 79th or 76th Street and walk south to admire the picturesque Conservatory Water, or cross East Drive and try to snag a table at the outdoor bar at the Loeb Boathouse to gaze at the lake over drinks. Grab a bus or taxi on Fifth Avenue (or walk through the park) to the **Museum of Modern Art** (*see p137*), for iconic art and design from the 19th and 20th centuries.

Evening

The dinner hour brings more dilemmas. Should you head back uptown for a global contemporary twist on soul food and live music at **Red Rooster** in Harlem (*see p167*)? Or downtown for cheap eats and a speakeasy-bar crawl of the East Village or the Lower East Side? It's simply a matter of taste.

Museum of Modern Art

BUDGET BREAK

Get the most bang for your buck
Budget $60-$70 per person
Getting around Ferry, walking, subway

Morning

It's no secret that the **Staten Island Ferry** provides thrilling panoramas of New York Harbor and the Statue of Liberty during its brief crossing. Before you embark on this free mini cruise, stop for breakfast at Brookfield Place, north along the Hudson River. A collection of inexpensive eateries in the **Hudson Eats** food court (*see p73*) includes Black Seed, where you can get an egg and cheese bagel for little more than a fiver. New York has several fine free museums, including the **National Museum of the American Indian** near the ferry terminal; others include the Museum at FIT in Chelsea and the American Folk Art Museum (2 Lincoln Square, Columbus Avenue, at 66th Street, 1-212 595 9533, folkartmuseum.org) on the Upper West Side.

Afternoon

Be sure to swing by the tiny but always fascinating **Mmuseumm** (*see p78*), exhibiting eccentric collections in an elevator shaft in nearby Tribeca. The free micro-museum keeps limited hours, but even when it's not open you can get a glimpse through peepholes in the door. Also near Chinatown, the Lower East Side has dozens of art galleries that cost nothing to peruse, including cutting-edge **Canada** and slick, high-profile **Sperone Westwater** (for both, *see p88*).

Evening

Nearby, you can pick up the subway from Prince Street to 28th Street, for a bite at **Made Nice** (*see p123*) in the Flatiron District. The nouveau cafeteria gives you a taste of Michelin-starred chef Daniel Humm's cuisine for a fraction of the cost of his lofty dining rooms. From here it's a short walk to premier alternative-comedy club **Upright Citizens Brigade Theatre** (*see p120*) in Chelsea. The laughs are on them for popular free late-night shows ASSSSCAT 3000 and Whiplash, and tickets for others are typically low.

National Museum of the American Indian

FAMILY DAY OUT

The Big Apple for the little ones
Budget $450-500 for a family of four
Getting around Walking, subway

Morning

Set the kids up for the day with porridge, pancakes, or scones in flavours such as pumpkin or ham and cheese, at Wonderland-themed café **Alice's Tea Cup** on the Upper West Side (102 West 73rd Street, at Columbus Avenue, 1-212 799 3006, www.alicesteacup. com) or Upper East Side (156 East 64th Street, at Lexington Avenue, 1-212 486 9200). **Central Park** (*see p148*) is truly a garden of delights for kids, with playgrounds, Central Park Zoo with its penguins and snow leopards, and seasonal attractions including an antique carousel and an ice-skating rink.

Afternoon

The nearby **American Museum of Natural History** (*see p150*), with its spectacular dinosaur specimens, animal dioramas and planetarium, is a must for a family visit to NYC. A handy location of burger chain **Shake Shack** (*see p151*) close to the museum is a good spot for lunch, though it can get busy at peak periods so it's a good idea to arrive early. If you have any energy left, catch the subway from the station outside the museum to the 42nd Street-Port Authority stop to check out Times Square's latest family attraction, **Gulliver's Gate** (*see p129*), an amazing scale-model microcosm representing 50 countries.

Gulliver's Gate

Evening

Although many Broadway shows are great for all ages, the **New Victory Theater** (*see p133*) stages international kid-centric productions, from opera and dance to circus-skills spectaculars. There's no shortage of fast-food options in the vicinity, but for some of the best pizza in the city that will appeal to connoisseurs and fussy children alike, walk a few blocks north to **Don Antonio by Starita** (*see p131*).

TWO BOROUGHS IN ONE DAY

A scenic river crossing and two hip hoods

Budget $140-$160 per person

Getting around Walking, return subway or taxi

Morning

It's hard to imagine that in the early years of this millennium, visitors who ventured into Brooklyn tended to be diehard urban explorers. These days, an excursion to the second borough is essential, and one of the nicest ways to get there is on foot. Start on the Lower East Side, which was home to the world's largest Jewish community in the early 20th century. In homage to the old country, start your day with the Shtetl sandwich – smoked sable and goat's milk cream cheese on a bialy – at **Russ & Daughters Cafe** (*see p91*).

For a window into how locals lived – and worked – in the 19th and early 20th centuries, the **Lower East Side Tenement Museum** (*see p88*) conducts tours of apartments once occupied by residents whose stories are told, some of whom operated businesses on the site. If you'd rather contemplate the provenance of impeccably selected vintage wares, head to **Edith Machinist** (*see p93*) and **David Owens Vintage Clothing** (*see p93*).

Afternoon

Before you trek to Brooklyn, you'll want to stop for lunch. The pastrami sandwiches at cavernous no-frills canteen **Katz's Delicatessen** (*see p91*) are legendary. When the Williamsburg Bridge was completed in 1903, it was the longest suspension bridge in the world. Soon after, it became known as the 'Jews' Highway' because it provided an exodus for Lower East Side residents into Brooklyn (Williamsburg retains a Hasidic community among its diverse demographic). Hoof it uphill on the two-way bike- and footpath straight up the centre, and you'll get an expansive Financial District skyline vista.

Evening

Like its counterpart across the East River, Williamsburg has a mix of indie boutiques, vintage shops and glossier businesses. But the neighbourhood is best known for its music scene. From the bridge, head north then back towards the river on North 9th Street to browse vinyl and maybe catch a free show at NYC's outpost of music emporium **Rough Trade** (*see p178*). There's no shortage of dinner options in the area, but the pasta at **Lilia** (*see p174*) is particularly divine. If you can still move after this bi-borough odyssey, end the night at one of New York's best clubs, **Output** (*see p180*), or catch a gig at one of the many music venues.

Diary

New Yorkers hardly struggle to find something to celebrate. As well as venerable city traditions, offbeat annual events, such as Brooklyn's Mermaid Parade or the Jazz Age Lawn Party on Governors Island, let you soak up the local vibe. In summer, take advantage of free performances in the city's green spaces. Before you set out, or plan a trip around an event, it's wise to call or check online first as dates, times and locations are subject to change. Of course, this is only a fraction of what's going on in the great metropolis each season – for the latest listings and more ideas, consult *Time Out New York* magazine or www.timeout.com/newyork.

Spring

Early spring is often chilly, and the season can be rainy, but it starts to warm up in late April and May. Green spaces such as Central Park (*see p148*), the Brooklyn Botanic Garden (*see p171*) and the New York Botanical Garden (*see p182*) are frothy with blossom, especially in April. Moderate weather, before the summer heat and humidity sets in, makes this a good time to explore the city on foot. It's also a busy time in the art world, with art fairs and events surrounding Armory Week. Seasonal flea markets open for business, along with other warm-weather staples such as Governors Island (*see p69*).

Sakura Matsuri

Early Mar Armory Show

www.thearmoryshow.com
Although its name pays homage to the 1913 show that introduced avant-garde European art to an American audience, this contemporary international art mart, held on Hudson River piers, debuted in 1999.

17 Mar St Patrick's Day Parade

www.nycstpatricksparade.org
Thousands of green-clad merrymakers strut down Fifth Avenue to the sounds of pipe bands.

Late Mar/early Apr Easter Parade

From 10am on Easter Sunday, participants gather on Fifth Avenue between 49th and 57th Streets to show off elaborately constructed hats – we're talking noggin-toppers shaped like the NYC skyline or the Coney Island Cyclone.

Mid-late Apr Tribeca Film Festival

www.tribecafilm.com

Launched in 2002, Robert De Niro's downtown festival draws more than 150,000 fans to screenings of independent movies and other events.

❤ Late Apr Sakura Matsuri (Cherry Blossom Festival)

www.bbg.org
The Brooklyn Botanic Garden celebrates more than 200 cherry trees in blossom with Japanese cultural offerings such as concerts, traditional dance, manga exhibitions, cosplay fashion shows and tea cere-monies.

Early May Five Boro Bike Tour

www.bikenewyork.org
Thousands of cyclists take over the city for a 40-mile, car-free Tour de New York. The route begins near Battery Park, moves up through Manhattan and makes a circuit of the boroughs before winding up at Staten Island's Fort Wadsworth for a festival.

Early/mid May Frieze Art Fair New York

www.frieze.com
The New York edition of the tent-tastic London art fair showcases a global array of around 200 galleries, plus site-specific works, on Randalls Island.

Late May/early June & early/mid Sept Washington Square Outdoor Art Exhibit

www.wsoae.org

In 1931, Jackson Pollock and Willem de Kooning propped up a few of their paintings on the sidewalk near Washington Square Park and called it a show. Now, twice a year, around 100 artists and artisans exhibit their wares in the surrounding streets.

Summer

Early summer typically brings blue skies and pleasantly warm temperatures, but late July and August can be uncomfortably hot and humid, although air-conditioning is ubiquitous. Since many wealthier residents escape to nearby resort areas such as the Hamptons, the city is quieter, especially on weekends, and it may be easier to score sought-after theatre tickets and restaurant reservations. There are usually good deals on accommodation too.

The season brings a roster of free outdoor music and theatre festivals, including **SummerStage**, **Shakespeare in the Park**, the **River to River Festival** and **Lincoln Center Out of Doors**, plus alfresco film screenings in several parks. On several Saturdays in August, the city closes a section of Park Avenue and other streets to traffic for strolling, biking and other activities. Those seeking traditional summer pleasures head to Rockaway Beach for sea and sand, or Coney Island for thrill rides and boardwalk amusements.

❤ Late May-Aug Shakespeare in the Park

www.shakespeareinthepark.org

The Public Theater offers the best of the Bard outdoors. Free tickets (two per person) are distributed at the Delacorte Theater at noon on the day of the performance. Around 8am is usually a good time to begin waiting, although the queue can start forming as early as 6am when big-name stars are on the bill.

❤ Late May-Sept SummerStage

www.summerstage.org

DJs, dance companies and more hit the main stage in Central Park – and green spaces across the five boroughs – for this popular, long-running and mostly free annual series.

June-Aug BRIC Celebrate Brooklyn! Festival

www.bricartsmedia.org

Since community arts organisation BRIC launched this series of outdoor performances to revitalise Prospect Park, it's become Brooklyn's premier summer fête, featuring music, dance, film and spoken word acts.

Early June Governors Ball Music Festival

www.governorsballmusicfestival.com

Catch big names in rock, pop and hip hop at this three-day outdoor festival in Randalls Island Park.

Early/mid June Big Apple Barbecue Block Party

www.bigapplebbq.org

Get your fill of the best 'cue around as the country's top pit masters gather in Madison Square Park for a two-day outdoor carnivore's paradise with live music.

Early/mid June Museum Mile Festival

www.museummilefestival.org

Several of the city's most prestigious art institutions on Fifth Avenue – including the Guggenheim and the Met – open their doors to the public free of charge, but you'll have to arrive early to stand a chance of getting in.

Early/mid June National Puerto Rican Day Parade

www.nprdpinc.org
Vejigantes (carnival dancers), colourful floats, and live salsa and reggaetón bands fill Fifth Avenue in this exuberant celebration of the city's largest Hispanic community and its culture.

Mid June Egg Rolls, Egg Creams & Empanadas Festival

www.eldridgestreet.org
The Museum at Eldridge Street's block party celebrates the convergence of Jewish, Chinese and Puerto Rican traditions on the Lower East Side, with klezmer and bomba music, acrobats, Chinese opera, tea ceremonies and plenty of the titular treats.

❤ Mid June & mid Aug Jazz Age Lawn Party

Young hepcats in period garb gather on the lawns of Colonels Row on Governors Island for Charleston contests, old-timey swimsuit competitions, vintage portraits and a DJ spinning 78rpm records, among other activities.

Mid/late June New York Philharmonic Concerts in the Parks

www.nyphil.org
Thousands of classical music lovers lay their picnic blankets on Central Park's Great Lawn, as well as in other green spaces across the city, for free evening performances.

Mid-late June River to River Festival

www.rivertorivernyc.com
Lower Manhattan organisations present dozens of free events – from visual art to all sorts of performances – at mainly waterfront venues.

❤ Mid/late June Mermaid Parade

www.coneyisland.com
Glitter-covered semi-nude revellers, aquatically adorned floats and classic cruisers fill Surf Avenue for this annual Coney Island art parade.

Late June NYC LGBT Pride March

www.nycpride.org
NYC's Pride parade, in commemoration of the 1969 Stonewall Riots, paints Fifth Avenue all the colours of the rainbow, with floats, drag queens and hundreds of marching organisations. After the march, there's a massive street fair with dancing and performances on the West Side piers.

Late June-mid July Midsummer Night Swing

www.midsummernightswing.org
Lincoln Center's Damrosch Park hosts three weeks of dance parties (Tue-Sat) including lessons, with bands playing salsa, Cajun, swing and other music.

July-Aug Warm Up

www.momaps1.org/warmup
Thousands of dance-music fanatics and alt-rock enthusiasts make the pilgrimage to Queens on summer Saturdays for sounds ranging from spiritually inclined soul to full-bore techno or dubstep in MoMA PS1's courtyard.

4 July Macy's Fourth of July Fireworks

www.macys.com/fireworks
At NYC's main Independence Day attraction, fireworks are launched from barges on the East River at around 9pm, but you'll need to arrive much earlier to secure a spot.

Late July Panorama

www.panorama.nyc

The organiser of California's Coachella music festival launched this East Coast counterpart held over three days. The sprawling multi-stage affair in Randalls Island Park attracts some of the biggest names in hip hop, indie rock, pop and beyond.

Late July-early Aug Lincoln Center Out of Doors

www.lcoutofdoors.org

Free dance, music, theatre, opera and more make up the programme over the course of three weeks at this family-friendly and ambitious festival.

Late July-late Aug Harlem Week

www.harlemweek.com

Harlem Day is the centrepiece of this massive culture fest, but 'Week' is now a misnomer – besides the street fair serving up music, art and food along 135th Street, a wealth of concerts, films, dance performances, fashion and sports events are on tap for around a month.

Late July/early Aug Summer Restaurant Week

www.nycgo.com/restaurantweek

Twice a year, for two weeks or more at a stretch, some of the city's finest restaurants dish out three-course prix-fixe lunches for under $30 and dinners for little more than $40.

Mid Aug Battery Dance Festival

batterydance.org

During one summer week, Battery Park City's Robert F Wagner, Jr Park comes to life with dozens of free dance performances, from contemporary premières to classical Indian Kuchipudi, against the backdrop of New York Harbor at sunset.

❤ Mid/late Aug Elements Music and Art Festival

www.elementsfest.nyc

Run by epic party-throwers BangOn!NYC, this annual bash features dozens of DJs and electronic music acts, plus circus-skills performers and arty spectacles, on the Brooklyn waterfront.

Late Aug-mid Sept US Open

www.usopen.org

Flushing, Queens, becomes the centre of the tennis universe when the USTA Billie Jean King National Tennis Center hosts the final Grand Slam event of the year.

Autumn

Warm weather typically lasts into September, but October brings cooler days, as well as vivid foliage in the city's streets and parks. Autumn is an important time on the cultural calendar, with new show openings on Broadway, blockbuster museum exhibitions, New York Fashion Week and prominent festivals such as the Brooklyn Academy of Music's **Next Wave Festival** and the **New York Film Festival**. At the end of October,

Mermaid Parade

Halloween is a big event in NYC, when the streets are populated with costumed revellers and families going door to door with trick-or-treating children. Autumn is the high season for hotels, so be sure to book accommodation well in advance if you're planning a trip during this time.

Sept-Dec Next Wave Festival
www.bam.org
Among the most highly anticipated of the city's autumn culture offerings, the Brooklyn Academy of Music festival showcases only the very best in avant-garde music, dance, theatre and opera.

Early Sept Electric Zoo
www.electriczoofestival.com
Don your Day-Glo shades and head to Randalls Island Park for this three-day outdoor EDM rager, featuring a wide range of artists both top name and underground.

Early Sept West Indian American Day Carnival
www.wiadcacarnival.org
This annual Caribbean parade along Brooklyn's Eastern Parkway is never short on costumed stilt dancers, floats blaring soca and calypso music, and vendors selling traditional island eats such as jerk chicken, curry goat and oxtail.

Mid Sept Brooklyn Book Festival
www.brooklynbookfestival.org
The city's largest (and free) literary fest takes over Brooklyn Borough Hall and Plaza every autumn for a full day of panels and readings, bibliophile swag and inordinate book buying, plus related city-wide events.

Mid-late Sept Feast of San Gennaro
www.sangennaro.org
Little Italy celebrates the martyred third-century bishop and patron saint of Naples at this 11-day festival, with live music and food stalls selling zeppole (custard- or jam-filled fritters) and sausages. On the official feast day, a statue of San Gennaro is carried in a Grand Procession outside the Most Precious Blood Church.

Late Sept New York Burlesque Festival
www.thenewyorkburlesquefestival.com
Co-produced by performer Angie Pontani, the 'Italian Stallionette', NYC's annual burlesque fest brings an international line-up of tassel twirlers, boylesque artists and circus-skills acts to several venues over four days.

Tompkins Square Park Halloween Dog Parade

💙 Late Sept–mid Oct New York Film Festival

www.filmlinc.com
The Film Society of Lincoln Center hosts the city's biggest event for film fans and industry folk alike, with more than two weeks of premières, features and short flicks from around the globe.

▶ *For more on Lincoln Center's cultural offerings, see p152.*

Mid Oct New York City Wine & Food Festival

www.nycwff.org
The Food Network's epicurean fête offers four belt-busting days of tasting events and celebrity-chef demos in various venues.

Mid Oct Open House New York Weekend

www.ohny.org
More than 200 of the city's coolest and most exclusive architectural sites, private homes and landmarks open their doors during a weekend of urban exploration.

Late Oct Tompkins Square Park Halloween Dog Parade

www.tompkinssquaredogrun. com/halloween
To see a plethora of puppies in adorable outfits, head to this canine costume parade, which has been an East Village institution for more than two decades.

💙 31 Oct Village Halloween Parade

www.halloween-nyc.com
The sidewalks lining Sixth Avenue are always packed with spectators for a themed procession of dancers, bands, puppets, floats and ordinary folks in arty, gruesome and jokey costumes.

Winter

As you'd expect, the main shopping thoroughfares, such as Fifth and Madison Avenues, are bustling in the run-up to Christmas, with festive lights, elaborate displays in department store windows and a giant tree at Rockefeller Center. Seasonal ice-skating rinks and outdoor holiday bazaars scattered around the city add to the festive atmosphere. Temperatures can be frigid and snow is fairly common, especially in January and February. The white wonderland is picturesque, particularly in Central Park and other large green spaces, though it quickly becomes dirty and slushy. A slew of holiday-themed shows, from traditional offerings such as the New York City Ballet's *Nutcracker* to Yuletide burlesque, hits the city, culminating in a whirl of (generally expensive) New Year's Eve events and parties. Although hotel rates tend to be high in December and early January, you may be able to get a bargain later in the month or in February.

Early Nov New York City Marathon

www.tcsnycmarathon.org
Around 50,000 runners hotfoot it through all five boroughs over a 26.2-mile course.

Early-mid Nov New York Comedy Festival

www.nycomedyfestival.com
This six-day laugh fest features both big names (Tracy Morgan, Marc Maron, Jerry Seinfeld and Amy Schumer in recent years) and up-and-comers.

Late Nov Macy's Thanksgiving Day Parade & Balloon Inflation

www.macys.com/parade
At 9am on Thanksgiving Day, the stars of this nationally televised

parade are the gigantic balloons, the elaborate floats and good ol' Santa Claus. The night before, you can watch the rubbery colossi take shape outside the American Museum of Natural History.

Late Nov/early Dec Rockefeller Center Tree-Lighting Ceremony

www.rockefellercenter.com

Proceedings start at 7pm, but this festive celebration is always mobbed, so get there early. Most of the two-hour event is devoted to celebrity performances, then the 30,000 LEDs covering the massive evergreen are switched on.

Mid Dec Unsilent Night

www.unsilentnight.com

To participate in composer Phil Kline's arty, secular answer to Christmas carolling, gather under the Washington Square Arch in Greenwich Village to pick up a cassette or CD of one of four different atmospheric tracks, or sync up via smartphone app. Everyone then presses play at the same time and marches through the streets, filling the air with a 45-minute piece.

Rockefeller Center Christmas Tree

31 Dec New Year's Eve in Times Square

www.timessquarenyc.org

Join a million others and watch the giant illuminated Waterford Crystal ball descend amid confetti and cheering. Arrive by 3pm or earlier to stake out a spot near the junction of Broadway and Seventh Avenue and be prepared to stay put. There are no public restrooms or food vendors, and leaving means giving up your spot. Celebrity performances are held across two stages, from 6pm.

1 Jan New Year's Day Marathon Benefit Reading

www.poetryproject.org

Around 140 of the city's best poets, artists and performers gather at St Mark's Church in-the-Bowery to recite their work.

Early/mid Jan No Pants Subway Ride

www.improveverywhere.com

The name says it all. Improv Everywhere's annual bare-legged expedition began as a mildly subversive, playful prank in 2002, with a handful of operatives in one car on the downtown 6 train, but it's grown into a well-publicised mass event.

Late Jan/early Feb Winter Restaurant Week

www.nycgo.com/restaurantweek

See Summer Restaurant Week.

Late Jan/Feb Chinese New Year

www.betterchinatown.com

Chinatown is charged with energy during the two weeks of the Lunar New Year. The key events are the parade down Mott Street and the firecracker ceremony, which is usually held in Sara D Roosevelt Park and includes lion dances and food and craft vendors.

New York
by Area

Downtown

The Big Apple's original core, Downtown Manhattan
is still NYC's financial, legal and political powerhouse.
The area is also home to some of the city's most exciting
restaurants and bars, arts and retail. Here, the network of
streets is largely off the rest of the island's orderly street
grid, and the landscape shifts from block to block. In the
Financial District, gleaming skyscrapers rub shoulders
with 18th-century landmarks; Soho's designer flagships
are only a short hop from Chinatown's frenetic food
markets; and the quiet brownstone-lined streets of the
West Village are just around the corner from the flashy
nightspots of the Meatpacking District.

Best sight

Ascend to the crown of the Statue of Liberty (p70) for a breathtaking vista.

Best restaurants

Katz's Delicatessen (p91) for classic pastrami on rye. Carbone (p104), with a retro mob supper club vibe. Glamorous French dining room Le Coucou (p79). High Street on Hudson (p106) for house-baked breads and seasonal all-day fare.

Must-see museums

National September 11 Memorial & Museum (p72), a suitably monumental tribute. The city's newest art temple, Whitney Museum of American Art (p107).

Best live music and laughs

Bowery Ballroom (p94), an elegant venue for indie bands. Comedy Cellar (p112), a popular spot for local and big-name talent. Rockwood Music Hall (p95) for emerging acts across three stages. Iconic jazz bar Village Vanguard (p111).

Best shops

Dear: Rivington (p101) for Japanese designers and vintage. Eclectic, ultra-hip fashion emporium Opening Ceremony (p82). Well-stacked institution Strand Book Store (p102). Discount department store Century 21 (p75).

Best cultural venues

Metrograph (p95), a boutique cinema with a lively restaurant. Public Theater (p103) for ambitious new plays and top cabaret venue Joe's Pub.

Best park

The High Line (p105), for views and art along the elevated promenade.

Best cocktails

Bespoke concoctions at Attaboy (p92). Bar Goto (p92) for Eastern-inflected drinks. BlackTail (p74), a homage to pre-revolution Cuba. Contemporary tiki bar Mother of Pearl (p101).

Financial District

Commerce has been the backbone of New York's prosperity since its earliest days as a Dutch colony. The southern tip of Manhattan evolved into the **Financial District** as banks established their headquarters near the port.

When the city's role as a shipping hub diminished during the 20th century, the **South Street Seaport** area fell into disuse, but it was redeveloped in the mid 1980s. It's now home to shops, restaurants and the **South Street**
Seaport Museum. A new mall and a seafood market helmed by top chef Jean-Georges Vongerichten are expected to open by mid 2018.

As more than a decade of construction nears completion, the **World Trade Center** is both a potent 9/11 memorial and a busy downtown shopping hub, home to the **One World Observatory**, the city's highest vantage point. A string of parks runs north along the Hudson River from Battery Park, providing expansive views of the **Statue of Liberty** and **Ellis Island**.

Sights & museums

Alexander Hamilton US Custom House/National Museum of the American Indian

1 Bowling Green, between State & Whitehall Streets (1-212 514 3700, www.nmai.si.edu). Subway R, W to Whitehall Street-South Ferry; 1 to South Ferry; 4, 5 to Bowling Green. **Open** *10am-5pm Mon-Wed, Fri-Sun; 10am-8pm Thur.* **Admission** *free.* **Map** *p69 E33.*

Cass Gilbert's magnificent Beaux Arts Custom House, completed in 1907, housed the Customs Service until 1973, when the federal government moved it to the newly built World Trade Center complex. Four monumental figures by Lincoln Memorial sculptor Daniel Chester French – representing Asia, America, Europe and Africa – flank the impressive entrance. The panels surrounding the elliptical rotunda dome were designed to feature murals, but the plan wasn't realised until the 1930s, when local artist Reginald Marsh was commissioned to decorate them under the New Deal's Works Progress Administration; the paintings depict a ship entering New York Harbor.

In 1994, the National Museum of the American Indian's George Gustav Heye Center, a branch of the Smithsonian, moved into the first two floors of the building. On the second level, the life and culture of Native Americans are illuminated in three galleries radiating out from the rotunda. In addition to a roster of changing shows, the permanent exhibition, 'Infinity of Nations', displays 700 of the museum's wide-ranging collection of Native American art and objects, from decorated baskets to elaborate ceremonial headdresses, organised by geographical region. On the ground floor, the Diker Pavilion

for Native Arts & Culture is the city's only dedicated showcase for Native American performing arts.

City Hall

City Hall Park, from Vesey to Chambers Streets, between Broadway & Park Row (1-212 788 2656, www.nyc.gov/cityhalltours). Subway J, Z to Chambers Street; R, W to City Hall; 2, 3 to Park Place; 4, 5, 6 to Brooklyn Bridge-City Hall. **Open** *Tours (individuals) noon Wed, 10am Thur; (groups) 10.30am Mon, Tue. Reservations required.* **Admission** *free.* **Map** *p69 E32.*

Designed by French émigré Joseph François Mangin and John McComb Jr, the fine, Federal-style City Hall was completed in 1812. Tours take in the rotunda, with its splendid coffered dome, the City Council Chamber and the Governor's Room, with its collection of American 19th-century political portraits and historic furnishings (including George Washington's desk). The Thursday morning tour must be booked in advance; alternatively, sign up for the first come, first-served Wednesday noon tour between 10am and 11.30am at the NYC tourism kiosk at the southern end of City Hall Park on the east side of Broadway, at Barclay Street.

Fraunces Tavern Museum

2nd & 3rd Floors, 54 Pearl Street, at Broad Street (1-212 425 1778, www.frauncestavernmuseum. org). Subway J, Z to Broad Street; 4, 5 to Bowling Green. **Open** *noon-5pm Mon-Fri; 11am-5pm Sat, Sun.* **Admission** *$7; $4 reductions; free under-6s.* **Map** *p69 E33.*

True, George Washington slept here, but there's little left of the original 18th-century tavern he favoured during the Revolution. Fire-damaged and rebuilt in the 19th century, it was reconstructed in its current Colonial Revival style in 1907. Step into a period

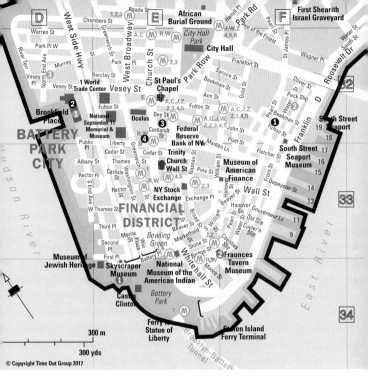

Map labels:

First Shearith Israel Graveyard

African Burial Ground

City Hall Park

City Hall

St Paul's Chapel

1 World Trade Center

Vesey St

Brookfield Place

National September 11 Memorial & Museum

Oculus

Federal Reserve Bank of NY

BATTERY PARK CITY

Trinity Church Wall St

NY Stock Exchange

Museum of American Finance

FINANCIAL DISTRICT

Wall St

Bowling Green

South Street Seaport

South Street Seaport Museum

Museum of Jewish Heritage

Skyscraper Museum

National Museum of the American Indian

Frances Tavern Museum

Castle Clinton

Battery Park

Ferry to Statue of Liberty

Staten Island Ferry Terminal

Hudson River

East River

Brooklyn-Battery Tunnel

300 m

300 yds

---

recreation of the Long Room, where Washington took tearful farewell of his troops after the British had been defeated and vowed to retire from public life. (Luckily, he had a change of heart six years later and became the country's first president.) The museum also contains a collection of 5,000 Revolutionary War objects, including muskets, prints and such Washington relics as a lock of his hair. And you can still raise a pint in the bar and restaurant, which is run by Dublin's Porterhouse Brewing Company.

Governors Island

1-212 440 2000, www.govisland. com. Subway R, W to Whitehall Street-South Ferry; 1 to South Ferry; 4, 5 to Bowling Green. Then take ferry from Battery Maritime Building at Slip no.7. Open May-early Oct 10am-6pm Mon-Fri; 10am-7pm Sat, Sun (see website for ferry schedule). Admission Ferry $2 round trip; $1 reductions; free under-13s. Free 10-11.30am Sat, Sun.

A seven-minute ferry ride takes you to this seasonal island sanctuary, a scant 800 yards from lower Manhattan. Because of its strategic position in the middle of New York Harbor, Governors Island was a military outpost and off-limits

♥ Statue of Liberty

*Liberty Island (1-212 363 3200, www.nps.gov/stli). Subway R, W to Whitehall Street-South Ferry; 1 to South Ferry; 4, 5 to Bowling Green. Then take Statue of Liberty ferry (1-201 604 2800, 1-877 523 9849, www.statuecruises.com), departing roughly every 30mins from gangway 4 or 5 in southernmost Battery Park. **Open** ferry runs 9.30am-3.30pm daily (extended hours in summer; see website). Purchase tickets online, by phone or at Castle Clinton in Battery Park. **Admission** $18.50; $9-$14 reductions; free under-4s.*

The sole occupant of Liberty Island, Liberty Enlightening the World stands 305 feet tall from the bottom of her base to the tip of her gold-leaf torch.

Intended as a gift from France on America's 100th birthday, the statue was designed by Frédéric Auguste Bartholdi (1834-1904). Construction began in Paris in 1874, her skeletal iron framework crafted by Gustave Eiffel (the man behind the Tower), but only the arm with the torch was finished in time for the centennial in 1876. In 1884, the statue was finally completed – only to be taken apart to be shipped to New York, where it was unveiled in 1886. It served as a lighthouse until 1902, and as a welcoming beacon for millions of immigrants. These 'tired... poor... huddled masses' were evoked in Emma Lazarus's poem 'The New Colossus', written in 1883 to raise funds for the pedestal and engraved inside the statue in 1903.

With a free Monument Pass, available only with ferry tickets reserved in advance, you can enter the pedestal and view the interior through a glass ceiling. Access to the crown costs an extra $3 and must be reserved in advance.

A half-mile across the harbour from Liberty Island is the 32-acre Ellis Island, gateway for over 12 million people who entered the country between 1892 and 1954. In the National Museum of Immigration (a former check-in depot), three floors of photos, interactive displays and exhibits pay tribute to the hopeful souls who made the voyage.

Statue of Liberty

to the public for 200 years. The verdant, 172-acre isle still retains a significant chunk of its military-era architecture, including Fort Jay, started in 1776, and Castle Williams, completed in 1812 and for years used as a prison. Today, as well as providing a peaceful setting for cycling (bring a bike, or rent one on arrival), the island hosts a programme of events, a, including the popular Jazz Age Lawn party (*see p60*). Sprawling green spaces include the Hammock Grove for shady reclining, and the Hills, constructed from the debris of demolished buildings. The tallest hill offers harbour panoramas from its 70ft summit. Food and drink options include pop-up beer gardens and a fleet of food trucks. There are even plans for a day spa.

One World Observatory

One World Trade Center, 285 Fulton Street, at Vesey & West Streets (1-844 696 1776, https:// oneworldobservatory.com). Subway A, C, 1, 2, 3 to Chambers Street; A, C, J, Z, 2, 3, 4, 5 to Fulton Street; E to World Trade Center; R, W to Cortlandt Street; R, W, 1 to Rector Street; 2, 3 to Park Place. **Open** *9am-8pm daily (extended hours in summer; see website).* **Admission** *$34; $28-$32 reductions; free under-6s, 9/11 family members and 9/11 rescue and recovery workers.* **Map** *p69 E32.*

Perched on floors 100 to 102 of the tallest skyscraper in the western hemisphere, One World Observatory has surpassed the Empire State Building as the highest observation deck in the city. Getting up there is an experience in itself – Sky Pod elevators, featuring a lightning-fast floor-to-ceiling simulation of New York City's development, whisk visitors to the top of the building in a mere minute. When you arrive on the 102nd floor, a high-tech two-minute video presentation whets your appetite for the main attraction

before screens rise to reveal the panoramic view. Two levels down, those not prone to vertigo can step on to the Sky Portal, a 14ft-wide circular disc displaying an HD real-time image of the street below. On the middle level, a restaurant, casual café and bar let you relax and take in the incredible vistas over a snack, cocktails or a full meal.

South Street Seaport Museum

12 Fulton Street, between South & Water Streets (1-212 748 8600, https://southstreetseaportmuseum. org). Subway A, C, J, Z, 2, 3, 4, 5 to Fulton Street. **Open** *11am-5pm Wed-Sun.* **Admission** *$12; $8 reductions; $6 under-18s.* **Map** *p69 F32.*

Founded in 1967, the South Street Seaport Museum celebrates the maritime history of New York City's 19th-century waterfront. In addition to rotating exhibitions, the institution has a fleet of historic vessels on Pier 16. The admission price includes a tour of the 1907 lightship *Ambrose* and the 19th-century cargo ship *Wavertree*. From late May until mid-October, visitors can book excursions along the East River on the 1885 schooner Pioneer. For the museum's gift shop, comprising Bowne Printers and Bowne & Co Stationers, *see p74*.

In the know
The bull's balls

On Bowling Green's northern side stands a three-and-a-half-ton bronze sculpture of a bull (symbolising the bull, or rising, share market). The statue was deposited without permission outside the Stock Exchange by guerrilla artist Arturo di Modica in 1989 and has since been moved by the city to its current location. The bull's enormous balls are often rubbed for good luck by tourists (and perhaps the occasional broker).

❤ National September 11 Memorial & Museum

Various entry points on Greenwich, Liberty & West Streets (1-212 312 8800, www.911memorial.org). Subway A, C, 1, 2, 3 to Chambers Street; A, C, J, Z, 2, 3, 4, 5 to Fulton Street; E to World Trade Center; R, W to Cortlandt Street; R, W, 1 to Rector Street; 2, 3 to Park Place. **Open** *Memorial plaza 7.30am-9pm daily. Museum 9am-8pm Mon-Thur, Sun; 9am-9pm Fri, Sat (hours vary seasonally; see website for updates).* **Admission** *Memorial plaza free. Museum $24; $12-$18 reductions; free under-6s, 9/11 family members, rescue workers & US military. Free 5-8pm Tue.* **Map** *p69 E32.*

Surrounded by a tree-shaded plaza, the memorial, Reflecting Absence, created by architects Michael Arad and Peter Walker, comprises two one-acre 'footprints' of the destroyed towers, with 30 foot man-made waterfalls cascading down their sides. Bronze parapets around the edges are inscribed with the names of the 2,983 victims of the 2001 attacks at the World Trade Center, the Pentagon and the passengers of United Flight 93, as well as those who lost their lives in the bombing on 26 February 1993.

The museum pavilion, designed by Oslo-based firm Snøhetta, rises between the pools. Its web-like glass atrium houses two steel trident-shaped columns salvaged from the base of the Twin Towers. Visitors descend to the vast spaces of the WTC's original foundations alongside a remnant of the Vesey Street staircase known as the Survivors' Stairs, which was used

by hundreds of people escaping the carnage. Massive pieces of twisted metal and a fallen segment of the North Tower's radio/TV antenna bring home the enormous scale of the disaster.

Around 1,000 artefacts, plus images, documents and oral histories chronicle events leading up to the attacks, commemorate the victims and document how the world changed after 9/11.

The adjacent Oculus, a dramatic bird-like structure designed by starchitect Santiago Calatrava, is the centrepiece of a multi-level Westfield shopping and dining complex spread across the WTC site.

Trinity Church Wall Street & St Paul's Chapel

Trinity Church Wall Street 75 Broadway, at Wall Street (1-212 602 0800, www.trinitywallstreet.org). Subway R, W, 1 to Rector Street; 2, 3, 4, 5 to Wall Street. **Open** *7am-6pm daily (churchyard closes at 4pm Oct-Mar).* **Admission** *free.* **Map** *p69 E33.*

St Paul's Chapel 209 Broadway, between Fulton & Vesey Streets (1-212 602 0800, www. trinitywallstreet.org). Subway A, C, J, Z, 2, 3, 4, 5 to Fulton Street. **Open** *10am-6pm daily.* **Admission** *free.* **Map** *p69 E32.*

Trinity Church was the island's tallest structure when it was completed in 1846 (the original burned down in 1776; a second was demolished in 1839). A set of gates on Broadway allows access to the surrounding cemetery, where cracked and faded tombstones mark the final resting places of dozens of past city dwellers, including such notable New Yorkers as founding father Alexander Hamilton and steamboat inventor Robert Fulton.

Six blocks to the north, Trinity's satellite, St Paul's Chapel, is more important architecturally. The oldest public building in New York still in continuous use (it dates from 1766), it is one of the nation's most valued Georgian structures.

Restaurants & cafés

Hudson Eats $-$$

Brookfield Place, 230 Vesey Street, between West Street & the Hudson River (1-212 978 1698, www. brookfieldplaceny.com). Subway A, C, 1, 2, 3 to Chambers Street; A, C, J, Z, 2, 3, 4, 5 to Fulton Street; E to World Trade Center; R, w to Cortlandt Street; R, W, 1 to Rector Street; 2, 3 to Park Place. **Open** *7am-9pm Mon-Fri; 10am-9pm Sat; 11am-7pm Sun.* **Map** *p69 D32* ❶ *Eclectic*

Carved out from the second floor of a monster retail complex, the glossy, 600-seat dining terrace upgrades food-court schlock with white-marble counters, 17ft-high windows offering gobsmacking waterfront views and over 14 chef-driven kiosks, including branches of Mighty Quinn's for Texas-meets-Carolina 'cue, Dos Toros for tacos and burritos, Num Pang for Cambodian sandwiches, and lox-and-bagel purveyor Black Seed.

Jack's Stir Brew Coffee $

222 Front Street, between Beekman Street & Peck Slip (1-212 227 7631, www.jacksstirbrew.com). Subway A, C, J, Z, 2, 3, 4, 5 to Fulton Street. **Open** *7am-6pm Mon-Fri; 8am-6pm Sat, Sun.* **Map** *p69 F32* ❷ *Café*

Java fiends convene at this award-winning caffeine spot that offers organic, shade-grown beans and a homey vibe. Coffee is served by espresso artisans with a knack for oddball concoctions, such as the super-silky Mountie latte, infused with maple syrup. **Other locations** 138 W 10th Street, between Greenwich Avenue & Waverly Place, West Village (1-212 929 0821); 10 Downing Street, between Bedford Street & Sixth Avenue, West Village (1-212 929 6011); 2 6th Avenue, between Walker & White Streets, Tribeca (1-212 519 6600).

North End Grill $$

104 North End Avenue, at Murray Street (1-646 747 1600, www. northendgrillnyc.com). Subway A, C to Chambers Street; E to World Trade Center; 2, 3 to Park Place. **Open** *11.30am-10pm Mon-Thur; 11.30am-10.30pm Fri; 11am-10.30pm Sat; 11am-8pm Sun.* **Map** *p69 D32* ❸ *American*

This instant classic has all the hallmarks of a Danny Meyer joint: effortless, affable service; a warm, buzzy space; and cooking that's easy and accessible. Eric Korsh puts a French-accented

BlackTail

spin on the seasonal menu (which incorporates produce from the eaterie's rooftop farm). The chef has introduced charcuterie and a raw bar dispensing lavish shellfish platters and a weeknight $1 oyster happy hour. Wood-fired grills and mesquite charcoal ovens impart a smoky finish to meat and poultry dishes.

Bars

♥ BlackTail

Pier A Harbor House, 22 Battery Place, between Little West Street & Hudson River Greenway (1-212 785 0153, www.blacktailnyc.com). Subway 4, 5 to Bowling Green. **Open** *5pm-2am daily.* **Map** *p69 E34* ❶

It's only a whiskey stone's throw away from the Dead Rabbit – Sean Muldoon and Jack McGarry's exceptionally successful cocktail bar on Water Street – but the sequel from the renowned team couldn't be further away in terms of theme. Where the original tavern looked to the Irish gangs of NYC's Five Points, this second outfit, located inside the Pier A Harbor House complex, channels Prohibition-era Cuba. A statue of Cuban lit hero José Martí stands at the bar, where the stools are modelled after those in Ernest Hemingway-frequented joints in

balmy Havana, and the expansive menu is loaded with more than 40 cocktails – contemporary takes on drinks from the classic 1920s to '50s era. Servers outfitted in straw fedoras and bright *guayaberas* weave between wicker chairs and potted palms with dishes like sugarcane-skewered Gulf shrimp and rum-glazed pork ribs.

Dead Rabbit Grocery & Grog

30 Water Street, at Broad Street (1-646 422 7906, www. deadrabbitnyc.com). Subway R, W to Whitehall Street-South Ferry; 1 to South Ferry. **Open** *11am-4am daily.* **Map** *p69 E33* ❷

At this time-capsule nook, you can drink like a boss – Boss Tweed, that is. Belfast bar vets Sean Muldoon and Jack McGarry have conjured up a rough-and-tumble 19th-century tavern in a red-brick landmark. Resurrecting long-forgotten quaffs is nothing new in NYC, but the Dead Rabbit's sheer breadth of mid 19th-century libations eclipses the competition, spanning 60-odd bishops, fixes, nogs and smashes. The ever-changing cocktail selection makes good use of seasonal produce and esoteric ingredients.

Shops & services

Bowne Printers/ Bowne & Co Stationers

209-211 Water Street, between Fulton & Beekman Streets (1-646 628 2707). Subway A, C, J, Z, 2, 3, 4, 5 to Fulton Street. **Open** *11am-7pm daily.* **Map** *p69 F32* ❶ *Gifts & stationery*

The South Street Seaport Museum shop comprises Bowne Printers and Bowne & Co Stationers. The re-creation of a 19th-century print shop doesn't just look the part: the platen presses – hand-set using antique letterpress and type from the museum's collection – also turn out stationery and cards. Next door, Bowne & Co Stationers, founded in 1775, sells hand-printed cards, prints, journals and other gifts.

Brookfield Place

*230 Vesey Street, between West Street & the Hudson River (1-212 978 1673, www.brookfieldplaceny.com). Subway A, C, 1, 2, 3 to Chambers Street; A, C, J, Z, 2, 3, 4, 5 to Fulton Street; E to World Trade Center; R, W to Cortlandt Street; R, W, 1 to Rector Street; 2, 3 to Park Place. **Open** 10am-8pm Mon-Sat; noon-6pm Sun (hours vary for some shops and restaurants). **Map** p69 D32* ❷
Mall

Directly across West Street from the World Trade Center, this sprawling office, retail and dining complex has the distinction of being the only mall with a view of the Statue of Liberty. Anchored by an outpost of Saks Fifth Avenue, it caters to the WTC's stylish tenants (the likes of Condé Nast) with a mix of luxe designer names like Gucci, Bottega Veneta and Burberry, contemporary fashion brands including DVF, Bonobos and Vince, plus cool Tribeca-born kids' shop Babesta and a 30,000sq ft French-food market, Le District. Refuelling options include chic food court Hudson Eats (*see p73*). Brookfield Place also hosts numerous free arts events in its Winter Garden atrium and waterfront plaza (see online calendar), which overlooks a marina.

BOWNE & Co STATIONERS.

❤ Century 21

*22 Cortlandt Street, between Broadway & Church Street (1-212 227 9092, www.c21stores.com). Subway A, C, J, Z, 2, 3, 4, 5 to Fulton Street; E to World Trade Center; R, W to Cortlandt Street. **Open** 7.45am-9pm Mon-Wed; 7.45am-9.30pm Thur, Fri; 10am-9pm Sat; 11am-8pm Sun. **Map** p69 E32* ❸ **Fashion**

A Marc Jacobs cashmere sweater for less than $200? Stella McCartney sunglasses for a mere $40? No, you're not dreaming – you're shopping at Century 21. You may have to rummage to unearth a treasure, but with savings of up to 65% off regular prices, it's worth it. In our experience, the smaller, more upscale, less chaotic Upper West Side location doesn't yield as many steals as the original.

Eataly

*4 World Trade Center, 101 Liberty Street, between Greenwich Street & Trinity Place, 3rd floor (1-212 897 2895, www.eataly.com). Subway A, C, 1, 2, 3 to Chambers Street; A, C, J, Z, 2, 3, 4, 5 to Fulton Street; E to World Trade Center; R, W to Cortlandt Street; R, W, 1 to Rector Street; 2, 3 to Park Place. **Open** 7am-11pm daily. **Map** p69 E32* ❹ **Food & drink**

The downtown location of the Italian food mega market is a 45,000sq ft foot complex on the third floor of 4 World Trade Center. Each Eataly location has a set theme, and this outpost's is bread, with a massive in-house bakery and a kiosk dedicated to the Italian flatbread known as *piadina*. There are four eateries, including the upscale Osteria Della Pace, with southern Italian fare and cocktails. Three casual restaurants, each with a different focus, share a large open dining area: Orto e Mare ('the garden and the sea'), Il Pesce (fresh seafood) and La Pizza & La Pasta (pretty obvious, no?). Some tables directly overlook the 9/11 Memorial.

Rubin Museum of Art

Union Square

27 W 16th St

Tenth Ave

High Line

W 14th St — A,C,E,L Ⓜ   1,2,3 Ⓜ   F,L,M Ⓜ

33 W 13th St

W 13th St

Fifth Ave

Sixth Ave

MEATPACKING
DISTRICT

Little W 12th St   W 12th St

32 Gansevoort St

Horatio St

Jane St

W 12th St

Greenwich Ave

W 12th St

W 11th St

W 10th St

W 9th St   **39**

Whitney Museum of American Art

WEST
VILLAGE

Washington St

Waverly Pl   **16**

W 4th St

15

W 8th St   **42**

University Pl

Bethune St   **41**

Bank St   **16**

Hudson St

Bleecker St

28

W 11th St

Greenwich St

Perry St   **40**

Charles St

Grove St   **43**

1

Waverly Pl   **34**

Washington Pl   **29**   **30**

GREENWICH

Washington Sq West

Washington Sq East

Greene St

West Side Hwy

50

46

45

W 10th St

Christopher St

Bedford St   **14**

Barrow St

Commerce St

Jones St   **38**   **13**
Cornelia St

Leroy St   **32**

Washington
Square

W 4th St

W 3rd St   **35**
12

Minetta Lane

New York
University

VILLAGE

La Guardia Pl

Seventh Ave South

Morton St

St Lukes Pl

Carmine St

Downing St

AIA New York Center for Architecture

14
36

Bleecker St

29

42

Leroy St

Clarkson St

W Houston St

W Houston St

MacDougal St

Sullivan St

6

Prince St

3

B,D,F,M Ⓜ

SOHO

Broadway

40

Greenwich St

Washington St

King St

Charlton St

Varick St

Ⓜ **1**

C,E

5

Spring St

Thompson St

Wooster St

Greene St

Mercer St

Broadway

R,W Ⓜ

Vandam St

Spring St

New York City
Fire Museum

Dominick St

Renwick St

30

34

Holland Tunnel

Canal St

Watts St

West
Drawing
Center

10

Haughwout
Building

Grand St

Hudson River

Watts St

Desbrosses St

Vestry St

Desbrosses St
1 Ⓜ

A,C,E Ⓜ

Canal St

5 Howard St

J,N,Q,R,W,Z,6 Ⓜ
Lispenard St

2

Walker St

West Side Hwy

Laight St

Hubert St

Beach St

Collister St
Ericsson Pl

St John's Ln

Varick St

White St

Mmuseumm

Franklin St

Broadway

31

North Moore St

Franklin St

Hudson St

West Broadway

Leonard St

Worth St

Harrison St

Jay St

Staple St

Greenwich St

Thomas St

Ⓜ

Duane St

7

TRIBECA

Reade St

1,2,3 Ⓜ

Church St

Chambers St

City Hall
Park

31

0 ——— 200 m

0 ——— 300 yds

© Copyright Time Out Group 2017

Warren St

North End Ave

River Terr

Park Pl W

Murray St

A,C Ⓜ   R,W Ⓜ

32

C   D   E

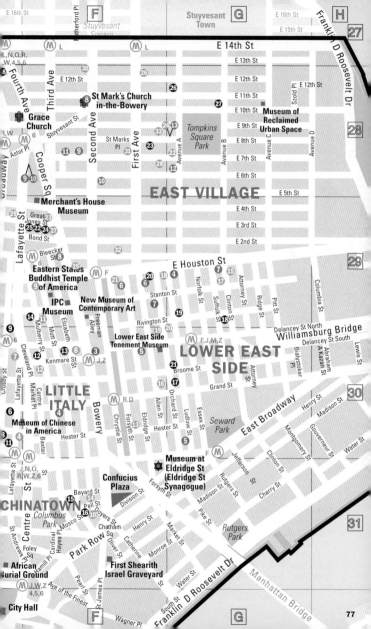

Mmuseumm

Soho & Tribeca

In the 1960s and '70s, artists colonised what had become a post-industrial wasteland south of Houston Street, squatting in abandoned warehouses. Eventually, they worked with the city to rezone and restore them. Others followed suit in the Triangle Below Canal, which was once the site of the city's main produce market. Today, those once-spartan loft spaces are among the most desirable real estate in the city. Many of the area's well-preserved factory buildings are occupied by designer stores – especially in retail mecca Soho – and high-end restaurants.

Sights & museums
Drawing Center

35 Wooster Street, between Broome & Grand Streets (1-212 219 2166, www.drawingcenter.org). Subway A, C, E, 1 to Canal Street. **Open** *noon-6pm Wed, Fri-Sun; noon-8pm Thur.* **Admission** *$5; $3 reductions; free under-12s. Free 6-8pm Thur.* **Map** *p76 E30.*

Established in 1977, the Drawing Center showcases the broadly defined art form in its three galleries. The non-profit standout assembles shows of museum-calibre legends such as Philip Guston, James Ensor and Willem de Kooning, but also 'Selections' surveys of newcomers. Art stars such as Kara Walker and Chris Ofili received some of their earliest NYC exposure here.

Mmuseumm

Cortlandt Alley, between Franklin & White Streets (no phone, www.mmuseumm.com). Subway J, N, Q, R, Z, 6 to Canal Street. **Open** *noon-6pm Sat, Sun (also May-Sept 6-9pm Thur, Fri).* **Admission** *Suggested donation $5).* **Map** *p76 E31.* Founded by a trio of indie filmmakers, this 60-square-foot repository in an abandoned Tribeca freight elevator showcases a mishmash of found objects and artefacts donated by hobbyists. Exhibits typically change annually, and have included such varied ephemera as religious objects catering to contemporary consumers (a gluten-free holy communion wafer, for example),

Le Coucou

Donald Trump-branded merchandise, fake vomit from around the world, and part of a collection charting the evolution of the coffee-cup lid, amassed by two architects. In 2015, the institution expanded with Mmuseumm 2, an even smaller shop-window space two doors down. Although Mmuseumm is only open at weekends (plus Thursday and Friday nights during the warmer months), viewers can also get a peek at the space when it's closed – look for the small peepholes in a metal door on the narrow throughway between Franklin and White Streets.

Restaurants & cafés

♥ Le Coucou $$$

138 Lafayette Street, between Canal & Howard Streets (1-212 271 4252, www.lecoucou.com). **Open** *7am-10.30am, 11.30am-2pm, 5-11pm Mon-Fri; 7am-2pm, 5-11pm Sat; 7am-2pm, 5-10pm Sun.* **Map** *p76 E30* ④ *French*
In an era of fast-casual poke and high-tech quinoa, restaurateur Stephen Starr and chef Daniel Rose did something new – by doing something old. With its vaulted ceilings, hand-blown chandeliers, gold-trimmed plates and 12-inch candles set at each table, the Chicago-born chef's lively stateside debut is more luxurious than his Parisian flagship, Spring. That's the handiwork of the Roman and Williams design company's power couple, Robin Standefer and Stephen Alesch, who've created a dreamy, grown-up dining room. Borrowing from Gallic restaurants of years past, particularly long-gone fine-dining great Lutèce, Rose is less concerned with tweaking French classics (which won him praise in Paris) than with cooking the rich-sauced fare outright: sweetbreads spooned with *crème de tomate*; airy pike quenelles in frothy sauce *américaine*; and halibut bathed in *beurre blanc*.

Dominique Ansel Bakery $

189 Spring Street, between Sullivan & Thompson Streets (1-212 219 2773, www.dominiqueansel.com). Subway C, E to Spring Street. **Open** *8am-7pm Mon-Sat; 9am-7pm Sun.* **Map** *p76 E30* ⑤ *Café*
Dominique Ansel honed his skills as executive pastry chef at Daniel

for six years before opening this innovative patisserie. In 2013, his croissant-doughnut hybrid, the Cronut, created a frenzy in foodie circles and put his ingenious creations into the spotlight. If you can't get your hands on a Cronut, which sell out early, try the DKA – a caramelised, flaky take on the croissant-like Breton speciality *kouign amann*. And his cotton-soft mini cheesecake, an ethereally light gâteau with a brûléed top, leaves the dense old New York classic sputtering in its dust.

The Dutch $$$

131 Sullivan Street, at Prince Street (1-212 677 6200, www.thedutchnyc. com). Subway C, E to Spring Street. **Open** *11.30am-3pm, 5.30-11pm Mon-Thur; 11.30am-3pm, 5.30-11.30pm Fri; 10am-3pm, 5.30-11.30pm Sat; 10am-3pm, 5.30-11pm Sun.* **Map** *p76 E29* **6** *American*
From the moment it opened, Andrew Carmellini's rollicking Soho eaterie seemed destined to join the ranks of neighbourhood classics. The virtuoso chef offers diners an exuberant gastro-tour of the American melting pot, including mini fried-oyster sandwiches on house-made buns and superb dry-aged steaks. That everything tastes good and somehow works well together explains why reservations are hard to come by. Wait for your table in the airy oak bar (with adjacent oyster room) with one of the extensive selection of American whiskeys.

Jack's Wife Freda $$

224 Lafayette Street, between Kenmare & Spring Streets (1-212 510 8550, www.jackswifefreda. com). Subway 6 to Spring Street. **Open** *8.30am-midnight Mon-Sat; 8.30am-10pm Sun.* **Map** *p76 E30* **7** *Café*
Keith McNally protégé Dean Jankelowitz (Balthazar, Schiller's

Liquor Bar) is behind this charming café. Decked out with dark-green leather banquettes, brass railings and marble counters, the classic yet cosy spot serves homey fare like Jankelowitz's grandmother's matzo ball soup made with duck fat, or skirt steak sandwich with hand-cut fries. In a prime shopping area, between Soho and Nolita, it's also a great brunch spot. **Other location** 50 Carmine Street, between Bedford & Bleecker Streets, West Village (1-646 669 9888).

Bars

Pegu Club

2nd Floor, 77 W Houston Street, at West Broadway (1-212 473 7348, www.peguclub.com). Subway B, D, F, M to Broadway-Lafayette Street; R to Prince Street. **Open** *5pm-2am Mon-Thur, Sun; 5pm-4am Fri, Sat.* **Map** *p76 E29* **3**
It's easy to miss the discreet entrance of this bar, which was inspired by a British officers' club in Burma. Once you've found it, you'll be glad you persevered. The sophisticated second-floor

destination, helmed by cocktail maven Audrey Saunders, focuses on classics culled from decades-old booze bibles. Gin is the key ingredient – these are serious drinks for grown-up tastes.

Shops & services

Soho's converted warehouses are packed with just about every major fashion brand you can think of, from budget and mid-priced international chains like H&M, COS and Topshop to A-list designer labels like Balenciaga, Chanel and Prada, plus stores selling home goods, cosmetics, food and more. Listed below is a selection of our favourite independent shops.

3x1

15 Mercer Street, between Howard & Grand Streets (1-212 391 6969, www.3x1.us). Subway A, C, E, J, N, Q, R, Z, 1, 6 to Canal Street. **Open** *11am-7pm Mon-Sat; noon-6pm Sun.* **Map** *p76 E30* ❺ *Fashion*
Denim obsessives who are always looking for the next 'It' jeans have another place to splurge: 3x1 creates entirely limited-edition styles sewn in the store. Designer Scott Morrison, who previously launched Paper Denim & Cloth and Earnest Sewn, fills the large, gallery-like space with a variety of jeans (prices start at $185 for women, $245 for men) and other denim pieces such as shorts and miniskirts. Watch the construction process take place in a glass-walled design studio in the middle of the boutique.

American Two Shot

135 Grand Street, between Crosby & Lafayette Streets (1-212 925 3403, www.americantwoshot.com). Subway J, N, Q, R, Z, 6 to Canal Street. **Open** *11am-8pm Mon-Fri; 11am-7pm Sat; noon-6pm Sun.* **Map** *p76 E30* ❻ *Fashion*

A whitewashed brick wall, neon signs and a retro collage create a cool, DIY aesthetic in this laid-back boutique for men and women owned by pals Stephanie Krasnoff and Olivia Wolfe. On the racks are indie NYC labels such as Samantha Pleet, Dusen Dusen and Rachel Antonoff (who happens to be a friend of *Girls'* Lena Dunham), plus '90s-focused vintage clothing courtesy of Babemania (www. babemania.nyc). An array of cards and small gift items at the front of the store contributes to the eclectic vibe, and you can hang out over organic juices and snacks from Brooklyn's Grass Roots Juicery.

Nili Lotan

188 Duane Street, between Greenwich & Hudson Streets (1-212 219 8794, www.nililotan.com). Subway 1, 2, 3 to Chambers Street. **Open** *11am-7pm Mon-Sat; noon-6pm Sun.* **Map** *p76 E31* ❼ *Fashion*
The sparsely hung women's garments in Israeli designer Nili Lotan's airy, all-white store and studio look like art pieces on display in a gallery. Perfectly cut, largely monochrome wardrobe staples such as silk camisoles and dresses, oversized cashmere sweaters, boy-cut trousers and crisply tailored menswear-inspired shirts appeal to minimalists with a penchant for luxury.

In the know
Neighbourhood portmanteaus

Soho and Tribeca are early examples of an NYC phenom: catchy, contracted neighbourhood names largely driven by real estate agents trying to generate buzz. Recent inventions include NoMad (North of Madison Square Park), Dumbo (Down Under the Manhattan Bridge Overpass) and even Rambo (Right Around the Manhattan Bridge Overpass).

❤ Opening Ceremony

33-35 Howard Street, between Broadway & Lafayette Street (1-212 219 2688, www.openingceremony. com). Subway J, N, Q, R, Z, 6 to Canal Street. **Open** *11am-8pm Mon-Sat; noon-7pm Sun.* **Map** *p76 E30* ❽ *Fashion*

The Olympics-referencing name reflects Opening Ceremony's multinational approach to fashion. The mega-concept store sprawls over two storefronts and four floors, with eye-catching installations and eclectic stock. The constantly rotating mix of labels veers from experimental to refined, and under-the-radar to iconic. You'll find the popular Opening Ceremony collection, including its limited-edition collaborations with other brands, and big names like Kenzo and Vans, but also some you might not recognise – for example, Adam Selman, who created sensational outfits for Rihanna before launching his own line; HVN, a line of vintage-looking print dresses designed by DJ Harley Viera-Newton, and Lorod, a classics-inspired brand. Cult shoes and accessories bump up the browse factor.

Rachel Comey

95 Crosby Street, between Prince & Spring Streets, 1-212 334 0455, www.rachelcomey.com). Subway N, R to Prince Street; 6 to Spring Street. **Open** *11am-7pm Mon-Sat; noon-6pm Sun.* **Map** *p76 E30* ❾ *Fashion*

A certain arty, indie sensibility in this NYC designer's output can be traced to her fine arts background and a stint creating stage gear for downtown bands. Comey has amassed a devoted following, and fans flock to this Soho flagship in a strikingly renovated former mechanic's garage. In addition to the complete collection of vintage-inspired women's clothing and the hugely popular footwear, the store also offers a line of unisex pieces.

Museum of Chinese in America

What Goes Around Comes Around

*351 West Broadway, between Broome & Grand Streets (1-212 343 1225, www.whatgoesaroundnyc.com). Subway A, C, E, 1 to Canal Street. **Open** 11am-8pm Mon-Sat; noon-7pm Sun. **Map** p76 E30* ❿
Fashion

A favourite among the city's fashion cognoscenti, this downtown vintage destination sells highly curated stock alongside its own retro label. Style mavens particularly recommend it for 1960s, '70s and '80s rock T-shirts, pristine Alaïa clothing and vintage fur coats.

Entertainment

Film Forum

*209 W Houston Street, between Sixth Avenue & Varick Street, Soho (1-212 727 8110, www.filmforum.org). Subway 1 to Houston Street. Tickets $14; $8 reductions. **No cards** (except for online purchases). **Map** p76 D30* ❶
Cinema

The city's leading taste-making venue for independent new releases and classic movies, Film Forum is programmed by festival-scouring staff who take their duties as seriously as a Kurosawa samurai. Born in 1970 as a makeshift screening space with folding chairs, Film Forum is still one of the few nonprofit cinemas in the United States – but thankfully its three screens are now furnished with comfortable seats.

Soho Rep

*46 Walker Street, between Broadway & Church Street, Tribeca (TheaterMania 1-212 352 3101, www.sohorep.org). Subway A, C, E, N, Q, R, W, Z, 6 to Canal Street; 1 to Franklin Street. Tickets $35-$55. **Map** p76 E31* ❷ *Theatre*

A few years ago, this Off-Off mainstay moved to an Off Broadway contract, but tickets for most shows have remained cheap. Artistic director Sarah Benson's programming is diverse and audacious: Recent productions include works by Young Jean Lee, David Adjmi, Branden Jacobs-Jenkins and the Nature Theater of Oklahoma.

Chinatown, Little Italy & Nolita

Take a walk in the area south of Broome Street and east of Broadway, and you'll feel as though you've entered a different continent. The streets of Manhattan's **Chinatown** are packed with exotic produce stands, herb emporiums, cheap jewellers, snack vendors and, of course, restaurants. As New York's largest Asian community continues to grow, it merges with neighbouring **Little Italy**. Squeezed between Chinatown's sprawl and the multiplying boutiques and hotspots of **Nolita** (North of Little Italy), the historically Italian district has long been shrinking, but you can still get a taste of the old neighbourhood in its classic (and neo-classic) cafés and red-sauce eateries.

Sights & museums

Museum of Chinese in America

*215 Centre Street, between Grand & Howard Streets (1-212 619 4785, www.mocanyc.org). Subway J, N, Q, R, Z, 6 to Canal Street. **Open** 11am-6pm Tue, Wed, Fri-Sun; 11am-9pm Thur. **Admission** $10; $5 reductions; free under-12s. Free 1st Thur of mth. **Map** p76 E30.*
Designed by prominent Chinese American architect Maya Lin,

MOCA reopened in an airy former machine shop in 2009. Its interior is loosely inspired by a traditional Chinese house, with rooms radiating off a central courtyard and areas defined by screens. The core exhibition traces the development of Chinese communities in the US from the 1850s to the present through objects, images and video. Innovative displays (drawers open to reveal artwork and documents, portraits are presented in a ceiling mobile) cover the development of industries such as laundries and restaurants in New York, Chinese stereotypes in pop culture, and the suspicion and humiliation Chinese-Americans endured during World War II and the McCarthy era. A mocked-up Chinese general store evokes the feel of these multi-purpose spaces, which served as vital community lifelines for men severed from their families under the 1882 Exclusion Act that restricted immigration. There's also a gallery for special exhibitions.

Restaurants & cafés

Black Seed $

170 Elizabeth Street, between Kenmare & Spring Streets (1-212 730 1950, www.blackseedbagels. com). Subway J, Z to Bowery. **Open** *7am-6pm daily.* **Map** *p76 F30* ⑧ *Café*

At this newfangled Nolita bagelry, from Mile End's Noah Bernamoff and the Smile impresario Matt Kliegman, the hand-rolled rounds merge two disciplines: they're honey-enhanced à la Bernamoff's native Montreal, but with an eggless, touch-of-salt bite to satisfy lifelong Gothamite Kliegman. Kettle-boiled and wood-fired, the small but mighty bagels are crowned with house-made toppings both classic (scallion cream cheese, silky cold-smoked salmon) and fanciful (salty tobiko caviar, crisp watermelon radishes). **Other locations** 176 First Avenue, between 10th & 11th Streets, East Village (1-646 484 5718); Hudson Eats, Brookfield Place, *see p73* .

Estela $$

47 E Houston Street, between Mott & Mulberry Streets (1-212 219 7693, www.estelanyc.com). Subway B, D, F, M to Broadway-Lafayette Street; 6 to Bleecker Street. **Open** *5.30pm-midnight Mon-Thur; 5.30pm-1am Fri; 11.30am-3pm, 5.30pm-1am Sat; 11.30am-3pm, 5.30pm-midnight Sun.* **Map** *p76 F29* ⑨ *American creative*

The fashionable cookie-cutter decor – exposed brick, globe lights, hulking marble bar – may suggest you've stumbled into yet another bustling rustic restaurant-cum-bar that's not worth the wait. But there's more to this Mediterranean-tinged spot than meets the eye: primarily, the talent of imaginative Uruguayan-born chef Ignacio Mattos. An ever-changing, mostly small-plates menu pivots from avant-garde towards intimate. Highlights might include beef tartare with tart

Nom Wah Tea Parlor

pickled elderberries – with a musty baseline note from fish sauce and crunchy sunchoke (Jerusalem artichoke) chips; egg with gigante beans and cured tuna; and a creamy panna cotta with honey.

Nom Wah Tea Parlor $

13 Doyers Street, between Bowery & Pell Street (1-212 962 6047, www.nomwah.com). Subway J, N, Q, R, W, Z, 6 to Canal Street; J, Z to Chambers Street. **Open** *10.30am-10pm daily.* **Map** *p76 F31* ⑩ *Chinese*

New York's first dim sum house, Nom Wah opened in 1920 and was owned by the same family for more than three decades. The current owner, Wilson Tang, has revamped it in a vintage style true to the restaurant's archival photographs. The most important tweaks, though, were behind the scenes: Tang updated the kitchen and did away with the procedure of cooking dim sum en masse. Now, each plate is cooked to order: ultra-fluffy oversized roasted-pork buns, flaky fried crêpe egg rolls and scallion pancakes. The Nolita offshoot has a fresh aesthetic with cartoon dumpling murals, white subway tiles and an open kitchen, serving some Nom Wah staples alongside more contemporary options such as a vegan noodle soup. **Other locations** 10 Kenmare Street, between Bowery & Elizabeth Street, Nolita (1-646 478 8242).

Parm $

248 Mulberry Street, between Prince & Spring Streets (1-212 993 7189, www.parmnyc.com). Subway N, R to Prince Street; 6 to Spring Street. **Open** *11.30am-10pm Mon-Thur, Sun; 11.30am-11pm Fri, Sat.* **Map** *p76 F29* ⑪ *Italian*

Mario Carbone and Rich Torrisi, two young fine-dining chefs, brought a cool-kid sheen to classic Italian sandwiches and red-sauce plates in 2010, when they debuted now-shuttered Torrisi Italian Specialties, a deli by day and haute eaterie by night. People lined up for their buzzworthy sandwiches. Although the original is no more, the superlative sandwiches, such as herb-rubbed roast turkey, classic cold cuts or chicken parmesan, are still served in these fetching diner digs and its branches. Together with partner Jeff Zalaznick, the duo now has several other restaurants, including the excellent Carbone (*see p104*). **Other locations** 250 Vesey Street, at North End Avenue, Tribeca (1-212 776 4927).

Pasquale Jones $$

187 Mulberry Street, between Kenmare & Broome Streets (no phone, www.pasqualejones.com). Subway 6 to Spring Street; J, Z to Bowery. **Open** *5.30-11pm Mon-Thur; noon-3pm, 5.30-11pm Fri, Sat; noon-3pm, 5.30-10pm Sun.* **Map** *p76 F30* ⑫ *Italian*

This pizzeria with fine-dining aspirations is a sequel to Ryan Hardy, Grant Reynolds and Robert Bohr's jaunty, wine-charged Soho spot Charlie Bird. Ambitious pies include the destination-making clam pizza, an elemental composition of juicy littlenecks, fire-roasted garlic and a whisper of cream. But Pasquale Jones also offers high-reaching mains like a gorgeous slow-roasted pork shank for two, and refreshingly out-of-the-box Italian wines served in hand-blown Zalto stems.

Spicy Village $

68B Forsyth Street, between Grand & Hester Streets (1-212 625 8299, www.spicyvillagenyc.com). **Open** *10am-11pm Mon-Sat. Subway B, D to Grand Street.* **No cards.** **Map** *p76 F30* ⑬ *Chinese*

A hole-in-the-wall temple to the cuisine of China's Henan heartland, Spicy Village is a pilgrimage site for adventurous eaters and regional cuisine purists. While the illustrated wall-mounted menu boasts noodle soups, dumplings, and, yes, soup dumplings, don't give them a second look. You're really here for the Big Tray Chicken, a red-hot plate of bone-in poultry chunks and potatoes marinated in Budweiser, MSG and a blend of chilli oil, star anise and Szechuan peppercorn. Can't stand the heat? Add an order of the house-made hand-pulled *hui mei* wheat noodles.

Xi'an Famous Foods $

45 Bayard Street, between Bowery & Elizabeth Street (no phone, www. xianfoods.com). Subway J, N, Q, R, W, Z, 6 to Canal Street. **Open** *11.30am-9pm Mon-Thur, Sun; 11.30am-9.30pm Fri, Sat.* **Map** *p76 F31* ⑭ *Chinese*

This cheap Chinese chainlet, which got the seal of approval from celebrity chef Anthony Bourdain, highlights the mouth-tingling cuisine of Xi'an, an ancient capital along China's Silk Road. Nosh on spicy noodles or a cumin-spiced burger for less than ten bucks.

Fawcett memorabilia). A garden-variety mojito is reimagined as a mini-glug of Cruzan white rum upturned into fizzy Sprite with lime and mint. Alternatively, you can help yourself to a self-service fridge stocked with beer and wine.

Bars

Genuine Liquorette

191 Grand Street, at Mulberry Street (1-646 726 4633, www. eatgenuine.com). Subway J, N, Q, R, W, Z, 6 to Canal Street; 6 to Spring Street. **Open** *6pm-midnight Tue, Wed; 6pm-2am Thur, Sat; 5pm-2am Fri.* **Map** *p76 F30* ④

Secreted beneath Little Italy burger joint Genuine Superette, Genuine Liquorette evokes a retro liquor store with a neon sign above the counter and price-marked bottles in backlit glass cabinets. The star attraction is the photogenic Cha-Chunkers, cocktails comprising soda cans with upturned mini liquor bottles perched in enlarged holes on top. Kitsch abounds (the loos are plastered with Farrah

Shops & services

Canal Street Market

265 Canal Street, between Broadway & Lafayette Street (no phone, www.canalstreet.market). Subway J, N, Q, R, W, Z, 6 to Canal Street. **Open** *11am-7pm Mon-Wed; 11am-8pm Thur-Sat; 11am-6pm Sun.* **Map** *p76 E30* ⑪ *Market*

The busy Chinatown thoroughfare is better known for tacky jewellery and souvenir shops, but the design-conscious wares at Canal Street Market are nothing less than tasteful. The sprawling white space houses nearly 30 rotating vendors selling everything from Brooklyn-made artisan chocolate and ceramics to candles hand-crafted in upstate New York. Eclectic on-site events include craft workshops,

pop-ups and exhibitions. At time of writing a mainly Asian-focused food court was in the works.

Creatures of Comfort
205 Mulberry Street, between Kenmare & Spring Streets (1-212 925 1005, www.creaturesofcomfort. us). Subway 6 to Spring Street; N, R to Prince Street. Open 11am-7pm Mon-Sat; noon-6pm Sun. Map p76 F30 *Fashion*

Jade Lai opened Creatures of Comfort in Los Angeles in 2005 and brought her cool-girl aesthetic east five years later. In the former home of the 12th police precinct, the New York store offers a similar collection of pricey, wearably nonconformist fashion. Rubbing shoulders on the racks with the eponymous house label are pieces by Lemaire, Acne Studios, A Détacher and Sofie D'Hoore, among others. Shoes and accessories – from Robert Clergerie, Woman by Common Projects, Pièce à Conviction and more – also reflect the boutique's effortless left-of-mainstream style.

Erica Weiner
173 Elizabeth Street, between Kenmare & Spring Streets (1-212 334 6383, www.ericaweiner.com). Subway C, E to Spring Street. Open noon-7pm daily. Map p76 F30 *Accessories*

Erica Weiner sells her own bronze, brass, silver and gold creations – many under $100 – alongside vintage and reworked baubles. Old wooden cabinets and stacked crates showcase rings and charm-laden necklaces, the latter dangling the likes of tiny pretzels and vintage NYC subway tokens (a quaint anachronism since the introduction of the MetroCard). Other favourites include brass ginkgo-leaf earrings and letterpress necklaces – the perfect gift for your favourite wordsmith.

McNally Jackson
52 Prince Street, between Lafayette & Mulberry Streets (1-212 274 1160, www.mcnallyjackson.com). Subway R, W to Prince Street; 6 to Spring Street. Open 10am-10pm Mon-Sat; 10am-9pm Sun. Map p76 F29 *Books & music*

This appealing indie bookstore has one of the city's most thoughtfully curated selections of non-fiction, novels, hard-to-find magazines, children's books and, most notably, poetry. The on-site café serves Stumptown coffee, organic tea and light fare. Readings and events – which have included such literary luminaries as Hari Kunzru, Martin Amis and Zadie Smith – take place in the comfortable downstairs space.

Sun's Organic Garden

79 Bayard Street, between Mott & Mulberry Streets (1-212 566 3260). Subway J, N, Q, R, W, Z, 6 to Canal Street. **Open** *10.30am-6.30pm Mon-Fri; 10.30am-5pm Sun.* **Map** *p76 F31* **⓯** *Food & drink*

Owner Lorna Lai knows tea the way a sommelier knows terroir. Curious sippers peruse the well-stocked shelves of the Hong Kong native's nook, which boasts more than a thousand jarred loose-leaf varieties from around the world, available by the ounce. Lai's house-made herbal blends are standouts, in exotic flavours like holy basil and bilberry.

Uniqulee

36 Mott Street, at Pell Street (1-212 323 2870, www.uniqulee.com). Subway J, N, Q, R, W, Z, 6 to Canal Street. **Open** *11am-8pm Mon-Thur; 11am-8.30pm Sat, Sun.* **Map** *p76 F31* **⓰** *Gifts & accessories*

Lee Chan's design store is the antithesis of Chinatown's stock-in-trade cheap gift emporiums. As the name asserts, Uniqulee focuses on one-of-a-kind finds. Vintage pieces span immaculately preserved jewellery and evening bags, an assortment of quirky key rings (including old hotel-room tags), toy soldiers, alarm clocks and classic cameras in working order. You'll also find stylish NYC-made ties and pocket squares, plus candles from Brooklyn company Apotheke.

Lower East Side

Once better known for bagels and bargains, the **Lower East Side** is now brimming with vintage and indie-designer boutiques, fashionable bars and eateries. However, development hasn't yet destroyed the character of this erstwhile centre of immigrant life. You can still explore remnants of the old Jewish neighbourhood that the Marx Brothers and George Gershwin called home, including a magnificently restored synagogue and recreated tenement apartments. The area is also home to dozens of comtemporary art galleries, such as the boundary-pushing **Canada** (333 Broome Street, between Bowery & Chrystle Street, 1-212 925 4631, www.canadanewyork. com), and **Sperone Westwater** (257 Bowery, between E Houston & Stanton Street, 1-212 999 7337, www.speronewestwater.com), which occupies a purpose-built showcase designed by starchitect Norman Foster.

Sights & museums

Lower East Side Tenement Museum

Visitors' centre, 103 Orchard Street, at Delancey Street (1-212 982 8420, www.tenement.org). Subway F to Delancey Street; J, M, Z to Delancey-Essex Streets. **Open** *Visitors' centre 10am-6.30pm Mon-Wed, Fri-Sun; 10am-8.30pm Thur. Tours See website for schedule.* **Admission** *$25; $20 reductions.* **Map** *p76 F30.*

This fascinating museum – a series of restored tenement apartments at 97 Orchard Street – is accessible only by guided tours. These start at the visitors' centre at 103 Orchard Street, and often sell out, so it's wise to book ahead. 'Hard Times' visits the homes of an Italian and a

German-Jewish clan; 'Sweatshop Workers' explores the apartments of two Eastern European Jewish families as well as a garment shop where many of the locals would have found employment; and 'Irish Outsiders' unfurls the life of the Moore family, who are coping with the loss of their child. 'Shop Life' explores the diverse retailers that occupied the building's storefronts, including a 19th-century German saloon. 'Live at the Tenement' lets you interact with actors channelling the original occupants (on select dates; see website). A new tour at 103 Orchard Street, 'Under One Roof', tells the stories of later immigrants to the neighbourhood. From mid March to December, the museum also conducts themed daily walking tours of the Lower East Side ($25-$45; $20-$40 reductions).

Museum at Eldridge Street

(Eldridge Street Synagogue)
*12 Eldridge Street, between Canal & Division Streets (1-212 219 0302, www.eldridgestreet.org). Subway F to East Broadway. **Open** 10am-5pm Mon-Thur, Sun; 10am-3pm Fri. **Admission** $14; $8-$10 reductions; free under-5s. Pay what you wish Mon. **Map** p76 F31.*

With an impressive façade that combines Moorish, Gothic and Romanesque elements, this opulent house of worship is now surrounded by dumpling shops and Chinese herb stores, but rewind about a century and you would have found delicatessens and *mikvot* (ritual bathhouses). For its first 50 years, the 1887 synagogue had a congregation of thousands and doubled as a mutual-aid society for new arrivals in need of financial assistance, healthcare and employment. But as Jews left the area and the congregation dwindled, the building fell into disrepair. A 20-year, $20-million facelift has restored its splendour; the soaring main sanctuary, designed by high-society interior decorators the Herter Brothers, features hand-stencilled walls and a resplendent stained-glass rose window with Star of David motifs. The renovations were completed in autumn 2010, with the installation of a second stained-glass window designed by artist Kiki Smith and architect Deborah Gans. The admission price includes a guided tour (see website for schedule).

New Museum of Contemporary Art

*235 Bowery, between Prince & Stanton Streets (1-212 219 1222, www.newmuseum.org). Subway F to Lower East Side-Second Avenue; J, Z to Bowery; R, W to Prince Street; 6 to Spring Street. **Open** 11am-6pm Tue, Wed, Fri-Sun; 11am-9pm Thur. **Admission** $18; $12-$15 reductions; free under-19s. Pay what you wish 7-9pm Thur. **Map** p76 F29.*

Having occupied various sites for 30 years, New York City's only contemporary art museum got its own purpose-built space in late 2007. Dedicated to emerging media and under-recognised artists, the New Mu also hosts a triennial for young talent. The seven-floor building is worth a look for the architecture alone – it's a striking, off-centre stack of aluminium-mesh-clad boxes designed by the cutting-edge Tokyo architectural firm SANAA. Two ongoing exterior installations by Chris Burden add to the drama: the artist's 36ft-high *Twin Quasi Legal Skyscrapers* (2013) perch on the roof and his 30ft-long *Ghost Ship* (2005) hangs on the façade. The museum's café is run by the folks behind the area's popular Hester Street Market, offering artisanal eats by a selection of local vendors.

Restaurants & cafés

Clinton Street Baking Company & Restaurant $$

4 Clinton Street, between E Houston & Stanton Streets (1-646 602 6263, www. clintonstreetbaking.com). Subway F to Lower East Side-Second Avenue or Delancey Street; J, M, Z to Delancey-Essex Streets. **Open** *8am-4pm, 5.30-11pm Mon-Fri; 9am-4pm, 5.30-11pm Sat; 9am-5pm Sun.* **No cards** *before 5.30pm.* **Map** *p76 G29* **15** *Café*

The warm buttermilk biscuits and fluffy plate-size pancakes at this pioneering little eatery are reason enough to face the brunch-time crowds. If you want to avoid the onslaught, the homey place is just as reliable for both lunch and dinner; drop in for the $16 beer and burger special (5.30-8pm Mon-Wed).

Dirt Candy $$

86 Allen Street, between Broome & Grand Streets (1-212 228 7732, www.dirtcandynyc.com). Subway F to Delancey Street; J, M, Z to Delancey-Essex Streets. **Open** *5.30-11pm Tue-Fri; 11am-3pm, 5.30-11pm Sat; 11am-3pm Sun.* **Map** *p76 F30* **16** *Vegetarian*

Vegetarian cuisine pioneer Amanda Cohen relocated her popular East Village restaurant to the Lower East Side with a ramped-up menu and a space three times the size of the 18-seat original. Emblazoned with a mural of greenery by graffiti artist Noah McDonough, the dining room is focused on the open kitchen at its heart, complete with a chef's counter. Each dish is anchored by one vegetable, but the chef's retooled offerings layer multiple ingredients, such as a portobello-mushroom mousse dish with sautéed Asian pears and cherries. Shareable plates include brussels-sprout tacos folded into lettuce wraps.

Ivan Ramen $$

25 Clinton Street, between E Houston & Stanton Streets (1-646 678 3859, www.ivanramen.com). Subway F to Lower East Side-Second Avenue or Delancey Street; J, M, Z to Delancey-Essex Streets. **Open** *12.30-10pm Mon-Thur, Sun; 12.30-11pm Fri, Sat.* **Map** *p76 G29* **17** *Japanese*

Ivan Orkin has never been one to play by the rulebook – the brash Long Islander first built his food-world fame 6,000 miles away in Tokyo, where he stirred up Japan's devout ramen congregation with his light, silky slurp bowls in 2007. Seven years later, he opened this narrow slip of a *ramen-ya* on the Lower East Side. The vibrant 65-seat parlour tangles together the noodle virtuoso's all-American roots and Japanophile leanings – a massive papier-mâché mural in front features a kaleidoscope of Dolly Parton, John Wayne, waving lucky cats and Technicolor geishas. Along with his seminal rye-flour noodles (in a choice of broth, including *shio* and *shoyu* varieties), the menu features specials that frequently cross cultures.

Wildair $$

142 Orchard Street, between Delancey & Rivington Streets (1-646 964-5624, www.wildair.nyc). Subway F to Delancey Street; J, M, Z to Delancey-Essex Streets. **Open** *6-11pm Tue-Thur; 6-11.30pm Fri, Sat.* **Map** *p76 G30* **20** *American*

The 45-seat restaurant is a sister to chef Jeremiah Stone and pastry chef Fabian von Hauske's understated avant-garde tasting-menu den, Contra (138 Orchard Street, 1-212 466 4633), two doors down. Wildair is even more relaxed, with sardine-packed bar tables and neighbourhood affability. And though Wildair's snacky à la carte menu has less sharp-edged experimentation than Contra's, there are low-key innovations

💙 Old-school delis

There are few things more synonymous with the city than the New York deli, serving dishes from the classic Jewish canon: corn-beef sandwiches, bagels with lox and cream cheese, matzo ball soup, chopped liver and other 'appetising' delicacies. The granddaddy of them all is cavernous, cafeteria-style **Katz's Delicatessen** (205 E Houston Street, at Ludlow Street, 1-212 254 2246, www.katzsdelicatessen.com, open 8am-10.45pm Mon-Wed, 8am-2.45am Thur, 8am-10.45pm Fri, Sun, *map p76 F29* 18) opened in 1888. You might get a kick out of the famous faces plastered to the panelled walls, or the spot where Meg Ryan faked it in *When Harry Met Sally...*, but the real stars are the thick-cut pastrami sandwiches and crisp-skinned all-beef hot dogs – the latter still less than five bucks.

Smoked-fish specialist **Russ & Daughters** debuted a café (127 Orchard Street, between Delancey & Rivington Streets, 1-212 475 4881, www.russanddaughterscafe. com, open 10am-10pm Mon-Fri; 8am-10pm Sat, Sun, *map p76 F30* 19) in its centennial year. The space takes design cues from the original shop a few blocks away, with tiled floors, clean-lined booths and back-lit art deco signage advertising 'pickles from the barrel' and 'egg cream'. There are some significant upgrades from the average old-school deli, however. Seltzer water is dispensed free of charge, but there's also a full bar and you can pair your schmaltz (fat) herring with a shot of vodka. Open-faced sandwich boards, such as the

Shtetl, which pairs melt-in-your-mouth sable with decadent goat's-milk cream cheese on a bagel or bialy, let you sample some of the store's famous fish.

Another much-loved family-run old timer, **Barney Greengrass** (*see p151*) was established in 1908, but has occupied its current Upper West Side location since 1929. And from the looks of it, the wallpaper dates from some two decades later. The self-styled 'Sturgeon King' combines two classic flavours with its pastrami salmon – cured fish with a sharp, peppery edge.

at play here. The simple bistro pleasure of breakfast radishes with soft-churned sweet butter are smacked with the briny funk of seaweed, and beef tartare is sultry with smoke courtesy of a haze of hardwood-kissed cheddar, with Brazil nuts adding pops of crunch. Entrée-size options are well-executed – a fat-bordered for-two Wagyu beef with charred Padrón peppers and shallots – but lack the brainy tick of the small plates.

Yonah Schimmel Knish Bakery $

*137 E Houston Street, between Eldridge & Forsyth Streets (1-212 477 2858, www. yonahschimmelknish.com). Subway F to Lower East Side-Second Avenue. **Open** 9.30am-7pm daily (extended hours in summer). **Map** p76 F29* 21 *Bakery/café*

Born from the namesake rabbi's pushcart, this neighbourhood stalwart has been doling out its carb-laden goodies since 1910. More than a dozen rotating varieties are available, including blueberry, chocolate-cheese and 'pizza', but traditional potato, kasha and spinach knishes are the most popular.

Bars

❤ Attaboy

*134 Eldridge Street, between Broome & Delancey Streets (no phone). Subway F to Delancey Street; J, M, Z to Delancey-Essex Streets. **Open** 6pm-4am daily. **Map** p76 F30* 5

Occupying the former location of Milk & Honey, the seminal cocktail den opened by late mixology pioneer Sasha Petraske, Attaboy is run by alums Sam Ross and Michael McIlroy. The tucked-away haunt is lighter and livelier than its forebear, but has kept the same bespoke protocol:

at the brushed-steel bar, drinks slingers stir off-the-cuff riffs to suit each customer's preference. Nostalgic boozers can seek solace in Petraske-era standard-bearers, like Ross's signature Penicillin, a still-inspiring blend of single-malt whisky, honey-ginger syrup and lemon.

❤ Bar Goto

*245 Eldridge Street, between E Houston & Stanton Streets (1-212 475 4411, www.bargoto. com). Subway F to Lower East Side-Second Avenue. **Open** 5pm-midnight Tue-Thur, Sun; 5pm-2am Fri, Sat. **Map** p76 F29* 6

When a sake-and-spirits temple with a Pegu Club-pedigreed barkeep lands on the Lower East Side, there's no avoiding the chorus of cocktail-geek fanfare to follow. Yet take a seat at Kenta Goto's glimmering black-and-gold boîte, lodged away from the Houston Street bedlam, and you'll find the noisy hype storm is curtailed by cool poise, from the hostess's graceful reception to silent servers weaving through tables. In the absence of distractions, focus directs to the well-lit bar, where Goto effortlessly stirs his Far East-whispered creations, drawing on his Japanese heritage as much as his lauded tenure at Audrey Saunders's cocktail trailblazer.

Suffolk Arms

*269 E Houston Street, at Suffolk Street (1-212 475 0400, www. suffolkarms.com). Subway F to Delancey Street. **Open** 5pm-3am Mon-Thur, Sun; 5pm-4am Fri, Sat. **Map** p76 G29* 7

There's hardly a name in New York's bar scene more polarising than Giuseppe González. The Bronx-born, Cornell-educated barman has worked behind the stick everywhere from Julie Reiner's Flatiron Lounge to Audrey

Saunders's Pegu Club to his own short-lived PKNY. With his sharp wit and sharper tongue, González has a straight-shooting MO that is, according to those who've worked with him, an acquired taste. It's no surprise, then, that this highly personal Lower East Side project, taking decor cues from humble English pubs (namely, the Churchill Arms in London), aims to make cocktail culture more accessible than ever for the average drinker while simultaneously challenging industry norms through both drink and design.

Shops & services

The Cast
*72 Orchard Street, between Broome & Grand Streets (1-212 228 2020, www.thecast.com). Subway B, D to Grand Street; F to Delancey Street; J, M, Z to Delancey-Essex Streets. **Open** noon-8pm Mon-Sat; noon-6pm Sun. **Map** p76 G30* ⓱ *Fashion*
Pass through an outpost of London Jewellery company the Great Frog to access this rock 'n' roll-inspired collection, focused on the trinity of well-cut denim, superior leather jackets based on classic motorcycle styles, and the artful T-shirts that launched the label in 2004. The shop caters to a range of budgets – the Terminal line of jackets for men and women starts at $395, but you'll pay at least $1,500 for a bespoke leather made in NYC. Supple skirts, trousers and a range of accessories are also available, plus vintage boots and records.

David Owens Vintage Clothing
*161 Rivington Street, between Clinton & Suffolk Streets (1-212 677 3301). Subway F to Lower East Side-Second Avenue. **Open** 11am-7pm daily. **Map** p76 G29* ⓲ *Fashion*

Unlike many vintage stores that traffic in 1980s and '90s garb, David Owens's eponymous boutique carries items exclusively from the '40s to the '70s. The space is stuffed to the gills with rare and unique pieces, such as a '30s printed dress with the original store tags attached and a '60s clutch made to look like a rolled-up *Harper's Bazaar* magazine. Men will find just as many interesting items, including pin-up girl ties and leather motorcycle jackets.

Edith Machinist
*104 Rivington Street, between Essex & Ludlow Streets (1-212 979 9992, www.edithmachinist.com). Subway F to Delancey Street; J, M, Z to Delancey-Essex Streets. **Open** noon-6pm Mon, Fri, Sun; noon-7pm Tue-Thur, Sat. **Map** p76 G29* ⓳ *Fashion/accessories*
An impeccable, eclectic assemblage of leather bags, shoes and accessories is the main draw of this vintage trove, but you'll also find a whittled-down collection of clothes, including a small men's section.

Russ & Daughters
*179 E Houston Street, between Allen & Orchard Streets (1-212 475 4880, www.russanddaughters. com). Subway F to Lower East Side-Second Avenue. **Open** 8am-8pm Mon-Fri; 8am-7pm Sat; 8am-5.30pm Sun. **Map** p76 F29* ⓴ *Food & drink*
The daughters in the name have given way to great-grandchildren, but this Lower East Side institution (established 1914) is still run by the same family. Specialising in smoked and cured fish and caviar, it sells about a dozen varieties of smoked salmon, eight types of herring (pickled, salt-cured, smoked and so on) and many other Jewish-inflected Eastern European delectables.

Filled bagels like the amazing Super Heebster (whitefish and baked salmon salad, horseradish cream cheese and wasabi flying-fish roe) are available to take away, but a new café (*see p91*) offers a more extensive menu and table service.

Tictail Market

90 Orchard Street, at Broome Street (1-917 388 1556, www.tictail.com). Subway F to Delancey Street; J, M, Z to Delancey-Essex Streets. **Open** *noon-9pm Mon-Sat; noon-6pm Sun.* **Map** *p76 G30* ㉑ *Fashion & accessories*

The bricks-and-mortar offshoot of the global online marketplace showcases a rotating selection of goods by independent designers and artists from around the world. Find everything from designed-in-NYC clothing to hand-crafted jewellery and limited-edition prints in the airy, laid-back space with weathered wooden and tiled floors and a tin ceiling.

Tictail Market

Entertainment

❤ Bowery Ballroom

6 Delancey Street, between Bowery & Chrystie Street, Lower East Side (1-212 260 4700, www. boweryballroom.com). Subway B, D to Grand Street; J, Z to Bowery; 6 to Spring Street. **Box office** *at Mercury Lounge (see right). Tickets $15-$35.* **Map** *p76 F30* ❸ *Live music*

Bowery Ballroom is probably the best venue in the city for seeing indie bands, either on the way up or holding their own. But it also brings in a diverse range of artists from home and abroad, and you can expect a clear view and bright sound from any spot in the venue. The spacious downstairs lounge is a great place to hang out between sets.

Mercury Lounge

217 E Houston Street, between Essex & Ludlow Streets, Lower East Side (1-212 260 4700, www. mercuryloungenyc.com). Subway F to Lower East Side-Second Avenue. **Box office** *noon-6 pm Thur-Sat. Tickets $8-$20.* **Map** *p76 G29* ❹ *Live music*

The unassuming, boxy Mercury Lounge is an old standby, with solid sound and sightlines (and a cramped bar in the front room). There are multiple band bills most nights, although they can seem stylistically haphazard and set times are often later than advertised. (It's a good rule of thumb to show up half an hour later than you think you should.) Some of the bigger shows sell out in advance; young hopefuls from years gone by to take the stage here include Mumford & Sons.

🖤 Metrograph

7 Ludlow Street, between Canal & Hester Streets, Lower East Side (1-212 660 0312, www.metrograph. com). Subway B, D to Grand Street; F to East Broadway. Tickets $15; $12 reductions. **Map** *p76 G30* ⑤ *Cinema*

Founded in 2016 by filmmaker and designer Alexander Olch, this retro-chic bi-level movie house has two theatres outfitted with comfortable seats fashioned out of reclaimed wood from Williamsburg's old Domino Sugar Refinery. And they're reserved at purchase, eliminating the need to arrive early to nab your preferred spot. The complex also contains a film bookstore and a posh candy shop. Upstairs, a full-service restaurant, the Commissary (featuring a menu inspired by Hollywood's old-time studio cafeterias), serves breakfast, lunch and dinner, plus a late-night menu. It also has two bars. But more important is the standout programming, which includes inspired retrospectives and imaginatively framed series.

🖤 Rockwood Music Hall

196 Allen Street, between E Houston & Stanton Streets, Lower East Side (1-212 477 4155, www. rockwoodmusichall.com). Subway F to Lower East Side-Second Avenue. **Open** *6pm-3am Mon-Fri; 3pm-3am Sat, Sun. Tickets free-$15 (1-drink minimum per set).* **Map** *p76 F29* ⑥ *Live music*

The cramped quarters are part of this club's appeal: there are no bad seats (or standing spots) in the house. You can catch multiple acts every night of the week on three separate stages, and it's likely that many of those performers will soon be appearing in much bigger halls. Multi-genre polymath Gabriel Kahane is a regular, as is bluegrass great Michael Daves.

Slipper Room

167 Orchard Street, at Stanton Street, Lower East Side (1-212 253 7246, www.slipperroom. com). Subway F to Lower East Side-Second Avenue. Shows vary Mon, Sun; 9pm Tue; 8pm, 10pm Wed; 8pm, 10pm, midnight Thur; 9.30pm, 10.30pm, midnight, 1am Fri, Sat. **Admission** *$10-$25.* **Map** *p76 F29* ❼ *Burlesque*

After being closed for extensive renovations for more than two years, the Slipper Room reopened with a better sound system, new lighting and a mezzanine, among other swank touches, and reclaimed its place as the city's premier burlesque venue. Among the jam-packed weekly schedule are such long-running shows as Mr. Choade's Upstairs Downstairs (which began in 1999).

East Village

The area east of Broadway between Houston and 14th Streets has a long history as a countercultural hotbed. From the 1950s to the '70s, St Marks Place (8th Street, between Lafayette Street & Avenue A) was a hangout for artists, writers, radicals and musicians. The grungy strip still fizzes with energy well into the wee hours, but these days it's packed with cheap eateries, tattoo parlours and shops selling T-shirts, tourist junk and pot paraphernalia. In **Tompkins Square Park**, which dates from 1834, bongo beaters, guitarists, multi-pierced teenagers, hipsters, local families and vagrants mingle. The entire area has a lively food and drink scene, and chic shops and restaurants have taken up residence on Bond and Great Jones Streets in the enclave also known as Noho.

Restaurants & cafés

Big Gay Ice Cream Shop $

125 E 7th Street, between First Avenue & Avenue A (1-212 533 9333, www.biggayicecream.com). Subway L to First Avenue. **Open** *1-10pm Mon-Thur, Sun; 1-11pm Fri, Sat (varies seasonally).* **Map** *p76 G28* ㉒ *Ice-cream*

Ice-cream truckers Doug Quint and Bryan Petroff now have two bricks-and-mortar shops in NYC, dispensing their quirky soft-serve creations. Toppings run the gamut from cayenne pepper to bourbon-butterscotch sauce, or opt for one of the signature combos like the Salty Pimp (vanilla ice-cream, dulce de leche, sea salt and chocolate dip) or the Bea Arthur (vanilla ice-cream, dulce de leche and crushed Nilla wafers). **Other locations** 61 Grove Street, at Seventh Avenue South, West Village (1-212 414 0222); 353 West 14th Street, between Eighth & Ninth Avenues, Meatpacking District (1-646 678 3231).

Bowery Market $

348 Bowery, between Great Jones & 4th Streets (no phone, www. theborerymarket.com). Subway B, D, F, M to Broadway-Lafayette Street; 6 to Bleecker Street. **Open** *10am-midnight daily (varies seasonally).* **Map** *p76 F29* ㉓ *Eclectic*

On the site of a defunct auto-body shop, this all-day, rain-or-shine outdoor marketplace features food vendors in corrugated-iron shacks. Choose from Italian-sandwich shop Alidoro; the Butcher's Daughter, serving health-minded fare like breakfast burritos, rice bowls and fresh-pressed juice; Mexican canteen Pulqueria, offering tacos and piña coladas; *nigiri* operation Sushi on Jones; and Greenpoint favourite Champion Coffee, pouring hot and iced coffees, teas and speciality drinks.

Crif Dogs $

113 St Marks Place, between First Avenue & Avenue A (1-212 614 2728, www.crifdogs.com). Subway L to First Avenue; 6 to Astor Place. **Open** *noon-2am Mon-Thur, Sun; noon-4am Fri, Sat.* **Map** *p76 G28* ㉔ *American*

You'll recognise this place by the giant hot dog outside, bearing the come-on 'Eat me'. Crif offers the best New Jersey-style dogs this side of the Hudson: handmade smoked-pork tube-steaks that are deep-fried until they're bursting out of their skins. While they're served in various guises, among them the Spicy Redneck (wrapped in bacon and covered in chilli, coleslaw and jalapeños), we're partial to the classic with mustard and kraut. If you're wondering why there are so many people hanging around near the public phone booth at night, it's because there's a trendy cocktail bar, PDT (*see p101*), concealed behind it.

DBGB Kitchen & Bar $$

299 Bowery, at E Houston Street (1-212 933 5300, www.dbgb. com/nyc). Subway B, D, F, M to Broadway-Lafayette Street; 6 to Bleecker Street. **Open** *5-11pm Mon-Thur; noon-1am Fri; 11am-1am Sat; 11am-11pm Sun.* **Map** *p76 F29* ㉕ *French*

This big, buzzy brasserie – chef Daniel Boulud's most populist venture – stands out for its kitchen-sink scope. Several kinds of sausage, from Thai-accented to Tunisienne, are served alongside burgers, offal and haute bistro fare. The best way to get your head around the schizophrenic enterprise is to bring a large group and try to sample as much of the range as possible, including ice-cream sundaes or sumptuous cakes for dessert.

Hearth $$

403 E 12th Street, at First Avenue (1-646 602 1300, www.restauranthearth.com). Subway L to First Avenue. **Open** *6-10pm Mon-Thur; 6-11pm Fri; 11am-2.30pm, 6-11pm Sat; 11am-3pm, 6-10pm Sun.* **Map** *p76 F28* ㉖ *American*

Upscale yet relaxed, Hearth skirts food trends with a hearty, health-conscious menu that includes offal, broths, grains and a substantial list of seasonal vegetables. Look for Italian-leaning main courses like beef-and-ricotta meatballs, polenta with pecorino, and whole roasted wild or sustainably grown fish. There is a small hearth in the restaurant, but the real warmth comes from the staff, who takes pains in helping you pick the right dish and are equally interested in finding out afterwards what you thought of it.

Il Buco Alimentari & Vineria $$

53 Great Jones Street, between Bowery & Lafayette Street (1-212 837 2622, www.ilbucovineria.com). Subway B, D, F, M to Broadway-Lafayette Street; 6 to Bleecker Street. **Open** *8am-11pm Mon-Thur; 8am-midnight Fri; 9am-midnight Sat; 9am-11pm Sun.* **Map** *p76 F29* ㉗ *Italian*

Il Buco has been a mainstay of the downtown dining scene since the 1990s and a pioneer in the sort of rustic Italian food now ubiquitous in the city. Owner Donna Lennard took her sweet time (18 years, to be exact) to unveil her first offshoot, Il Buco Alimentari & Vineria. It was worth the wait: the hybrid bakery, food shop, café and trattoria is as confident as its decades-old sibling, with sure-footed service, the familial bustle of a neighbourhood pillar, and heady aromas of wood-fired short ribs and salt-crusted fish drifting from an open kitchen. If you like the rustic style of the restaurants, you can purchase Italian hand-blown glass, artisan-made kitchenware and vintage finds from the retail shop Il Buco Vita. **Other locations** Il Buco, 47 Bond Street, between Bowery & Lafayette Street, East Village (1-212 533 1932); Il Buco Vita, 2nd floor, 51 Bond Street, between Bowery & Lafayette Street, East Village (1-917 946 3085).

Kyo Ya $$$

94 E 7th Street, between First Avenue & Avenue A (1-212 982 4140). Subway 6 to Astor Place. **Open** 6-11pm Tue-Sat; 6-10pm Sun. **Map** p76 F28 ㉓ *Japanese*
This ambitious Japanese speakeasy is marked only by an 'Open' sign, but in-the-know diners still find their way inside. The food, presented on beautiful handmade plates, is gorgeous: *maitake* mushrooms are fried in the lightest tempura batter and delivered on a polished stone bed. Sushi is pressed with a hot iron on to sticky vinegar rice. The few desserts are just as ethereal as the savoury food.

Lafayette $$

380 Lafayette Street, at Great Jones Street (1-212 533 3000, www.lafayetteny.com). Subway B, D, F, M to Broadway-Lafayette Street; 6 to Bleecker Street. **Open** 8am-10.30pm Mon-Wed; 8am-11pm Thur-Sat; 8am-10pm Sun. **Map** p76 E29 ㉙ *French*
Ace culinary crew Andrew Carmellini, Josh Pickard and Luke Ostrom – the winning team behind

---

In the know
Spin the Alamo

Astor Place is marked by a steel cube that has sat on a traffic island by the entrance to the 6 train since 1968. With a little elbow grease, the cube, whose proper title is *Alamo*, will spin on its axis.

---

blockbusters Locanda Verde and the Dutch – followed up with this souped-up, all-day French bistro, marking Carmellini's return to his Francophile roots (exemplified by runs at Café Boulud and Lespinasse). The changing menu focuses on the country's rustic south. In the spacious, mahogany-floored eaterie, a zinc-hooded rotisserie twirls roast chicken, while an in-house bakery churns out Provençal staples like *pain de campagne*, and pretty people gab over their niçoise salads. While some dishes fail to excite, it's a solid choice for brunch.

Momofuku Ssäm Bar $$

207 Second Avenue, at 13th Street (no phone, www.momofuku. com). Subway L to First or Third Avenue; L, N, Q, R, W, 4, 5, 6 to 14th Street-Union Square. **Open** 11.30am-3.30pm, 5pm-midnight Mon-Thur, Sun; 11.30am-3.30pm, 5pm-1am Fri, Sat. **Map** p76 F28 ㉚ *Korean*
Chef David Chang has gone from East Village rebel to awards-circuit veteran, piling up accolades and expanding his empire across the city. Ssäm Bar, his second modern Asian restaurant, shares the pared-down wood decor and utilitarian seating as its nearby predecessor, Momofuku Noodle Bar. Try the wonderfully fatty pork-belly steamed bun with hoisin sauce and cucumbers, or one of the ham platters. But you'll need to come with a crowd to sample the house speciality, *bo ssäm* (a slow-roasted pork shoulder that is consumed wrapped in lettuce leaves, with a dozen oysters and other accompaniments); it serves six to ten people and must be ordered in advance. Across the street at Momofuku Milk Bar (251 E 13th Street, at Second Avenue, 1-347 577 9504, www.milkbarstore. com) pastry wizard Christina Tosi conjures up inventively homey

St Marks Place

sweets such as Crack Pie (toasted oat crust with an addictively buttery filling) and Cereal Milk soft serve ice cream.

Oiji $$

119 First Avenue, between 7th Street & St Marks Place (1-646 767 9050, www.oijinyc.com). Subway 6 to Astor Place. **Open** *6-10.30pm Mon-Thur; 6-11.30pm Fri, Sat; 5-10pm Sun.* **Map** *p76 F28* ③① *Korean*
Honey-buttered potato crisps are just one of the instantly craveable takes on cultish South Korean junk food at Oiji, helmed by fine-dining vets Brian Kim and Tae Kyung Ku. Craggy Korean fried chicken is reborn as arguably the most ethereal chicken cutlet ever, trading grease traps of batter for a delicately crisp tapioca coating.

Prune $$

54 E 1st Street, between First & Second Avenues (1-212 677 6221, www.prunerestaurant.com). Subway F to Lower East Side-Second Avenue. **Open** *5.30-11pm Mon-Fri; 10am-3.30pm, 5.30-11pm Sat, Sun.* **Map** *p76 F29* ③② *American creative*

Tiny, well-lit Prune is still as popular as it was the day it opened. Gabrielle Hamilton's French mother developed this fearless chef's palate early on. Expect creative dishes like Manila clams with hominy and smoked paprika butter, and rack of lamb with fried mint, fried aubergine (eggplant) and fresh feta. This is the area's go-to brunch spot, so beware: the wait for a table can stretch over an hour.

Superiority Burger $

430 E 9th Street, between Avenue A & First Avenue (1-212 256 1192, www.superiorityburger.com). Subway L to First Avenue. **Open** *11.30am-10pm Mon, Wed, Thur-Sun.* **Map** *p76 F28* ③③ *Vegetarian*
In a white-tiled slip of an East Village eatery, former James Beard Award-winning Del Posto pastry great and erstwhile punk-rock drummer Brooks Headley offers his uberpopular veggie burger. Tofu cabbage wraps, vegetarian sloppy joes and gelato are also on the menu, but seating is in short supply.

Bars

Ghost Donkey

4 Bleecker Street, between Bowery & Elizabeth Street (1-212 254 0350, www.ghostdonkey.com). Subway B, D, F, M to Broadway-Lafayette Street; F to Lower East Side-Second Avenue; 6 to Bleecker Street. **Open** *5pm-2am daily.* **Map** *p76 F29* ⑧

This Latin-spirited cocktail haunt straddles the line between speakeasy and dive bar. For the sliver of a bar – festooned with red lights that cast a glow over everything – head barmen Nacho Jimenez and Eben Freeman have built a menu that emphasises mescal but isn't committed to the liquor. Instead it touches on stuff like Nicaraguan rum and tiger-nut *horchata*, and yes, some of the creations are served in ceramic donkey cups. The standout cocktail is the namesake El Burro Fantasma, a for-two option that packs a punch of mescal and chilli, soothed slightly with pink grapefruit and Aperol. The proper accompaniment to the bar's cocktails is a hefty portion of haute nachos, in varieties like cojito cheese with black truffles or chorizo with tripe.

Jimmy's No.43

43 E 7th Street, between Second & Third Streets (1-212 982 3006, www.jimmysno43.com). Subway F to Lower East Side-Second Avenue; 6 to Astor Place. **Open** *2pm-2am Mon-Thur; 1pm-4am Fri, Sat; 1pm-midnight Sun.* **Map** *p76 F28* ⑨

You could easily miss this worthy subterranean spot if it weren't for the sign painted on a doorway over an inconspicuous set of stairs. Descend them and you'll encounter mismatched wooden tables, burnt-yellow walls displaying taxidermy and medieval-style arched passageways that lead to different rooms. Beer is a big attraction here, with about a dozen quality selections on tap (and more in the bottle). A short menu of changing bar eats (burgers, tacos, seasonal vegetables) is also available.

Mayahuel

304 E 6th Street, between First & Second Avenues (1-212 253 5888, www.mayahuelny.com). Subway F to Lower East Side-Second Avenue; 6 to Astor Place. **Open** *6pm-2am daily.* **Map** *p76 F28* ⑩

Tequila and its cousin, mezcal, are the focus at this haute cantina. The inventive cocktail menu features Green Gloves, a spicy mix of jalapeño-infused tequila blanco, green chartreuse, celery and lime; and the smoky but sweet Ron's Dodge Charger, made with *chile de árbol*-infused mescal, pineapple, agave nectar and smoked salt. The craftsmanship in the drinks is equalled in the shareable Mexican snacks and small plates, such as popcorn dolled up with cotija cheese, ancho chilli and lime.

McSorley's Old Ale House

15 E 7th Street, between Second & Third Avenues (1-212 473 9148, https://mcsorleysoldalehouse. nyc). Subway F to Lower East Side-Second Avenue. **Open** *11am-1am Mon-Sat; 1pm-1am Sun.* **No cards.** **Map** *p76 F28* ⑪

Ladies should probably leave the Blahniks at home. In traditional Irish-pub fashion, McSorley's floor has been thoroughly scattered with sawdust to take care of the spills and other messes that often accompany the consumption of large quantities of cheap beer. Established in 1854, McSorley's became an institution by remaining steadfastly authentic and providing only two options: McSorley's Dark Ale and McSorley's Light Ale. A fascinating cast of characters has raised a glass here, from Tammany Hall politicians to purported regular Harry Houdini (look for his handcuffs above the bar).

❤ Mother of Pearl

95 Avenue A, at 6th Street (1-212 614 6818, www.motherofpearlnyc. com). Subway F to Lower East Side-Second Avenue. **Open** *5pm-2am Mon-Thur; 3pm-2am Fri, Sat.* **Map** *p76 G28* ⑫

Ravi DeRossi (Death & Co) recruited longtime cohort Jane Danger (the NoMad) to rehash the throwback pours shaped by 1940s tiki culture. Without a single standard-issue offering on the menu – no mai tais here – Mother of Pearl is a postmodern Polynesian affair. The Shark Eye plays on a Demerara dry float, swapping the usual rum for curaçao and bourbon in a novelty ceramic shark's head cup. The cosy teal-and-white den is rife with time-warp nods to the Pacific isles, including retro floral-patterned banquettes, hand-carved totem pole stools and mother-of-pearl light fixtures. The effect is somewhat dreamlike, enhanced by a lo-fi pop soundtrack ranging from the Velvet Underground to St. Vincent.

PDT

113 St Marks Place, between First Avenue & Avenue A (1-212 614 0386, www.pdtnyc.com). Subway L to First Avenue; 6 to Astor Place. **Open** *6pm-2am Mon-Thur, Sun; 6pm-3am Fri, Sat.* **Map** *p76 G28* ⑬

The word is out about 'Please Don't Tell', the faux speakeasy inside gourmet hot dog joint Crif Dogs (*see p97*), so it's a good idea to reserve a booth in advance. Once you arrive, you'll notice people lingering outside an old wooden phone booth near the front. Slip inside, pick up the receiver and the host opens a secret panel to the dark, narrow space. The serious cocktails surpass the gimmicky entry: try the house old-fashioned, made with bacon-infused bourbon, which leaves a smoky aftertaste.

Shops & services

❤ Dear: Rivington

37 Great Jones Street, between Bowery & Lafayette Street (1-212 673 3494, www.dearrivington.com). Subway B, D, F, M to Broadway-Lafayette; 6 to Bleecker Street. **Open** *11am-7pm Mon-Sat; noon-6pm Sun.* **Map** *p76 F29* ㉒ *Fashion*

A utilitarian white space provides a stage for Moon Rhee and Hey Ja Do's installation-like displays, incorporating industrial furniture, manufacturing relics and other curios. Hanging on an assortment of period rolling racks, the duo's own line of one-of-a-kind garments is interspersed with select pieces by the likes of Comme des Garçons and Yohji Yamamoto; the Dear label combines a Japanese minimalist aesthetic with Victorian and 1950s influences, often incorporating salvaged trimmings like beaded collars and lace. Pristine vintage handbags and accessories are scattered around the store and arranged in old display cases. The lower level showcases contemporary ceramics, antique furnishings and decorative objects.

Fun City Tattoo

94 St Marks Place, between First Avenue & Avenue A (1-212 353 8282, www.funcitytattoo.com). Subway R, W to 8th Street-NYU; 6 to Astor Place. **Open** *noon-10pm daily.* **No cards.** **Map** *p76 F28* ㉓ *Tattoo parlour*

Jonathan Shaw started inking locals from his apartment in the mid-1970s (when tattooing was illegal) before opening this store in the 1990s. The legendary figure has retired, but his New York City institution – which has served the likes of Johnny Depp, Jim Jarmusch, Dee Dee Ramone and Sepultura's Max Cavalera – continues its operations. Fun City's artists can do most anything, from lettering and Japanese to American traditional.

The Future Perfect

55 Great Jones Street, between Bowery & Lafayette Street (1-212 473 2500, www.thefutureperfect.com). Subway 6 to Bleecker Street. **Open** *10am-7pm Mon-Fri; noon-5pm Sat.* **Map** *p76 F29* ❷ *Homewares*

Championing avant-garde interior design, this innovative store specialises in artist-made, limited-edition and one-of-a-kind pieces. The Future Perfect is the exclusive US stockist of Dutch designer Piet Hein Eek's elegant woodwork and pottery, but it also showcases local talent. Look out for beautifully simple hand-thrown and -glazed bowls by Jason Miller and spare gold jewellery and branching metal light fixtures by Lindsey Adelman.

Great Jones Spa

29 Great Jones Street, at Lafayette Street (1-212 505 3185, www. greatjonesspa.com). Subway 6 to Astor Place. **Open** *9am-10pm daily.* **Map** *p76 F29* ❷ *Health & beauty*

Harnessing the wellbeing-boosting properties of water, Great Jones is outfitted with a popular wet lounge complete with subterranean pools, saunas, steam rooms and a three-and-a-half-storey waterfall. Access to the 15,000sq ft paradise is complimentary with spa services over $100 – treat yourself to a divinely scented body scrub, a massage or one of the many indulgent packages. Alternatively, a three-hour pass costs $55.

Obscura Antiques & Oddities

207 Avenue A, between 12th & 13th Streets (1-212 505 9251, www. obscuraantiques.com). Subway L to First Avenue. **Open** *noon-8pm Mon-Sat; noon-7pm Sun.* **Map** *p76 G28* ❷ *Gifts & souvenirs/ homewares*

Housed inside a former funeral home, this eccentric shop, immortalised in a Science Channel reality TV series, specialises in bizarre items like medical and scientific antiques, human skulls and taxidermied animals dating from the 19th century. Owners Evan Michelson and Mike Zohn scour flea markets, auctions and even museums for rare artefacts such as jarred piranhas, 1920s decorative 'boudoir dolls' and a mummified cat.

Rue St Denis

170 Avenue B, between 10th & 11th Streets (1-212 260 3388, www. ruestdenis.com). Subway L to First Avenue. **Open** *noon-8pm Mon-Fri; noon-7.30pm Sat, Sun.* **Map** *p76 G28* ❷ *Fashion*

Jean-Paul Buthier searches the US and Europe for unworn dead-stock garb, from long-closed factories and stores. Film, TV and Broadway costume departments frequently source pieces here. Menswear is the speciality – the back room is filled with pristine suits from the 1950s to the '90s, organised by era – but ladies will also find plenty to ogle.

❤ Strand Book Store

828 Broadway, at 12th Street (1-212 473 1452, www.strandbooks. com). Subway L, N, Q, R, W, 4, 5, 6 to 14th Street-Union Square. **Open** *9.30am-10.30pm Mon-Sat; 11am-10.30pm Sun.* **Map** *p76 E28* ❷ *Books & music*

Established in 1927, the Strand has a mammoth collection of more than two million discount volumes (both new and used), and the store is made all the more daunting by its chaotic, towering shelves and sometimes crotchety staff. You can find just about anything here, from that out-of-print Victorian book on manners to the kitschiest of sci-fi pulp. Note that the rare book room upstairs closes at 6.15pm. There's a seasonal Strand kiosk on the edge of Central Park at Fifth Avenue and 60th Street (Apr-Dec 10am-dusk, weather permitting).

Obscura Antiques & Oddities

Entertainment

Danspace Project

*St Mark's Church in-the-Bowery,
131 E 10th Street, at Second Avenue,
East Village (information 1-212 674
8112, tickets 1-866 811 4111, www.
danspaceproject.org). Subway L
to Third Avenue; 6 to Astor Place.
Tickets free-$25. **Map** p76 F28* 8
Dance

A space is only as good as its
executive director, and Judy
Hussie-Taylor has injected new
life into Danspace's programming
by creating the Platform series,
in which artists curate seasons
based on a particular idea.
Moreover, the space itself – a
high-ceilinged sanctuary – is
very handsome. Ticket prices are
reasonable, making it easy to take
a chance on unknown work.

Joe's Pub

*Public Theater, 425 Lafayette
Street, between Astor Place & E
4th Street, East Village (1-212 967
7555, www.joespub.com). Subway
R, W to 8th Street-NYU; 6 to Astor
Place. **Box office** 2-6pm Mon, Sun;
2-7.30pm Tue-Sat. Tickets $15-$50
($12 food or 2-drink minimum).
Map p76 F28* 9 *Live music*

One of the city's premier small
spots for sit-down audiences,
Joe's Pub brings in impeccable
talent of all genres and origins.
While some well-established
names play here, Joe's also lends
its stage to up-and-comers (this
is where Amy Winehouse made
her US debut), drag acts and
cabaret performers (Justin Vivian
Bond is a mainstay). The food
menu – a mix of snacks, shareable
plates and main courses – has
been revitalised by prominent
chef Andrew Carmellini.

❤ Public Theater

*425 Lafayette Street, between Astor
Place & 4th Street, East Village
(1-212 539 8500, tickets 1-212 967
7555, www.publictheater.org).
Subway R, W to 8th Street-NYU; 6
to Astor Place. **Box office** 2-6pm
daily. Tickets $15-$95. **Map** p76
F28* 10 *Theatre*

Under the guidance of the civic-
minded Oskar Eustis, this local
institution – dedicated to producing
the work of new American
playwrights, but also known
for its Shakespeare in the Park
productions – has regained its place
at the forefront of the Off Broadway
world. The ambitious, multicultural
programming ranges from new
works by major playwrights to the
annual Under the Radar festival for
emerging artists. The company's
home building, a renovated Astor
Place landmark, has five stages.

Greenwich Village & West Village

Anchored by **New York University**, **Greenwich Village**, along with its western adjunct the **West Village**, is one of the most picturesque parts of the city. The stomping ground of the Beat Generation is no longer a cheap-rent bohemian paradise, but it's still a pleasant place for idle wandering, dining in excellent restaurants and hopping between bars, jazz clubs and cabaret venues. Great for people-watching, **Washington Square Park** attracts a disparate cast of characters that takes in hippies, students, chess players and street musicians. The Washington Arch, a modestly sized replica of Paris's Arc de Triomphe built in 1895 to honour George Washington, leads to the park's large central fountain. The **Meatpacking District**, which since the 1980s has evolved from gritty industrial zone to gay cruising spot to hedonistic consumer playground, has a flashier feel. It's also the starting point for the hugely popular **High Line** elevated park, and the 2015 opening of the **Whitney Museum** has brought a welcome injection of culture to the neighbourhood.

Restaurants & cafés

Blue Hill $$$

75 Washington Place, between Washington Square West & Sixth Avenue (1-212 539 1776, www. bluehillfarm.com). Subway A, B, C, D, E, F, M to W 4th Street. **Open** *5-11pm Mon-Sat; 5-10pm Sun.* **Map** *p76 E28* ㉞ *American creative*
More than a mere crusader for sustainability, Dan Barber is also one of the most talented cooks in town, building his menu around whatever's at its peak on the family farm in Great Barrington, Massachusetts, and the not-for-profit Stone Barns Center for Food and Agriculture in Westchester, New York (home to a sibling restaurant), among other suppliers. The tastefully understated dining room is tucked discreetly on the lower level of a townhouse just off Washington Square Park. Choose from the ever-changing four-course daily menu or six-course tasting menu. The evening may begin with a sophisticated seasonal spin on a pig's liver terrine and move on to a sweet slow-roasted parsnip 'steak' with creamed spinach and beet ketchup, or grass-fed lamb. Wine pairings are available.

Caffe Reggio $

119 MacDougal Street, at W 3rd Street (1-212 475 9557, www. caffereggio.com). Subway A, B, C, D, E, F, M to W 4th Street. **Open** *9am-3am Mon-Thur, Sun; 9am-4am Fri, Sat.* **Map** *p76 E29* ㉟ *Café*
Legend has it that the original owner of this classic café introduced Americans to the cappuccino in 1927 and, apart from its acquired patina, we bet the interior hasn't changed much since then. Although it's traded in the coal-fuelled espresso machine for a sleeker Caffe Sacco model, you can still admire the old custom chrome-and-bronze contraption on the bar. Sip espresso and tuck into a house-made tiramisu under the Italian Renaissance-style paintings.

❤ Carbone $$$

181 Thompson Street, between Bleecker & Houston Streets (no phone, www.carbonenewyork. com). Subway C, E to Spring Street. **Open** *noon-2pm, 5.30-11.30pm Mon-Fri; 5-11.30pm Sat, Sun.* **Map** *p76 E29* ㊱ *Italian*
Red sauce revivalists Rich Torrisi and Mario Carbone honour Gotham's legendary Italian joints

💙 High Line

1-212 500 6035, www.thehighline. org. **Open** *usually 7am-10pm daily (hours vary seasonally; see website for updates).* **Map** *p76 C28.*

Originally a freight-bearing railway stretching from 34th Street to Spring Street, the High Line fell into disuse after World War II as trucks replaced trains. A southern chunk was torn down beginning in the 1960s, and, after the last train ground to a halt in 1980, local property owners lobbied for its destruction. However, thanks to the efforts of railroad enthusiast Peter Obletz and, later, the Friends of the High Line, the industrial relic was saved and transformed into an elevated public park.

Running from Gansevoort Street in the Meatpacking District to 34th Street and Eleventh Avenue, the slender, sinuous green strip was designed by landscape architects James Corner Field Operations and architects Diller Scofidio + Renfro. As well as trees, flowers and landscaped greenery, the High Line has several interesting features along the way, plus a programme of public art. Commanding an expansive river

view, the 'sun deck' between 14th and 15th Streets has wooden deck chairs on the original tracks, plus a water feature with benches for cooling your feet. From around late April until late October, you can stop for a glass of wine at open-air café **Terroir** at the Porch. Nearby, the promenade cuts through the former loading dock of the old Nabisco factory, now home to the shops and restaurants of Chelsea Market (chelseamarket. com).

As you head north, look out for the Empire State Building to the east. After cutting through Chelsea's gallery district, the park skirts under-construction complex Hudson Yards, which over the next few years will be populated with gardens, a cultural centre, restaurants and retailers, including a Neiman Marcus department store. Opening late 2018, the Spur, a block-long section extending over the avenue at 30th Street contains the park's largest open space. It features the High Line Plinth, inspired by the Fourth Plinth in London's Trafalgar Square and showcasing temporary art installations.

(Rao's, Bamonte's) with their high-profile revamp of historic Rocco's Ristorante. Suave, tuxedo-clad waiters – Bronx accents intact, but their burgundy threads designed by Zac Posen – tote an avalanche of complimentary extras: chunks of chianti-infused parmesan, olive-oil-soaked 'Grandma Bread' and slivers of smoky prosciutto. Follow updated renditions of classic pasta, such as a spicy, über-rich rigatoni vodka, with mains like sticky cherry-pepper ribs and lavish takes on tiramisu for dessert.

❤ High Street on Hudson $$

*637 Hudson Street, at Horatio Street (1-917 388 3944, www. highstreetonhudson.com). Subway A, C, E to 14th Street; L to Eighth Avenue. **Open** 8am-10pm Mon-Thur, Sun; 8am-10.30pm Fri, Sat. **Map** p76 C28* ③⑦ *American*

Bread is no mere afterthought at High Street on Hudson, the day-to-night sibling to chef Eli Kulp and Ellen Yin's lauded Philadelphia restaurant, High Street on Market. Beautiful loaves – potent New World ryes, hearty German-style *vollkornbrot*, and *anadama miche* enriched with molasses – are for sale, along with equally great baked goods, near the venue's street-facing windows. In the morning, a buttery biscuit, popping with black pepper and subdued with sage, hugs a cloud-soft egg, malted sausage and melty aged cheddar in the kitchen's gorgeous send-up of a breakfast sandwich. The lunch menu's grilled cheese is served on doorstop slabs of roasted potato bread. When the lights dim, sandwiches and pastries make way for composed dishes spotlighting local produce and, naturally, grains. Charred rutabaga is pureed into a smooth-as-silk houumos, while soured grains lend a fermented funk to a dish of Long Island duck.

Kesté Pizza & Vino $$

*271 Bleecker Street, between Cornelia & Jones Streets (1-212 243 1500, www.kestepizzeria. com). Subway 1 to Christopher Street-Sheridan Square. **Open** 11.30am-11pm Mon-Thur; 11.30am-11.30 pm Fri, Sat; 11.30am-10.30pm Sun. **Map** p76 D29* ③⑧ *Pizza*

If anyone can claim to be an expert on Neapolitan pizza, it's Kesté's Roberto Caporuscio: as president of the US branch of the Associazione Pizzaiuoli Napoletani, he's the top dog for the training and certification of *pizzaioli*. At his intimate, 40-seat space, it's all about the crust – blistered, salty and elastic, it could easily be eaten plain. Add ace toppings such as sweet-tart San Marzano tomato sauce, milky mozzarella and fresh basil, and you have one of New York's finest pies. **Other locations** 77 Fulton Street, between Cliff & Gold Streets, Financial District (1-212 693 9030).

Num Pang Sandwich Shop $

*28 E 12th Street, between Fifth Avenue & University Place (1-646 791 0439, www.numpangnyc.com). Subway L, N, Q, R, W, 4, 5, 6 to 14th Street-Union Square. **Open** 11am-9pm Mon-Sat; noon-8pm Sun. **Map** p76 E28* ③⑨ *Cambodian*

At this small shop, the rotating varieties of *num pang* (Cambodia's answer to the Vietnamese *banh mi*) include pulled *duroc* pork with spiced honey, peppercorn catfish, and roasted cauliflower, each stuffed into crusty baguettes. There's limited seating, so if you can't find a space at the counter, get it to go and eat in Union or Washington Square Park. **Other locations** throughout the city.

💜 Whitney Museum of American Art

99 Gansevoort Street, between Washington & West Streets (1-212 570 3600, www.whitney. org). Subway A, C, E to 14th St; L to Eighth Avenue. **Open** *10.30am-6pm Mon, Wed-Thur, Sun; 10.30am-10pm Thur, Fri.* **Admission** *$25; $18 reductions; free under-19s. Pay what you wish 7-10pm Fri.* **Map** *p76 C28.*

Founded by sculptor and art patron Gertrude Vanderbilt Whitney in 1931, the Whitney Museum of American Art holds more than 22,000 works created by around 3,000 American artists during the 20th and 21st centuries, including Willem de Kooning, Edward Hopper, Jasper Johns, Georgia O'Keeffe and Claes Oldenburg. In 2015, the institution moved into a nine-storey, steel-and-glass building designed by Renzo Piano, roughly three times the size of its old Upper East Side premises. Now there's plenty of space to showcase selections from the permanent collection, including such iconic works as Alexander Calder's *Circus* and Jasper Johns' *Three Flags*, alongside temporary shows such as the prestigious and controversial Whitney Biennial, held in odd-numbered years.

An 8,500-square-foot public plaza beneath the High Line leads to the cantilevered glass entrance. Inside, you'll find a ground-floor restaurant helmed by dining guru Danny Meyer (plus a café with seasonal outdoor seating on the eighth floor) and a free-admission lobby gallery. Four elevators, commissioned from Richard Artschwager before his death in 2013, have a dual function as passenger lifts and an art installation, entitled *Six in Four,* using six themes that have featured in the artist's work since the 1970s – door, window, table, basket, mirror and rug.

The art isn't restricted to the museum's interior. The dramatic, asymmetrical structure features a series of outdoor terraces that rise like steps above the High Line. On the fifth, sixth and seventh floors you can take in alfresco sculptures and installations while admiring views of the Hudson River and city landmarks, including the Empire State Building and 1 World Trade Center.

RedFarm $

529 Hudson Street, between Charles & W 10th Streets (1-212 792 9700, www.redfarmnyc.com). Subway 1 to Christopher Street-Sheridan Square. **Open** *5-11.45pm Mon-Fri; 11am-2.30pm, 5-11.45pm Sat; 11am-2.30pm, 5-10pm Sun.* **Map** *p76 D28* ⓴ *Chinese*

The high-end ingredients and whimsical plating at Ed Schoenfeld's interpretive Chinese restaurant have helped to pack the dining room since opening night. Chef Joe Ng is known for his dim sum artistry, including Katz's pastrami-stuffed egg rolls and shrimp dumplings decorated with 'eyes' and pursued on the plate by a sweet-potato Pac-Man.

Spotted Pig $$

314 W 11th Street, at Greenwich Street (1-212 620 0393, www.thespottedpig.com). Subway A, C, E to 14th Street; L to Eighth Avenue. **Open** *noon-2am Mon-Fri; 11am-2am Sat, Sun.* **Map** *p76 D28* ⓵ *Eclectic*

With a creaky interior that recalls an ancient pub, this Anglo-Italian hybrid from Ken Friedman and James Beard Award-winning chef April Bloomfield is still hopping more than a decade after opening. The gastropub doesn't take reservations and a wait can always be expected. The burger is a must-order: a secret blend of ground beef grilled rare, covered with gobs of pungent roquefort and accompanied by a tower of shoestring fries tossed with rosemary. Bloomfield's predilection for offcuts, in dishes like the crispy pig's ear salad, helped usher in the city's pork-and-offal era.

▶ *There's more offal-inspired cuisine by April Bloomfield at White Gold Butchers, see p154.*

Stumptown Coffee Roasters $

30 W 8th Street, at MacDougal Street (1-855 711 3385, www.stumptowncoffee.com). Subway A, B, C, D, E, F, M to W 4th Street. **Open** *7am-8pm daily.* **Map** *p76 E28* ⓶ *Café*

The lauded Portland, Oregon, outfit expanded its New York holdings – which include a branch inside the Ace Hotel (*see p190*) – with this stand-alone café. The wood-panelled counter and old-fashioned cabinetry nod to classic coffee houses, but purists can savour single-origin espresso from a La Marzocco GS3 machine and slow brews prepared via java-geek speciality drips like Chemex pour-overs, ceramic filter-cone Bee House drippers or a siphon vacuum brewer. The low-key hangout offers the chain's full line of around ten seasonal coffees, plus pastries and sandwiches.

Via Carota $$

51 Grove Street, between Bleecker Street & Seventh Avenue South (no phone, www.viacarota.com). Subway 1 to Christopher St-Sheridan Square. **Open** *11am-midnight Mon-Wed, Sun; 11am-1am Thur-Sat.* **Map** *p76 D28* ⓷ *Italian*

The soulful Italian plates served at this glass-fronted gastroteca, the first joint effort from chef power couple Jody Williams and Rita Sodi, prove that simple food can be anything but basic. Pastas are satisfying but safe – what really stands out is *verdure*. The seasonally changing selection might include fuss-free provincial stunners such as *barbabietola*, a toss of tender beets and pickled apples flecked with fragrant thyme and tangy pebbles of goat's-milk feta. You can make an excellent meal here on vegetable dishes alone, but then you'd miss out on the house *svizzerina*, a bunless, hand-chopped round of New York

Chumley's

strip steak that arrives flash-seared and nearly naked, save a few husk-on garlic cloves and a salty, rosemary-licked pool of fat. The chefs operate with an unflappable disregard for 'cool' that nearly borders on subversive – the knick-knacky room is garnished with more bowls of fruit than a Nancy Meyers movie kitchen.

Bars

Chumley's

86 Bedford Street, between Barrow & Grove Streets (1-212 675 2081, chumleysnewyork.com). Subway 1 to Christopher Street-Sheridan Square. **Open** *5.30-10pm Mon-Thur; 5.30-10.30pm Fri, Sat.* **Map** *p76 D29* ⓮

Behind a heavy, unmarked wooden door – the same one that once welcomed New York literati like William Faulkner, ee cummings and Edna St Vincent Millay – lies the landmark speakeasy that social activist Leland Stanford Chumley opened back in 1922. Following a chimney collapse in 2007, the bar was in limbo for the better part of a decade before Sushi Nakazawa restaurateur Alessandro Borgognone partnered with longtime owner Jim Miller and revamped the historic space. Brown-spirit cocktails are as cosy as the dimly lit, wood-panelled environs. The Basement of Thieves is a pretty-in-purple froth of a drink that offsets the peppery kick of Cutty Sark Prohibition whiskey with crème de violette, sweet blackberry and a shake of egg white. Even the food touts the bar's history: a towering double cheeseburger stacked with crispy shallots and smeared with bone marrow, is dubbed the 86'd Burger, after lore that the term was born at Chumley's. Police would warn bartenders to '86' drunken guests through the front entrance – 86 Bedford Street – before coming through the alley door during Prohibition-era raids.

Stonewall Inn

53 Christopher Street, at Waverly Place (1-212 488 2705, www. thestonewallinnnyc.com). Subway 1 to Christopher Street-Sheridan Square. **Open** *2pm-4am daily.* **Map** *p76 D28* ⓯

This National Historic Landmark is the site of the 1969 gay rebellion against police harassment, and has since become a cultural bastion for the community. Special nights range from dance soirées and drag shows to burlesque performances and bingo gatherings.

White Horse Tavern

567 Hudson Street, at 11th Street (1-212 989 3956). Subway 1 to Christopher Street-Sheridan Square. **Open** *11am-1.30am Mon-Thur, Sun; 11am-3am Fri, Sat.* **No cards.** *Map p76 D28* ⑯

Popular lore tells us that in 1953, Dylan Thomas knocked back 18 straight whiskies here before expiring in his Chelsea Hotel residence – a portrait of him now hangs in the middle room, above his favourite table in the corner. Now the old-school bar and its adjacent outdoor patio play host to a yuppie crowd and clutches of tourists, drawn by the outdoor seating, a fine selection of beers – and the legend.

Shops & services

Aedes Perfumery

7 Greenwich Avenue, between Christopher & 10th Streets (1-212 206 8674, www.aedes.com). Subway A, B, C, D, F, M to W 4th Street; 1 to Christopher Street-Sheridan Square. **Open** *noon-8pm Mon-Sat; 1-7pm Sun.* **Map** *p76 D28* ㉙ *Health & beauty*

Decked out like a 19th-century boudoir, this perfume collector's den devotes itself to ultra-sophisticated fragrances and high-end skincare lines, such as Diptyque, Santa Maria Novella and its own glamorously packaged range of fragrances, candles and room sprays. Hard-to-find scents, such as Serge Lutens perfumes, line the walls.

CO Bigelow Chemists

414 Sixth Avenue, between 8th & 9th Streets (1-212 533 2700, www. bigelowchemists.com). Subway A, B, C, D, F, M to W 4th Street; 1 to Christopher Street. **Open** *7.30am-9pm Mon-Fri; 8.30am-7pm Sat; 9am-5pm Sun.* **Map** *p76 D28* ㉚ *Health & beauty*

Established in 1838, Bigelow is the oldest apothecary in the US. Its appealingly old-school line of toiletries includes such tried-and-trusted favourites as Mentha Lip Shine, Rose Salve and Bay Rum After-Shave Balm. The spacious, chandelier-lit store is packed with natural and homeopathic remedies, organic skincare products and drugstore essentials – and the place still fills prescriptions.

Doyle & Doyle

412 W 13th Street, between Ninth Avenue & Washington Street (1-212 677 9991, www.doyledoyle.com). Subway A, C, E to 14th Street; L to Eighth Avenue. **Open** *noon-7pm Mon-Wed, Fri-Sun; noon-8pm Thur.* **Map** *p76 C28* ㉛ *Accessories*

Whether your taste is art deco or nouveau, Victorian or Edwardian, Elizabeth and Irene Doyle are bound to have that one-of-a-kind piece you're looking for, including engagement and eternity rings. The gemologist sisters, who specialise in vintage and antique jewellery, have also launched their own collection of new heirlooms.

Murray's Cheese

254 Bleecker Street, between Sixth & Seventh Avenues (1-212 243 3289, www.murrayscheese.com). Subway A, B, C, D, E, F, M to W 4th Street. **Open** *8am-9pm Mon-Sat; 9am-7pm Sun.* **Map** *p76 D29* ㉜ *Food & drink*

In the know
Dylan's village

Bob Dylan resided at 94 MacDougal Street (on a row of historic brownstones near Bleecker Street) through much of the 1960s, performing in Washington Square Park and at clubs such as **Café Wha?** (www.cafewha.com) and the **Bitter End** (www.bitterend.com).

💜 Greenwich Village jazz joints

Greenwich Village was already an established bohemian bastion when jazz clubs began to take root in the 1930s, including the city's first integrated nightclub, Café Society. It was here that Billie Holiday debuted the haunting anti-lynching ballad *Strange Fruit* in 1939. Café Society was only in operation for a decade, but there are several old-school joints in the neighbourhood that are still jumpin' today.

Promoter Max Gordon opened the legendary **Village Vanguard** (178 Seventh Avenue South, at Perry Street, 1-212 255 4037, www. villagevanguard.com, *map p76 D28* ⑯) in 1935, and ran it until his death in the '80s. Initially featuring an eclectic roster of folk and blues, Gordon made the switch to heavier jazz bills in the late '50s. The hallowed room welcomed the likes of Miles Davis, Cecil Taylor and Bill Evans. You can catch glimpses of the venue's history on the walls, which are covered with black and white photos, as you settle in for one of the intimate daily shows. Staples include Grammy Award-winning Vanguard Jazz Orchestra, which has performed on Mondays since 1966.

A relatively recent arrival on the Village jazz scene, **Smalls** (183 W 10th Street, between Seventh Avenue South & W 4th Street, 1-646 476 4346, www. smallslive.com, *map p76 D28* ⑮) convincingly channels an old-school hole-in-the-wall jazz joint in its cosy, bare-bones basement space. The booking also skews retro, yet not stubbornly so. You'll hear classic hardbop as well as more adventurous, contemporary approaches. During the week, the cover charge also gains you admittance to nearby **Mezzrow**, another intimate subterranean room, outfitted with a gleaming Steinway piano.

Established in 1981, **Blue Note** (131 W 3rd Street, between MacDougal Street & Sixth Avenue, Greenwich Village, 1-212 475 8592, www.bluenote.net, *map p76 E29* ⑪) spotlights jazz titans such as Roy Hargrove, Cassandra Wilson and Chick Corea. An extensive dinner and late-night menu enhances the daily performances, while the Sunday brunch series is one of the best show deals in the city ($35 including food and one drink).

For the last word in curd, New Yorkers have been flocking to Murray's since 1940 to sniff out the best international and domestic cheeses. The helpful staff will guide you through hundreds of stinky, runny, washed-rind and aged comestibles.

Rag & Bone
*425 W 13th Street, at Washington Street (1-212 249 3331, www.rag-bone.com). Subway A, C, E to 14th Street. **Open** 10am-8pm Mon-Sat; 11am-7pm Sun. **Map** p76 C27* ❸❸ *Fashion*

This large downtown outpost of the enduringly hip brand, which began as a denim line in 2002, was once a meat factory, and it retains much of that industrial vibe, with unfinished concrete floors, brick walls and an original Dave's Quality Veal sign. Sip a latte from the in-store Jack's Stir Brew Coffee before or after browsing the impeccably cut jeans, classic T-shirts, luxurious knitwear and well-tailored jackets for men and women. **Other locations** throughout the city.

Entertainment

🖤 Comedy Cellar
*117 MacDougal Street, between Bleecker Street & Minetta Lane, Greenwich Village (1-212 254 3480, www.comedycellar.com). Subway A, B, C, D, E, F, M to W 4th Street. Shows 7.30pm, 9.30pm, 11.30pm Mon-Thur, Sun; 7pm, 8.45pm, 10.30pm, 12.15am Fri, Sat. **Admission** $14-$24 (2-item minimum). **Map** p76 E29* ❶❷ *Comedy*

Claustrophobes, beware: it gets crowded down here, especially at weekends, thanks to the immense popularity of this Village standby. Big names from Louis CK to Aziz Ansari may drop by for a set, and on any given night you can expect to see local greats whose acts are more X-rated than at other clubs (and who will distract you from your bachelorette-partying neighbours). **Other location** Comedy Cellar at the Village Underground, 130 W 3rd Street, between Sixth Avenue & MacDougal Street, Greenwich Village (1-212 777 7745).

IFC Center
*323 Sixth Avenue, at W 3rd Street, Greenwich Village (1-212 924 7771, www.ifccenter.com). Subway A, B, C, D, E, F, M to W 4th Street. Tickets $15; $10-$11 reductions. **Map** p76 D29* ❶❸ *Cinema*

In 2005, the long-darkened 1930s Waverly was reborn as a five-screen arthouse cinema, showing the latest indie hits, along with choice midnight cult items and occasional foreign classics. You may come face to face with the directors or the actors on the screen, as many introduce their work on opening night and stick around for post-screening Q&As.

Le Poisson Rouge
*158 Bleecker Street, at Thompson Street, Greenwich Village (1-212 505 3474, www.lepoissonrouge.com). Subway A, B, C, D, E, F, M to W 4th Street. **Box office** 5pm-close daily. Tickets free-$40 **Map** p76 E29* ❶❹ *Live music*

Tucked into the basement of the long-gone Village Gate, a legendary performance space that hosted everyone from Miles Davis to Jimi Hendrix, this cabaret-style space was opened in 2008 by a group of young music enthusiasts with ties to both the classical and the indie rock worlds. The booking policy reflects both camps, often on a single bill. A wide range of great music might span a feverish Saharan guitarist (Bombino), noisy art-rock luminaries (Deerhoof) or young classical stars (pianist Simone Dinnerstein).

Rockefeller Center

Midtown

Soaring office towers, crowded pavements and taxi-choked streets – that's the image most people have of the busy midsection of Manhattan. The area between 14th and 59th Streets is home to some of the city's best-known landmarks, including iconic skyscrapers like the Empire State Building and the Chrysler Building, the dazzling electronic spectacle that is Times Square, and Rockefeller Center with its picturesque seasonal ice-skating rink. Fifth Avenue, the dividing line between Midtown West and Midtown East, is continuously clogged with shoppers from all over the world. More residential neighbourhoods such as the Flatiron District, Hell's Kitchen and Murray Hill offer worthwhile restaurants and shops.

Best sights

Empire State Building (*p135*), the city's emblematic skyscraper. Gulliver's Gate (*p129*), the whole world in miniature.

Time-travel tipples

Speakeasy-style Raines Law Room (*p125*). Traditional tavern Old Town Bar (*p125*). Fine & Rare (*p142*) for nightcaps with live jazz.

Essential culture

Ars Nova (*p133*) for innovative multidisciplinary fare. Chelsea gallery district (*p119*), with hundreds of art spaces. Broadway theatre (*p130*), from long-running musicals to contemporary drama. Comedy sketch shows with starry guests at Upright Citizens Brigade Theatre (*p120*).

Best restaurants

The classic Grand Central Oyster Bar & Restaurant (*p141*). Eleven Madison Park (*p123*) for progressive tasting menus in a grand art deco dining room. Contemporary haute-Mexican cuisine at Cosme (*p122*). Don Antonio by Starita (*p131*) for pedigree pizza.

Best shops

Stylish eight-floor emporium ABC Carpet & Home (*p125*). Atmospheric vintage trove Mantiques Modern (*p118*). Classic department store Bergdorf Goodman (*p136*). Delightfully old-fashioned JJ Hat Center (*p138*). Fine and Dandy for dapper gents' accessories (*p132*).

Must-see museum

Museum of Modern Art (*p137*) for 20th-century masterpieces, film and more.

Chelsea

The corridor between 14th and 29th Streets west of Sixth Avenue emerged as the nexus of New York's gay life in the 1990s, though it's since been eclipsed by **Hell's Kitchen** to the north. Chelsea's cityscape shifts from leafy side streets lined with pristine 19th-century brownstones to an eclectic array of striking industrial and contemporary architecture on the far west side. In recent years, the local buzz has shifted to the previously neglected Hudson-hugging strip that has evolved into the city's main gallery district. The **High Line** (*see p105*) snakes through this area.

Sights & museums

Museum at FIT

Building E, Seventh Avenue, at 27th Street (1-212 217 4558, www.fitnyc. edu/museum). Subway 1 to 28th Street. **Open** *noon-8pm Tue-Fri; 10am-5pm Sat.* **Admission** *free.* **Map** *p116 D26.*
The Fashion Institute of Technology owns one of the largest and most impressive clothing collections in the world, with some 50,000 garments and accessories dating from the 18th century to the present. Under the directorship of fashion historian Dr Valerie Steele, the museum showcases a rotating selection from the permanent collection, and hosts a programme of temporary exhibitions focusing on individual designers or spotlighting fashion from cultural angles.

Rubin Museum of Art

150 W 17th Street, at Seventh Avenue (1-212 620 5000, www. rmanyc.org). Subway A, C, E to 14th Street; L to Eighth Avenue; 1 to 18th Street. **Open** *11am-5pm Mon, Thur; 11am-9pm Wed; 11am-10pm Fri; 11am-6pm Sat, Sun.* **Admission** *$15; $10 reductions; free under-13s. Free 6-10pm Fri.* **Map** *p116 D27.*

Dedicated to the art of the Himalayan region, the Rubin is a very stylish museum – a fact that falls into place when you learn that the six-storey space was once occupied by fashion store Barneys. The ground-floor Indian- and Tibetan-inflected café used to be the accessories department, and retail lives on in the colourful gift shop. In the galleries, rich-toned walls are classy foils for the serene statuary and intricate, multicoloured textiles. Rotating selections from the permanent collection of more than 3,000 pieces from the second century to the present day are highlighted in 'Gateway to Himalayan Art'. A recreation of a Tibetan Buddhist shrine room lets visitors see sculptures, paintings, textiles, furnishings and ritual objects in context. The Rubin's temporary shows often extend beyond the museum's primary focus to contemporary art and photography.

Restaurants & cafés

Cookshop $$

156 Tenth Avenue, at 20th Street (1-212 924 4440, www. cookshopny.com). Subway C, E to 23rd Street. **Open** *8am-11pm Mon-Fri; 10am-11pm Sat; 10am-10pm Sun.* **Map** *p116 C27* ❶ *American creative*

Chef Marc Meyer and his wife Vicki Freeman want their restaurant to be a platform for sustainable ingredients from independent farmers. True to this mission, the ingredients are consistently top-notch, and the menu changes daily. While organic ingredients alone don't guarantee a great meal, Meyer knows how to let the flavours speak for themselves, and Cookshop scores points for getting the house-made ice-cream to taste as good as Ben & Jerry's. The buzzing art world favourite is always packed for its excellent weekend brunch.

Empire Diner $

210 Tenth Avenue, at 22nd Street (1-212 335 2277, www.empire-diner. com). Subway C, E to 23rd Street. **Open** *8am-1am daily.* **Map** *p116 C26* ❷ *American*

This iconic 1940s Fodero dining car – immortalised by Woody Allen in the 1979 movie *Manhattan* – has changed hands several times in recent years. Inside the restored vintage digs, chef John DeLucie serves classic American cuisine, including macaroni and cheese with Black Diamond cheddar and parmesan breadcrumbs, a double-patty burger with herbed French fries, and sourdough-pretzel fried chicken with chilli-mustard sauce.

Bars

The Eagle

554 W 28th Street, at Eleventh Avenue (1-646 473 1866, www. eaglenyc.com). Subway C, E to 23rd Street. **Open** *10pm-3am Mon; 10pm-4am Mon-Sat; 5pm-4am Sun.* **No cards.** **Map** *p116 C26* ❶

You don't have to be a kinky leather daddy to enjoy this manly spot, but it certainly doesn't hurt. The gay fetish bar is home to an array of beer blasts, foot-worship fêtes and leather soirées, plus simple pool playing and cruising nights. Thursdays are gear night, so be sure to dress the part or you might not get past the doorman. In summer, the rooftop is a surprising oasis.

Half King

505 W 23rd Street, between Tenth & Eleventh Avenues (1-212 462 4300, www.thehalfking.com). Subway C, E to 23rd Street. **Open** *11am-4am Mon-Fri; 9am-4am Sat, Sun.* **Map** *p116 C26* ❷

Don't let their blasé appearance fool you – the creative types gathered at the yellow pine bar in this unpretentious pub are probably as excited as you are to catch a glimpse of the part-owner, author Sebastian Junger. While you're waiting, order one of the 15 draught beers – including several local brews – or a seasonal cocktail.

Sid Gold's Request Room

165 W 26th Street, between Sixth & Seventh Avenues (1-212 229 1948, www.sidgolds.com). Subway C, E to 23rd Street; 1 to 28th Street. **Open** *5pm-2am Mon-Fri; 7pm-1am Sat, Sun.* **Map** *p116 D26* ❸

The campy joint effort of Beauty Bar proprietor Paul Devitt and Loser's Lounge founder (and Psychedelic Furs ivory tickler) Joe McGinty, Sid's has the kind of downtown clout that draws New York notables (Parker Posey, Andrew Rannells), without the velvet-rope snootiness. Instead, a pink-bow-tied gent cheerfully ushers you through the velvet curtains separating the tamer front bar from the razzly-dazzly clubhouse in the back, an anything-goes sanctuary of Hemingway daiquiris and Celine Dion belt-alongs. At 9pm nightly (except for Fridays, when Happy Hour Karaoke starts at 6pm) game guests flip through karaoke-style songbooks, decamp from lowly lit half-moon booths and take to the stage, accompanied by a pianist on a Baldwin baby grand. The bar's Monday-night series brings in a rotating cast of performers.

Mantiques Modern

Shops & services

❤ Mantiques Modern

146 W 22nd Street, between Sixth & Seventh Avenues (1-212 206 1494, www.mantiquesmodern. com). Subway 1 to 23rd Street. **Open** *10.30am-6.30pm Mon-Fri; 11am-7pm Sat, Sun.* **Map** *p116 D26* ❶ *Gifts & souvenirs/ homewares*

Walking into this two-level shop is like stumbling on the private collection of a mad professor. Specialising in industrial and modernist art, objects, furnishings and accessories from the 1880s to the 1980s, it's a fantastic repository of beautiful and bizarre items, from kinetic sculptures and early 20th-century wooden artists' mannequins to a Soviet World War II telescope. Pieces by famous designers like Hermès sit side by side with natural curiosities. Skulls (in metal or Lucite), crabs, animal horns and robots are recurring themes.

Printed Matter

231 Eleventh Avenue, at 26th Street (1-212 925 0325, www. printedmatter.org). Subway C, E to 23rd Street; 7 to 34th Street-Hudson Yards. **Open** *11am-7pm Mon-Wed, Sat; 11am- 8pm Thur, Fri; noon-6pm Sun.* **Map** *p116 B26* ❷ *Books & music*

This non-profit organisation is devoted to artists' books – from David Shrigley's deceptively naïve illustrations to provocative photographic self-portraits by Matthias Herrmann. Works by little-known talents share shelf space with those by veterans such as Yoko Ono and Edward Ruscha.

Story

144 Tenth Avenue, at 19th Street (1-212 242 4853, www.thisisstory. com). Subway A, C, E to 14th Street; L to Eighth Avenue. **Open** *11am-8pm Mon-Wed, Fri, Sat; 11am-9pm Thur 11am-7pm Sun.* **Map** *p116 C27* ❸ *Accessories/ fashion/homewares*

Every four to eight weeks, Story shuts down and reopens with a totally new theme. Combining the editorial style of a magazine with splashy installations, the store collaborates with a different commercial partner for each cycle, changing not only the products but the entire interior, and hosting related events. Motifs have included 'Fresh Story' with delivery service Jet.com, spotlighting high-tech kitchen gadgets, cleanses, vegetable cookery books and Charlotte Olympia accessories, and 'Love Story', featuring chocolates and other tokens of affection. 'Your Story' focused on cult NYC brands and products favoured by YouTube personalities, from Vintage Twin reworked flannel shirts to sweets from Dylan's Candy Bar. Whatever the theme, you're bound to find an appealing mix of goods, engaging displays and NYC-specific merch.

❤ Chelsea gallery district

From West 18th Street to West 29th Street, mainly between Tenth and Eleventh Avenues, converted industrial buildings are crammed with around 300 art spaces. Here, you'll find group shows by up-and-comers, blockbuster exhibitions from big names and a slew of provocative work.

The highest concentration of major art-world players is on W 24th Street, including the mammoth showroom of early Chelsea adopter **Larry Gagosian**. The highest concentration of major art-world players is on W 24th Street, including the mammoth showroom of early Chelsea adopter **Mary Boone Gallery** (541 W 24th Street, 1-212 752 2929, www.maryboonegallery. com), which continues to produce hit shows featuring young artists, as well as luminaries like Ai Weiwei and Barbara Kruger. Also on this stretch, **Luhring Augustine** (No. 531, 1-212 206 9100, www.luhringaugustine. com) has an impressive index of artists, including Rachel Whiteread, Christopher Wool and Pipilotti Rist. **Matthew Marks Gallery** (No. 523, 1-212 243 0200, www.matthewmarks. com), which opened in 1991, was a driving force behind Chelsea's transformation into an art destination (there's a second location at 522 W 22nd Street). Blue-chip **Gladstone Gallery** (No.515, 1-212 206 9300, www.gladstonegallery.com) focuses on daring conceptual art.

Around the corner, **Yossi Milo** (245 Tenth Avenue, between 24th & 25th Streets, 1-212 414 0370, www.yossimilo.com) has an impressive roster of emerging and established photographers. The international artists at **Cheim & Read** (547 W 25th Street, 1-212 242 7727, www.cheimread.com) include such superstars as Diane Arbus and Jenny Holzer.

A few blocks south, powerhouse foundation **Dia**, which also has a huge art centre upstate in Beacon, New York, keeps two spaces on W 22nd Street (Nos.541, 546, www. diaart.org). It also maintains the outdoor art installation *7000 Oaks* by German artist Joseph Beuys on the same street. The piece, comprising 18 pairings of basalt stones and trees, is a spin-off of a five-year international effort, begun in 1982 at Germany's 'Documenta 7' exhibition, to enact social and environmental change by planting 7,000 trees.

The elegant **Tanya Bonakdar Gallery** (521 W 21st Street, 1-212 414 4144, www.tanyabonakdargallery. com) represents such prominent names as New York City Waterfalls maestro Olafur Eliasson. **David Zwirner** dominates W 19th Street (Nos. 519, 525 & 533, 1-212 727 2070, www.davidzwirner.com), mixing museum-quality shows of historical figures with a head-turning array of contemporary artists.

Note that galleries are generally closed or operate on an appointment-only basis on Mondays, and are open 10am-6pm Tuesday to Saturday. In summer, however, many keep different hours and close at weekends. Some may shut up shop for two weeks or a month at a stretch in July or August, so you're advised to call before visiting.

Museum of Sex

Entertainment

Joyce Theater

175 Eighth Avenue, at 19th Street, Chelsea (1-212 242 0800, www. joyce.org). Subway A, C, E to 14th Street; 1 to 18th Street; L to Eighth Avenue. Tickets $10-$76. Map p116 D27 ❶ *Dance*

This intimate space houses one of the finest theatres – we're talking about sightlines – in town. Companies and choreographers that present work here, among them Ballet Hispanico, Parsons Dance and Doug Varone, tend to be somewhat traditional. Regional ballet troupes, such as Aspen Santa Fe Ballet, appear here too.

The Kitchen

512 W 19th Street, between Tenth & Eleventh Avenues, Chelsea (1-212 255 5793, www.thekitchen.org). Subway A, C, E to 14th Street; L to Eighth Avenue. Box office 2-6pm Tue-Sat; 1hr before performance. Tickets free-$25. Map p116 C27 ❷ *Theatre*

The Kitchen, led by Tim Griffin, offers some of the best experimental dance around: inventive, provocative and rigorous. Some of the artists

who have presented work here are the finest in New York, such as Sarah Michelson (who has served as a guest curator for specific programmes), Dean Moss and Jodi Melnick.

❤ Upright Citizens Brigade Theatre

307 W 26th Street, at Eighth Avenue, Chelsea (1-212 366 9176, www.ucbtheatre.com). Subway C, E to 23rd Street; 1 to 28th Street. Shows daily, times vary. Admission free-$10. No cards. Map p116 D26 ❸ *Comedy*

UCBT is the most visible catalyst in New York's current alternative comedy boom. The improv troupes and sketch groups here are some of the best in the city. Stars of *Saturday Night Live* and writers for late-night talk-shows gather on Sunday nights to wow crowds in the long-running ASSSSCAT 3000. Other premier teams include the Stepfathers (Friday) and the Curfew (Saturday). Wildly popular Whiplash (Monday), hosted by Leo Allen and Aparna Nancherla, features the city's best rising comedians, but it's the surprise VIPs (name-check: Chris Rock, Louis CK and David Cross) who keep audiences hooked. Arrive early for a good seat – the venue has challenging sightlines. UCBEast (153 E Third Street, East Village, 1-212 366 9231) brings the same sort of cheap, raw and rowdy shows featured on the West Side, though this space focuses as much on sketch and stand-up as it does improv.

Gramercy & Flatiron

Lying east of **Chelsea**, this area is known for its distinctive architecture, especially around **Madison Square Park**, an elegant green space that hosts revolving outdoor art installations (www. madisonsquarepark.org). The famous wedge-shaped **Flatiron Building** was the world's first steel-frame skyscraper when it was completed in 1902. Some of the city's best eateries, from contemporary taverns to decadent fine dining rooms, have taken root here, and **Union Square** is home to a popular farmers' market. A key to **Gramercy Park**, the gated square at the southern end of Lexington Avenue (between 20th & 21st Streets), is the preserve of residents of the surrounding homes (and members of a couple of venerable private clubs).

Sights & museums
Museum of Sex
*233 Fifth Avenue, at 27th Street (1-212 689 6337, www.museumofsex. com). Subway R, W, 6 to 28th Street. **Open** 10am-9pm Mon-Thur, Sun; 11am-11pm Fri, Sat. **Admission** $17.50-$20.50; $15.50-$18.50 reductions. Under-18s not admitted. **Map** p116 E26.*
Situated in the former Tenderloin district, which was bumping and grinding with dance halls and brothels in the 1800s, the Museum of Sex explores its subject within a cultural context. In the three-level space, rotating highlights of the collection of more than 20,000 objects range from the tastefully erotic to the outlandish. You may see kinky art courtesy of Picasso and Keith Haring, one of Hugh Hefner's smoking jackets or a highly uncomfortable-looking 1890s anti-onanism device. The permanent installation 'Jump for Joy' lets you frolic in a 'Bouncy Castle of Breasts', and the changing exhibitions have covered such subjects as hardcore porn and 'The Sex Lives of Animals'. The large gift shop stocks books and arty sex toys.

National Museum of Mathematics (MoMath)
*11 E 26th Street, between Fifth & Madison Avenues (1-212 542 0566, www.momath.org). Subway R, W, 6 to 23rd Street. **Open** 10am-5pm daily (10am-2.30pm 1st Wed of each mth). **Admission** $16; $10 reductions. **Map** p116 E26.*
Designed for visitors of all ages, the country's first Museum of Mathematics replaces lectures and textbooks with nearly 40 eclectic, interactive exhibits covering such topics as algebra and geometry. Think a ride on a square-wheeled trike could never be smooth? Find out just how bump-free it can be when you take said tricycle over a sunflower-shaped track, where the petals create strategically placed catenaries – curves used in geometry and physics – that make a level ride possible. Elsewhere, you can pass 3D objects (or even your own body) through the laser-light 'Wall of Fire', and the lasers will display the objects as two-dimensional cross-sections (a cone becomes a triangle and circle, for instance). Or collaborate with a pair of fellow visitors to pan, zoom and rotate your own video cameras to create a single composite image, which can be manipulated into a bevy of interesting 'Feedback Fractals' (or fragmented shapes).

Restaurants & cafés

ABC Kitchen $$

35 E 18th Street, between Broadway
& Park Avenue South (1-212 475
5829, www.abckitchennyc.com).
Subway L, N, Q, R, W, 4, 5, 6 to 14th
Street-Union Square. **Open** *noon-*
3pm, 5.30-10.30pm Mon-Wed;
noon-3pm, 5.30-11pm Thur; noon-
3pm, 5.30-11.30pm Fri; 11am-3pm,
5.30-11.30pm Sat; 11am-3pm,
5.30-10pm Sun. **Map** *p116 E27* ❸
Eclectic

The *haute* green cooking at Jean-
Georges Vongerichten's artfully
decorated restaurant at premier
interior store ABC Carpet & Home
is based on the most gorgeous
ingredients from up and down
the East Coast. The local, seasonal
bounty finds its way into dishes like
a mushroom pizza, topped with
parmesan, oregano and a farm egg,
or roasted black sea bass infused
with chillies and herbs. A signature
sundae of salted caramel ice-cream,
candied peanuts and popcorn with
chocolate sauce reworks the kids'
classic to thrill a grown-up palate.
ABC delivers one message overall:
food that's good for the planet
needn't be any less flavourful or
stunning to look at. The store is also

In the know
Mysteries of the metronome

It's not uncommon to see passers-by
perplexed by the Metronome, a
massive sculptural installation
attached to 1 Union Square South
that bellows steam and generates
a barrage of numbers on a digital
read-out. Although they appear
strange, they're not random
numbers – the 15-digit display
is actually a clock indicating the
time relative to midnight. There's a
detailed explanation at the website
of Kristin Jones and Andrew Ginzel,
the artists responsible; see www.
jonesginzel.com.

---

home to the team's Latin-accented
ABC Cocina and vegetable-focused
ABCV restaurant.

City Bakery $

3 W 18th Street, between Fifth &
Sixth Avenues (1-212 366 1414,
www.thecitybakery.com). Subway
L, N, Q, R, W, 4, 5, 6 to 14th Street-
Union Square. **Open** *7.30am-6pm*
Mon-Fri; 8.30am-6pm Sat;
9am-6pm Sun. **Map** *p116 E27* ❹
Café

Pastry genius Maury Rubin's loft-
size City Bakery is jammed with
shoppers loading up on creative
baked goods such as maple
bacon biscuits and unusual salad
bar choices (grilled pineapple
with ancho chilli, for example).
There's also a small selection of
soups, pizzas and hot dishes. But
never mind all that: the thick,
incredibly rich hot chocolate with
fat house-made marshmallows
is justly famed, and the moist
'melted' chocolate-chip cookies are
divinely decadent.

❤ Cosme $$

35 E 21st Street, between
Broadway & Park Avenue South
(1-212 913 9659, www.cosmenyc.
com). Subway 6 to 23rd Street.
Open *noon-2.30pm, 5.30-11pm*
Mon-Thur; noon-2.30pm,
5.30pm-midnight Friday;
11.30am-2.30pm, 5.30pm-midnight
Sat; 11.30am-2.30pm, 5.30-11pm
Sun. **Map** *p116 E26* ❺ *Mexican*

Enrique Olvera is the megawatt
talent behind acclaimed Mexico
City restaurant Pujol. The elegant,
high-gear small plates served at
his first stateside debut – a bare-
concrete dining room – are pristine,
pricey and market-fresh. Tacos
make a solitary appearance on
the menu, in a generous portion
of duck *carnitas*, cooked to the
sinful midpoint of unctuous fat
and seared flesh. Single-corn
tortillas pop up frequently, from a
complimentary starter of crackly

blue-corn tortillas with chilli-kicked pumpkin-seed butter to dense, crispy tostadas dabbed with bone-marrow salsa and creamy tongues of sea urchin. But it's the face-melting, savoury-sweet, Instagrammed-to-death husk meringue, with its fine hull giving way to a velvety, supercharged corn mousse, that cements Olvera's status as a premier haute-Mex ambassador.

Eisenberg's Sandwich Shop $

174 Fifth Avenue, at 22nd Street (1-212 675 5096, www. eisenbergsnyc.com). Subway R, W to 23rd Street. **Open** *6.30am-8pm Mon-Fri; 9am-6pm Sat; 9am-5pm Sun.* **Map** *p116 E26* ❻ *Deli*
Since 1929, this slender Flatiron joint has dished out diner fare like hamburgers and egg creams with the kind of (earned) swagger unique to New York's restaurant institutions. Workers from nearby offices and visitors sidle up to the counter for retro classics. The corned beef and chopped liver sandwich and the spectacularly cheesy Reuben belong in the pantheon of the city's deli stalwarts.

❤ Eleven Madison Park $$$$

11 Madison Avenue, at E 24th Street (1-212 889 0905, www. elevenmadisonpark.com). Subway N, R, 6 to 23rd Street. **Open** *5.30-10pm Mon-Wed; 5.30-10.30pm Thur; noon-1pm, 5.30-10.30pm Fri-Sun.* **Map** *p116 E26* ❼ *American creative*
Michelin-starred chef Daniel Humm and impresario Will Guidara helm this vast art-deco jewel, which began life as a brasserie before evolving into one of the city's most rarefied and progressive eateries. The service is famously mannered, and the room among the city's most grand.

But the heady, epic seasonal tasting menus that pay homage to NYC history are the true heart of Eleven Madison Park, a format that spotlights Humm's auteur instincts.

Hill Country $$

30 W 26th Street, between Broadway & Sixth Avenue (1-212 255 4544, www.hillcountryny. com). Subway R, W to 28th Street. **Open** *11.30am-10pm Mon-Wed, Sun; 11.30am-11pm Thur-Sat.* **Map** *p116 E26* ❽ *American barbecue*
Owner Marc Glosserman's grandfather was the mayor of Lockhart, a Texas town known for its barbecue, and the cooking here is true to the restaurant's namesake region. Dishes feature sausages imported from barbecue stalwart Kreuz Market and two options for brisket: go for the 'moist' (read: fatty) version for full flavour. Beef shoulder emerges from the smoker in 20lb slabs, and hefty tips-on pork ribs have just enough fat to imbue them with proper flavour. Daily rotating desserts, such as jelly-filled cupcakes with peanut butter frosting, live out some kind of *Leave It to Beaver* fantasy, though June Cleaver wouldn't approve of the two dozen tequilas and bourbons on offer. Regular live music in the downstairs bar includes country, folk and roots acts.

Made Nice $

8 W 28th Street, between Broadway & Fifth Avenue (no phone, www. madenicenyc.com). Subway R, W to 28th Street. **Open** *11am-10pm Mon-Sat.* **Map** *p116 E26* ❾ *American*
Daniel Humm and Will Guidara, the duo behind Eleven Madison Park and the NoMad, are responsible for this nearby counter-service concept. From an open kitchen, Humm & Co serves deconstructed versions of dishes from the pair's more

upscale restaurants. Dishes like salmon-frisée salad with a soft-boiled egg and potato croutons, and confit pork shoulder with warm grains, roasted carrots and bacon, are inspired by similar flavour configurations at EMP and the NoMad. Single-digit-priced glasses of wine are available, as well as an on-tap beer collaboration with Evil Twin Brewing and house-made sodas. The bright, casual space, with a mural by street artist Shepard Fairey and disposable plates and cutlery, may lack ambiance for an evening meal, but makes a great quick lunch stop.

Union Square Cafe $$$

101 E 19th Street, at Park Avenue South (1-212 243 4020, www. unionsquarecafe.com). Subway L, N, Q, R, W, 4, 5, 6 to 14th Street-Union Square. **Open** *11.45am-10pm Mon-Thur; 11.45am-11pm Fri; 10am-11pm Sat; 10am-10pm Sun.* **Map** *p116 E27* ❿ *American creative*

The original Union Square Cafe, the beloved flagship of the formidable Danny Meyer empire, opened on East 16th Street in 1985, long before a Shake Shack patty ever sizzled on a griddle top. A rent spike prompted a move three blocks north to a two-storey space that's nearly double the size. The light and lofty setting, designed by architect David Rockwell, features little nods to the original: cherry-wood service stations, dark-green wainscotting, and quirky, colourful paintings lining the walls. The service is as well trained and personable as ever and a warm, convivial spirit still dominates the dining room. But the most crucial holdover is in the kitchen, where executive chef Carmen Quagliata – who headed the original USC for a decade – can still be found overseeing staples like ricotta gnocchi and lunchtime tuna burgers. Quagliata builds on those familiar comforts with new dishes that fit effortlessly with the oldies, with farmers' market produce still in evidence.

Union Square Cafe

Next door, **Daily Provisions** (103 E 19th Street, between Irving Place & Park Avenue South, 1-212 488 1505, www.dailyprovisionsnyc.com) is a casual, quick-service annex, serving Quagliata-created sandwiches such as a club-sandwich riff on USC's herb-rubbed rotisserie chicken, plus house-baked pastries, Joe coffee, beer and wine, at marble counters or to take away.

Bars

♥ Old Town Bar

45 E 18th Street, between Broadway & Park Avenue South (1-212 529 6732, www.oldtownbar.com). Subway L, N, Q, R, W, 4, 5, 6 to 14th Street-Union Square. **Open** *11.30am-1am Mon-Fri; noon-1am Sat; noon-midnight Sun.* **Map** *p116 E27* ❹

Amid the swank food and drink sanctums around Park Avenue South, this classic tavern remains a shrine to unchanging values. Grab a sweet wooden booth or belly up to the long bar and drain a few pints alongside the regulars who gather on stools 'south of the pumps' (their lingo for taps). If you work up an appetite, skip the much-praised burger in favour of the chilli dog: a grilled and scored all-beef Sabrett hot dog with spicy house-made beef-and-red-kidney-bean chilli. (Note that the kitchen closes at 11.30pm Monday to Saturday and 10pm on Sunday.)

♥ Raines Law Room

48 W 17th Street, between Fifth & Sixth Avenues (no phone, www.raineslawroom.com). Subway F, M to 14th Street; L to Sixth Avenue. **Open** *5pm-2am Mon-Thur; 5pm-3am Fri, Sat; 7pm-1am Sun.* **Map** *p116 E27* ❺

There's no bar at this louche lounge. In deference to its name (which refers to an 1896 law that was designed to curb liquor consumption), drinks are prepared in a half-hidden back room known as 'the kitchen', surrounded by gleaming examples of every tool and gizmo a barkeep could wish for. From this gorgeous tableau comes an austere cocktail list. Kick back in the plush, upholstered space to sip classics, and variations thereof.

Shops & services

♥ ABC Carpet & Home

888 Broadway, at 19th Street (1-212 473 3000, www.abchome.com). Subway L, N, Q, R, W, 4, 5, 6 to 14th Street-Union Square. **Open** *10am-7pm Mon-Wed, Fri, Sat; 10am-8pm Thur; 11am-6.30pm Sun.* **Map** *p116 E27* ❹ *Homewares*

Most of ABC's extensive carpet range is housed in the store across the street at no.881 – except the rarest rugs, which reside on the sixth floor of the main store. Browse everything from hand-embroidered cushions, contemporary ceramics and Tibetan crafts to jewellery and natural skincare on the bazaar-style ground floor, as well as women's clothing (both independent-designer and vintage) on the Mezzanine. The upper floors showcase furniture spanning every style, from slick European minimalism to antique oriental and mid-century modern, and kitchenware is in the basement.

Fishs Eddy

889 Broadway, at 19th Street (1-212 420 9020, www.fishseddy.com). Subway R, W to 23rd Street. **Open** *9am-9pm Mon-Thur; 9am-10pm Fri, Sat; 10am-8pm Sun.* **Map** *p116 E27* ❺ *Homewares*

Penny-pinchers frequent this barn-like space for sturdy dishware and glasses – surplus stock or recycled from restaurants, ocean liners and hotels (plain white side plates start at a mere $1.99). But there are plenty of affordable, freshly minted goods too, many with novelty patterns. Add spice to mealtime with glasses adorned with male or female pole-dancers. Dinnerware and mugs printed with the Manhattan skyline, or sugar and butter dishes with Brooklyn-accented labels ('shuguh', 'buttah'), make excellent NYC souvenirs.

Showplace Antique & Design Center

40 W 25th Street, between Fifth & Sixth Avenues (1-212 633 6063, www.nyshowplace.com). Subway F, M to 23rd Street. Open 10am-6pm Mon-Fri; 8.30am-5.30pm Sat, Sun (individual vendors vary). Map p116 E26 ❻ *Fashion/homewares*
Set over four expansive floors, this indoor market houses around 200 high-quality dealers. The warren of stalls specialises in everything from classical antiquities and Asian art to vintage toys, early-20th-century radios, designer clothing and collectable handbags. The top floor has a more open layout showcasing furniture as well as decorative objects, jewellery and accessories. Note that some dealers may knock off early, so it's best not to visit at the end of the day.

Union Square Greenmarket

From 16th to 17th Streets, between Union Square East & Union Square West (1-212 788 7476, www.grownyc. org/greenmarket). Subway L, N, Q, R, 4, 5, 6 to 14th Street-Union Square. Open 8am-6pm Mon, Wed, Fri, Sat. Map p116 E27 ❼ *Market*
Shop elbow-to-elbow with top chefs for locally grown produce, handmade breads and baked goods, preserves and cheeses at the city's flagship farmers' market on the periphery of Union Square Park. From around mid November until Christmas, a holiday market sets up shop here too.

Entertainment

Metropolitan Room

34 W 22nd Street, between Fifth & Sixth Avenues, Flatiron District (1-212 206 0440, www. metropolitanroom.com). Subway F, M, W, R to 23rd Street. Shows vary. Admission $10-$40 (2-drink minimum). Map p116 E26 ❹
Cabaret
The Metropolitan Room occupies a comfortable middle zone on the city's cabaret spectrum: less expensive than the fancier supper clubs but more polished than the cheaper spots. Regular performers range from emerging jazz vocalists to established cabaret artists such as Marilyn Maye, Baby Jane Dexter and Annie Ross.

Herald Square & Garment District

Seventh Avenue is the main drag of the **Garment District** (roughly from 34th to 40th Streets, between Broadway & Eighth Avenue), where designers feed America's multi-billion-dollar clothing industry. The world's largest store, **Macy's**, looms over **Herald Square** (at the junction of Broadway and Sixth Avenue). To the east, the spas, restaurants and karaoke bars of **Koreatown** line 32nd Street, between Broadway and Fifth Avenue.

Restaurants & cafés

Keens Steakhouse $$$

72 W 36th Street, at Sixth Avenue (1-212 947 3636, www.keens.com). Subway B, D, F, M, N, Q, R, W to 34th Street-Herald Square. Open 11.45am-10.30pm Mon-Fri; 5-10.30pm Sat; 5-9.30pm Sun. Map p116 D25 ⓫ *Steakhouse*
The ceiling and walls are hung with pipes, some from such long-ago Keens regulars as Babe Ruth, JP

Morgan and Teddy Roosevelt. Even in these non-smoking days, you can catch a whiff of the restaurant's history. Bevelled-glass doors, two working fireplaces and a forest's worth of dark wood suggest a time when 'Diamond Jim' Brady piled his table with bushels of oysters, slabs of seared beef and troughs of ale. Established in 1885, Keens still offers a three-inch-thick mutton chop, and the porterhouse (for two or three) holds its own against any steak in the city.

Mandoo Bar $

2 W 32nd Street, between Fifth Avenue & Broadway (1-212 279 3075, www.mandoobarnyc.com). Subway B, D, F, M, N, Q, R, W to 34th Street-Herald Square. **Open** *11.30am-10pm daily.* **Map** *p116 E25* **12** *Korean*

If the staff members filling and crimping dough squares in the front window don't give it away, we will – this wood-wrapped industrial-style spot elevates *mandoo* (Korean dumplings) above mere appetiser status. Several varieties of the tasty morsels are filled with such delights as subtly piquant kimchi, juicy pork, succulent shrimp and vegetables. Try them miniaturised, as in the Baby Mandoo, swimming in a soothing beef broth or atop soupy ramen noodles.

Shops & services

Kee's Chocolates

315 W 39th Street between Eighth & Ninth Avenues (1-212 967 8088, www.keeschocolates.com). Subway A, C, E to 42nd Street-Port Authority. **Open** *9am-6.30pm Mon-Fri; 10am-5pm Sat.* **Map** *p116 D24* **8** *Food & drink*

Every piece of Kee Ling Tong's exquisite confectionery is tempered and dipped by hand to create a thick, smooth shell that encloses either silky cream filling, fluffy mousse or rich ganache. The 48 bonbon flavours rotate daily, and crème brûlée, passionfruit and Thai chilli are among the most popular. But all of them, including green tea, key lime, blood orange and black sesame, are worth investigating. The turtles – dark or milk chocolate layered with pecans and creamy caramel – are the best we've tasted. **Other location** HSBC, 452 Fifth Avenue, between 39th & 40th Streets, Murray Hill (1-212 525 6099).

Macy's

151 W 34th Street, between Broadway & Seventh Avenue (1-212 695 4400, www.visitmacysusa. com). Subway B, D, F, M, N, Q, R, W to 34th Street-Herald Square; 1, 2, 3 to 34th Street-Penn Station. **Open** *10am-10pm Mon-Sat; 11am-9pm Sun.* **Map** *p116 D25* **9** *Department store*

It may not be as glamorous as New York's other famous stores, but for sheer breadth of stock, the 34th Street behemoth is hard to beat. Mid-price fashion for all ages, big beauty names and housewares have traditionally been the store's bread and butter, but a recent redesign introduced luxury boutiques including Gucci and Burberry. The cosmetics department has been luxed-up with high-end brands such as Laura Mercier and Tom Ford fragrances.

▶ *If you need tourist guidance, stop by the store's Official NYC Information Center.*

Nepenthes New York

307 W 38th Street, between Eighth & Ninth Avenues (1-212 643 9540, www.nepenthesny.com). Subway A, C, E, 1, 2, 3 to 34th Street-Penn Station. **Open** *noon-7pm Mon-Sat; noon-5pm Sun.* **Map** *p116 D24* **10** *Fashion*

Times Square

Well-dressed dudes with an eye on the Japanese style scene will already be familiar with this Tokyo fashion retailer. The narrow Garment District shop – its first US location – showcases expertly crafted urban-rustic menswear from house label Engineered Garments, such as plaid flannel shirts and workwear-inspired jackets. There is also a small selection of women's clothing.

Entertainment

Madison Square Garden

Seventh Avenue, between 31st & 33rd Streets, Garment District (1-212 465 6741, www.thegarden. com). Subway A, C, E, 1, 2, 3 to 34th Street-Penn Station. **Box office** *10am-6pm Mon-Sat (extended hours on show days). Tickets vary.* **Map** *p116 D25* **5** *Live music*

Some of music's biggest acts – Lady Gaga, Eric Clapton, Kanye West – come out to play at the world's most famous basketball arena, home to the Knicks and also hockey's Rangers. Whether you'll actually be able to get a look at them depends on your seat number or the quality of your binoculars. While the storied venue is undoubtedly a part of the fabric of New York, it's too vast for a rich concert experience. However, a three-year renovation restored the striking circular ceiling and brought new seating and food from top New York City chefs, among other improvements.

Theater District & Hell's Kitchen

Times Square is the gateway to the **Theater District**, the zone located roughly between 41st Street and 53rd Street, from Sixth Avenue to Ninth Avenue. Forty of the opulent show houses here – those with more than 500 seats – are designated as being part of **Broadway** (plus the Vivian Beaumont Theater, uptown at **Lincoln Center**; *see p152*). Just west is **Hell's Kitchen**, which had a tough, crime-ridden reputation until the 1980s. In recent years, the area emerged as a gay nightlife hotspot, and with the construction of **Hudson Yards** – a massive mixed-use development including residential towers, shops, restaurants and a park – in its southern fringes, it's still evolving. Ninth Avenue, with its cornucopia of cheap ethnic eateries, is a good bet for a pre- or post-theatre bite.

Sights & museums

♥ Gulliver's Gate

216 West 44th Street, between Seventh & Eighth Avenues (no phone, gulliversgate.com). Subway A, C, E to 42nd Street-Port Authority; N, Q, R, S, 1, 2, 3, 7 to 42nd Street-Times Square. **Open** *10am-7pm Mon-Thur, Sun (last entry 5.30pm); 10am-10pm Fri, Sat (last entry 8.30pm).* **Admission** *$36; $27 reductions.* **Map** *p116 D24.*

Times Square's newest attraction is an interactive miniature world spanning an entire city block and comprising more than 300 incredibly detailed scale models (1:87). Representing 50 nations, the scenes were created (roughly) in the region they depict, so the mini NYC – complete with landmarks such as Times Square itself with tiny LED billboards – was built in Brooklyn, while Europe was made in Rimini, Italy. The exhibition covers the iconic global attractions you'd expect – Niagara Falls, the Taj Mahal, the Eiffel Tower, the Parthenon, the Great Wall of China – but there's plenty of humour across the displays, too (mummies on the attack in Egypt, for instance,

and the Loch Ness Monster in Scotland). Geography and time periods are a bit fluid. Kids will delight in the many moving elements, including animals and vehicles – there are more than 1,000 trains, 10,000 cars and trucks, plus an entire working airport. Visitors can even have themselves scanned and 3D printed to become 'model citizens', and peer into the command centre to see the inner workings of the computer-controlled microcosm.

Intrepid Sea, Air & Space Museum

USS Intrepid, Pier 86, Twelfth Avenue & 46th Street (1-212 245 0072, www.intrepidmuseum.org). Subway A, C, E to 42nd Street-Port Authority, then M42 bus to Twelfth Avenue or 15min walk; 7 to 34th Street-Hudson Yards, then 15min walk. **Open** *Apr-Oct 10am-5pm Mon-Fri; 10am-6pm Sat, Sun. Nov-Mar 10am-5pm daily.* **Admission** *$33; $24-$31 reductions; free under-5s, active & retired US military.* **Map** *p116 B23.*

Commissioned in 1943, this 27,000-ton, 898ft aircraft carrier survived torpedoes and kamikaze attacks in World War II, served during the Vietnam War and the Cuban Missile Crisis, and recovered two space capsules for NASA. It was decommissioned in 1974, then resurrected as a museum. On its flight deck and portside aircraft elevator are top-notch examples of American military might, including the US Navy F-14 Tomcat (as featured in Top Gun), an A-12 spy plane and a fully restored Army AH-1J Sea Cobra gunship helicopter. Visitors can board a 1950s guided-nuclear-missile submarine, or experience flight simulators (for an extra charge). The Space Shuttle Pavilion houses the prototype NASA orbiter Enterprise (OV-101), along with related artefacts, photos and video.

In the know
Desperate characters

Since 2016, following complaints that costumed street performers in Times Square were hassling visitors a bit too aggressively for tips, Spider-Man, Elmo, and even the now-famous Naked Cowboy must remain within designated 'activity' zones indicated by teal-painted areas in the pedestrian plazas.

❤ Broadway shows

The Book of Mormon

Eugene O'Neill Theatre, 230 W 49th Street, between Broadway & Eighth Avenue, Theater District (Telecharge 1-212 239 6200, www. bookofmormonbroadway.com). Subway C, E, 1 to 50th Street; N, Q, R, S, W, 1, 2, 3, 7 to 42nd Street-Times Square; N, R, W to 49th Street. Box office 10am-8pm Mon-Sat; noon-6pm Sun. Tickets $99-$477. Map p116 D23 ➐

This gleefully obscene and subversive satire may be the funniest show to grace the Great White Way since *The Producers* and *Urinetown*. Writers Trey Parker and Matt Stone of *South Park*, along with composer Robert Lopez (*Avenue Q*), find the perfect blend of sweet and nasty for this tale of mismatched Mormon proselytisers on a mission in Uganda.

Dear Evan Hansen

Music Box Theatre, 239 W 45th Street, between Broadway & Eighth Avenue, Theater District (Telecharge 1-212 239 6200, www. dearevanhansen.com). Subway N, Q, R, S, W, 1, 2, 3, 7 to 42nd Street-Times Square. Box office 10am-8pm Mon-Sat; noon-6pm Sun. Tickets $119-$499. Map p116 D24 ➒

An awkward and unpopular high school student gets thrust into social relevance after a classmate's suicide in this captivating, Tony Award-winning original musical, which delivers a direct electric jolt to the heart. Benj Pasek and Justin Paul's score combines well-crafted lyrics with an exciting pop sound, and Steven Levenson's book gives all the characters shaded motives.

Hamilton

Richard Rodgers Theatre, 226 W 46th Street W, between Broadway & Eighth Avenue, Theater District (Ticketmaster 1-877 250 2929, www. hamiltonbroadway.com). Subway N, Q, R, S, W, 1, 2, 3, 7 to 42nd Street-Times Square; N, R, W to 49th Street. Box office 10am-8pm Mon-Sat; noon-6pm Sun. Tickets $179-$849. Map p116 D23 ⓫

Composer-lyricist Lin-Manuel Miranda forges a ground-breaking bridge between hip hop and musical storytelling with this sublime collision of radio-ready beats and an inspiring immigrant slant on Founding Father Alexander Hamilton. A brilliant, diverse cast takes back American history and makes it new. Good luck getting tickets: even with a top price of $849, the highest in Broadway history, it's still the hottest show in town.

Kinky Boots

Al Hirschfeld Theatre, 302 W 45th Street, between Eighth & Ninth Avenues, Theater District (Telecharge 1-212 239 6200, www. kinkybootsthemusical.com). Subway A, C, E to 42nd Street-Port Authority; N, Q, R, S, W, 1, 2, 3, 7 to 42nd Street-Times Square. Box office 10am-8pm Mon-Sat; noon-6pm Sun. Tickets $87-$399. Map p116 C24 ⓬

Harvey Fierstein and Cyndi Lauper's fizzy crowd-pleaser, in which a sassy-dignified drag queen kicks an English shoe factory into gear, feels familiar at every step. But it's been manufactured with solid craftsmanship and care (Lauper is a musical-theatre natural), and is boosted by a heart-strong cast. The overall effect is nigh irresistible.

The Lion King

Minskoff Theatre, 200 W 45th Street, between Broadway & Eighth Avenue, Theater District (Ticketmaster 1-866 870 2717, www.lionking.com). Subway A, C, E to 42nd Street-Port Authority; N, Q, R, S, W, 1, 2, 3 to 42nd Street-Times Square. **Box office** *10am-8pm Mon-Sat; 11am-7pm Sun. Tickets $89-$249.* **Map** *p116 D24* ⑬

Director-designer Julie Taymor surrounds the Disney movie's mythic plot and Elton John-Tim Rice score with African rhythm and music. Through elegant puppetry, Taymor populates the stage with a menagerie of African beasts; her staging has expanded a simple cub into the pride of Broadway.

Wicked

Gershwin Theatre, 222 W 51st Street, between Broadway & Eighth Avenue, Theater District (Ticketmaster 1-877 250 2929, www.wickedthemusical.com). Subway C, E, 1 to 50th Street. **Box office** *10am-8pm Mon-Sat; noon-6pm Sun. Tickets $62-$242.* **Map** *p116 D23* ⑯

Based on novelist Gregory Maguire's 1995 riff on *The Wizard of Oz*, *Wicked* is a witty pre-quel to the classic children's book and movie. The show's combination of pop dynamism and sumptuous spectacle has made it the most popular show on Broadway. Teenage girls, especially, have responded to the story of how a green girl named Elphaba comes to be known as the infamous Wicked Witch of the West.

Ripley's Believe It or Not!

234 W 42nd Street, between Seventh & Eighth Avenues (1-212 398 3133, www.ripleysnewyork.com). Subway A, C, E to 42nd Street-Port Authority; N, Q, R, S, 1, 2, 3, 7 to 42nd Street-Times Square. **Open** *9am-1am daily (last entry midnight).* **Admission** *$30; $23-$25 reductions; free under-4s.* **Map** *p116 D24.*

Times Square might be a little whitewashed these days, but you can get a feel for the old freak show at this repository of the eerie and uncanny. Marvel at such bizarre artefacts as a six-legged cow and the world's largest collection of shrunken heads, and get a close-up view of the dazzling LED-illuminated centennial ball, which was dropped from 1 Times Square on New Year's Eve 2007.

Restaurants & cafés

❤ Don Antonio by Starita $$

309 W 50th Street, between Eighth & Ninth Avenues (1-646 719 1043, www.donantoniopizza.com). Subway C, E to 50th Street. **Open** *11.30am-11pm Mon-Thur; 11.30am-11.30pm Fri, Sat; 11.30am-10.30pm Sun.* **Map** *p116 D23* ⑬ *Italian/pizza*

It may not be trendy, but this pedigreed eatery, a collaboration between Kesté's (*see p106*) talented Roberto Caporuscio and his decorated Naples mentor, Antonio Starita, is the real deal for pizza aficionados. Start with tasty bites like the *fritattine* (a deep-fried spaghetti cake oozing prosciutto cotto and mozzarella sauce). The main event should be the habit-forming Montanara Starita, which gets a quick dip in the deep fryer before hitting the oven to develop its puffy, golden crust. Topped with tomato sauce, basil and intensely smoky buffalo mozzarella, it's a worthy addition to the pantheon of classic New York pies.

Gotham West Market $-$$

*600 Eleventh Avenue, between 44th & 45th Streets (1-212 582 7940, www.gothamwestmarket.com). A, C, E to 42nd Street-Port Authority. **Open** 7.30am-11pm Mon-Thur, Sun; 7.30am-midnight Fri, Sat. **Map** p116 C24* **14** *Eclectic*

This hip take on a food court is perfect for lunch or a quick pre-theatre bite. The 15,000sq ft retail-dining mecca is divided into nine culinary stalls as well as a full-service NYC Velo bike shop. Dine-in or take-out options include Ivan Ramen Slurp Shop, where Tokyo noodle guru Ivan Orkin offers his famed *shio*, *shoyu* and other varieties; El Colmado tapas bar from Seamus Mullen of Tertulia; a cocktail-and-charcuterie-focused outpost of the Cannibal; and ultra-popular Brooklyn ice-cream shop Ample Hills Creamery. Seating is at chefs' counters or communal tables.

Bars

Atlas Social Club

*753 Ninth Avenue, between 50th & 51st Streets (1-212 762 8527, www.atlassocialclub.com). Subway C, E to 50th Street. **Open** 4pm-4am daily. **Map** p116 C23* **6**

This gay bar, designed to look like a cross between an old-school athletic club and a speakeasy, is one of the more relaxed options on the Hell's Kitchen scene – at least when it's not packed to the gills, which it can be at weekends. Be sure to check out the bathrooms, which are brightly papered with vintage beefcake and sports magazines.

Rum House

*228 W 47th Street, between Seventh & Eighth Avenues (1-646 490 6924, www.edisonrumhouse.com). Subway N, R, W to 49th Street. **Open** noon-4am daily. **Map** p116 D23* **7**

Not long ago, the rakish, 1970s vintage piano bar in the Edison Hotel seemed destined to go the way of the Times Square peep show. But the team behind Tribeca mixology den Ward III ushered in a second act, introducing key upgrades (including serious cocktails) while maintaining the charmingly offbeat vibe. Sip dark, spirit-heavy tipples, such as a funky old-fashioned riff that showcases a sultry aged rum, while listening to live music (9.30pm-12.30am nightly).

Shops & services

Domus

*413 W 44th Street, at Ninth Avenue (1-212 581 8099, www.domusnewyork.com). Subway A, C, E to 42nd Street-Port Authority. **Open** noon-8pm Tue-Sat; noon-6pm Sun. **Map** p116 C24* **11** *Homewares*

Scouring the globe for unusual design products is nothing new, but owners Luisa Cerutti and Nicki Lindheimer take the concept a step further; each year they visit a far-flung part of the world to forge links with and support co-operatives and individual craftspeople. The beautiful results, such as vivid pillows screen-printed in Morocco, carved soapstone boxes from Vietnam or handwoven Tunisian bath towels, reflect a fine attention to detail and a sense of place. It's a great place to pick up reasonably priced gifts.

❤ Fine and Dandy

*445 W 49th Street, between Ninth & Tenth Avenues (1-212 247 4847, www.fineanddandyshop.com). Subway C, E to 50th Street. **Open** noon-8pm Mon-Sat; 1-8pm Sun. **Map** p116 C23* **12** *Accessories*

Decked out with collegiate memorabilia, vintage barware and rare books (also for sale), this Hell's

Kitchen shop is a prime location for the modern gent to score of-the-moment retro accoutrements like bow ties, pocket squares, suspenders (braces) and spats. House-label printed ties are hung in propped-open vintage trunks, and patterned socks are displayed in old briefcases. A line of made-to-measure shirts is also available, plus fun souvenirs such as a mock college pennant emblazoned with 'Hell's Kitchen'.

Entertainment

💜 Ars Nova

511 W 54th Street, between Tenth & Eleventh Avenues, Hell's Kitchen (1-212 352-3101, OvationTix 1-866 811 4111, www.arsnovanyc.com). Subway C, E, 1 to 50th Street. **Box office** *30mins before show. Tickets $15-$50.* **Map** *p116 C22* ⑥ *Theatre*
Committed to presenting innovative new theatre, music and comedy, this offbeat space has been a boon to developing artists since it opened in 2002. Along with smart full productions, Ars Nova also presents an eclectic monthly special called Showgasm and the annual ANT Fest for emerging talents.

Carolines on Broadway

1626 Broadway, between 49th & 50th Streets, Theater District (1-212 757 4100, www.carolines. com). Subway N, R, W to 49th Street; 1 to 50th Street. Shows vary. **Admission** *varies (2-drink minimum).* **Map** *p116 D23* ⑧ *Comedy*
Even comics who are regulars at the city's other stand-up rooms have to work extra hard to get stage time at this venerable institution. Carolines is the best place to see marquee names, including sitcom-ready stars, familiar faces from the '80s comedy boom and cable-special ravers. You'll never see anything less than professional here.

Feinstein's/54 Below

254 W 54th Street, between Broadway & Eighth Avenue, Theater District (1-646 476 3551, www.54below.com). Subway B, D, E to Seventh Avenue; C, E, 1 to 50th Street; R, W to 57th Street. Shows vary. **Admission** *$25-$95 ($20-$30 food/drink minimum).* **Map** *p116 D22* ⑩ *Cabaret*
This killer supper club below the legendary Studio 54 space offers an evocative speakeasy atmosphere, excellent tech and a calendar stuffed with major talents. The schedule is dominated by Broadway stars (such as Patti LuPone, Lea Salonga and Ben Vereen), but there's also room for edgier performers such as Nellie McKay and rising songwriters – not to mention Great American Songbook standard bearer Michael Feinstein, whose name was added to the venue's in 2015.

New Victory Theater

209 W 42nd Street, between Seventh & Eighth Avenues, Theater District (1-646 223 3010, www. newvictory.org). Subway N, Q, R, S, W, 1, 2, 3, 7 to 42nd Street-Times Square. **Box office** *11am-5pm Mon, Sun; noon-7pm Tue-Sat. Tickets $16-$55.* **Map** *p116 D24* ⑭ *Theatre*
New York's only full-scale young people's theatre stages innovative productions from around the world.

Offerings span everything from reworkings of classic plays and puppetry to contemporary circus troupes and hip hop-inspired dance. The New Victory often collaborates with Autism Friendly Spaces on special adaptations, ensuring all kids can enjoy the experience of live theatre. Shows often sell out, so buy tickets well ahead.

Pershing Square Signature Center

480 W 42nd Street, at Tenth Avenue, Hell's Kitchen (1-212 244 7529, www.signaturetheatre.org). Subway A, C, E to 42nd Street-Port Authority. **Box office** *11am-6pm Tue-Sun. Tickets $25-$65.* **Map** *p116 C24* **⑮** *Theatre*

The award-winning Signature Theatre Company, founded by the late James Houghton in 1991, focuses on exploring and celebrating playwrights in depth, with whole seasons devoted to works by individual living writers. Over the years, the company has delved into the oeuvres of August Wilson, John Guare, Horton Foote and many more. Special programmes are designed to keep prices low. In 2012, the troupe expanded hugely into a new home – a theatre complex designed by Frank Gehry, with three major spaces and ambitious long-term commission programmes, cementing it as one of the city's key cultural institutions.

Fifth Avenue & Around

The city's central thoroughfare is the main route for public processions, such as the St Patrick's Day Parade (*see p58*) and the LGBT Pride March (*see p60*). But even without floats or marching bands, the sidewalks of Fifth Avenue are teeming with shoppers and sightseers. A number of landmarks and first-rate cultural institutions are on, or in the vicinity of, the strip.

Sights & museums

New York Public Library

476 Fifth Avenue, at 42nd Street (1-917 275 6975, www.nypl.org). Subway B, D, F, M to 42nd Street-Bryant Park; 7 to Fifth Avenue. **Open** *Sept-June 10am-6pm Mon, Thur-Sat; 10am-8pm Tue, Wed; 1-5pm Sun. July, Aug 10am-6pm Mon, Thur-Sat; 10am-8pm Tue, Wed (see website for gallery hours).* **Admission** *free.* **Map** *p116 E24.*

Guarded by the marble lions Patience and Fortitude, this austere Beaux Arts edifice, designed by Carrère and Hastings, was completed in 1911. The building was renamed in honour of philanthropist Stephen A Schwarzman in 2008, but Gothamites still know it as the New York Public Library (although the city-wide library system comprises 92 locations). Free hour-long tours (11am, 2pm Mon-Sat; 2pm Sun, except July & Aug) take in the Rose Main Reading Room on the third floor, which at 297ft long and 78ft wide is almost the size of a football field. Specialist departments include the Map Division, containing some 433,000 maps and 20,000 atlases and books, and the Rare Books Division boasting Walt Whitman's personal copies of the first (1855) and third (1860) editions of *Leaves of Grass*. The library also stages major exhibitions and events, including the excellent 'Live from the NYPL' series of talks and lectures from big-name authors and thinkers (see the website for the schedule).

Rockefeller Center

From 48th to 51st Streets, between Fifth & Sixth Avenues (tours & Top of the Rock 1-212 698 2000, www.rockefellercenter.com). Subway B, D, F, M to 47-50th Streets-Rockefeller Center. **Open** *Tours every 30mins 10am-8pm (last tour 7.30pm). Observation deck*

❤ Empire State Building

350 Fifth Avenue, between 33rd & 34th Streets (1-212 736 3100, www. esbnyc.com). Subway B, D, F, M, N, Q, R to 34th Street-Herald Square. **Open** *8am-2am daily (last elevator 1.15 am).* **Admission** *86th floor $34; $27-$31 reductions; free under-6s. 102nd floor $20 extra.* **Map** *p116 E25.*

Financed by General Motors executive John J Raskob at the height of New York's skyscraper race, the Empire State Building sprang up in little more than a year, weeks ahead of schedule. Since opening in 1931, the Indiana limestone and granite tower has been immortalised in countless photos and films, from the original *King Kong* to *Sleepless in Seattle*. The building contains 2.7 million square feet of office space, and has more than 130 antennas powering the region's broadcasting industry. But for NYC visitors, it's all about the view. At 1,454 feet from its base to the top of its spire, the iconic skyscraper is the city's second-tallest building. Its enclosed

102nd-floor observatory is 1,250 feet above the street, just a few feet lower than One World Observatory at the World Trade Center, and the roomier panoramic deck on the 86th floor, at 1,050 feet, retains its status as the highest outdoor lookout point. On a clear day, the view extends past the five boroughs to surrounding states New Jersey, Pennsylvania, Connecticut and Massachusetts. The building's marble-clad lobby features a faithful aluminium-and-gold reproduction of the art deco ceiling mural, depicting the sky with industrial-themed celestial bodies. After dark, the tower is illuminated with flashy LEDs. The colour scheme often honours holidays, charities or special events.

▶ *To cut down waiting time, purchase tickets online and visit between 8am and 10am or after 9pm. Alternatively, springing for an express pass ($60, or $80 for both the 86th and 102nd floors) allows you to cut to the front of the line.*

8am-midnight daily (last elevator 11pm). **Admission** *Rockefeller Center tours $25 (under-6s not admitted). Observation deck $34; $28-$32 reductions; free under-6s.* **Map** *p116 E23.*

Constructed under the aegis of industrialist John D Rockefeller in the 1930s, this art deco complex is inhabited by NBC, Simon & Schuster and other large companies, as well as Radio City Music Hall, Christie's auction house, and an underground shopping arcade. Guided tours of the entire complex are available daily, and there's a separate tour of NBC Studios at 30 Rockefeller Plaza (1-212 664 3700; $33, $29 reductions), home to iconic show *Saturday Night Live*.

The buildings and grounds are embellished with works by several well-known artists; look out for Isamu Noguchi's stainless-steel relief, *News*, above the entrance to 50 Rockefeller Plaza, and José Maria Sert's mural *American Progress* in the lobby of 30 Rockefeller Plaza (also known as the GE Building). But the most breathtaking sights are those seen from the 70th-floor Top of the Rock observation deck (combined tour/observation deck tickets are available). From around mid-October to April, the Plaza's sunken courtyard, featuring Paul Manship's bronze statue of Prometheus, becomes a picturesque, if crowded, ice-skating rink.

St Patrick's Cathedral

Fifth Avenue, between 50th & 51st Streets (1-212 753 2261, www.saintpatrickscathedral. org). Subway B, D, F, M to 47-50th Streets-Rockefeller Center; E, M to Fifth Avenue-53rd Street. **Open** *6.30am-8.45pm daily.* **Admission** *free.* **Map** *p116 E23.*

One of the largest Catholic churches in America, St Patrick's counts presidents, business leaders and movie stars among its past and present parishioners. The recently cleaned Gothic-style façade features intricate white-marble spires, but equally impressive is the interior, including the Louis Tiffany-designed altar, solid bronze baldachin, and the rose window by stained-glass master Charles Connick.

Shops & services

Bracketed by Saks Fifth Avenue and Bergdorf Goodman, the prime shopping stretch of Fifth Avenue is chock-a-block with luxury designer flagships (Gucci, Prada, Tiffany & Co, Valentino) and mall-level brands (Abercrombie & Fitch, Gap, Uniqlo), not to mention a 24-hour, subterranean Apple Store (www.apple.com), entered via a 32-foot glass cube. The parade of big names continues east along 57th Street.

♥ Bergdorf Goodman

754 Fifth Avenue, between 57th & 58th Streets (1-212 753 7300, www.bergdorfgoodman.com). Subway E, M to Fifth Avenue-53rd Street; N, Q, R to Fifth Ave-nue-59th Street. **Open** *10am-8pm Mon-Sat; 11am-7pm Sun.* **Map** *p116 E22* ⑬ *Department store*

Synonymous with understated luxury, Bergdorf's is known for designer clothes and accessories. On the fourth floor, Linda's is an elegant 'boutique' created by the store's fashion director, Linda Fargo, and stuffed with her personal picks: a mix of fresh-from-the-catwalk designs, vintage pieces and global finds, such as beauty products and handmade items. The fifth floor is dedicated to younger, trend-driven labels. It's also worth venturing to the seventh floor for Kentshire's amazing cache of vintage designer jewellery. In the basement, the wide-ranging beauty department includes unusual skincare and fragrance lines such as L'Officine

💜 Museum of Modern Art (MoMA)

11 W 53rd Street, between Fifth & Sixth Avenues (1-212 708 9400, www.moma.org). Subway E, M to Fifth Avenue-53rd Street. **Open** *Sept-June 10.30am-5.30pm Mon-Thur, Sat, Sun; 10.30am-8pm Fri. July, Aug 10.30am-5.30pm Mon-Wed, Sat, Sun; 10.30am-8.30pm Thur; 10.30am-8pm Fri.* **Admission** *(incl admission to film programmes) $25; $14-$18 reductions; free under-17s; free 4-8pm Fri.* **Map** *p116 E23.*

Founded in the late 1920s by a trio of arts patrons that included Mrs John D Rockefeller, Jr, MoMA is the world's orginal – and greatest – modern art museum, home to some of the most impressive artworks from the 19th, 20th and 21st centuries. Since 1939, the institution has occupied its current Midtown building, which early this century underwent a two-year renovation based on a design by Japanese architect Yoshio Taniguchi. Another expansion project, which will extend the museum into adjoining sites, is on the horizon, but the time frame hadn't been determined at time of writing. MoMA also collaborates on contemporary exhibitions with its Queens-based affiliate MoMA PS1 (*see p182*).

MoMA's permanent collection encompasses six curatorial departments: Architecture and Design; Drawings and Prints; Film; Media and Performance Art; Painting and Sculpture; and Photography. Among the many highlights are Picasso's *Les Demoiselles d'Avignon*, Van Gogh's *The Starry Night* and Dalí's *The Persistence of Memory*, as well as masterpieces by Giacometti, Hopper, Matisse, Monet, O'Keeffe, Pollock, Rothko, Warhol and many others. With a little forward planning, you can take in a film in one of the lower-level theatres as well (included in the price of admission).

Outside, the Philip Johnson-designed Abby Aldrich Rockefeller Sculpture Garden contains works by Calder, Rodin and Moore. If you want to contemplate the scene over an excellent meal, book a table at the Michelin-starred restaurant the Modern, overlooking the garden.

▶ *If you find the prices too steep at the Modern, dine in the bar, which shares the kitchen.*

Radio City Music Hall

Universelle Buly, which resurrects early-19th-century French apothecary recipes, and Roja, created by renowned perfumer Roja Dove and including an exclusive Bergdorf scent. The men's store is across the street at 745 Fifth Avenue.

♥ JJ Hat Center
*310 Fifth Avenue, between 31st & 32nd Streets (1-212 239 4368, www. jjhatcenter.com). Subway B, D, F, M, N, Q, R, W to 34th Street-Herald Square. **Open** 10am-7pm Mon-Fri; 10am-6pm Sat; noon-5pm Sunday. **Map** p116 E25 ⑭ Accessories*
Traditional hats may currently be back in fashion, but this venerable shop, in business since 1911, is oblivious to passing trends. Dapper gents sporting the shop's wares will help you choose from more than 10,000 fedoras, pork pies, caps and other styles on display in the splendid, chandelier-illuminated, wood-panelled showroom. Prices start at around $45 for a wool-blend cap.

Saks Fifth Avenue
*611 Fifth Avenue, between 49th & 50th Streets, (1-212 753 4000, www. saksfifthavenue.com). Subway E, M to Fifth Avenue-53rd Street. **Open** 10am-8.30pm Mon-Sat; 11am-7pm Sun. **Map** p116 E23 ⑮ Department store*
Although Saks has more than 40 locations nationwide, the Fifth Avenue flagship is the original, established in 1924 by New York retailers Horace Saks and Bernard Gimbel. The store features all the big names in fashion, from Armani to Zac Posen, including an expansive luxury shoe salon on the eighth floor and a recently overhauled contemporary-designer realm on the fifth floor. The opulent beauty hall is fun to peruse, and customer service is excellent, though some people might find it too aggressive. **Other Location** Saks Fifth Avenue Off 5th, 125 E 57th Street, between Lexington & Park Avenues, Midtown (1-212 634 0730).

Entertainment

Carnegie Hall
*154 W 57th Street, at Seventh Avenue, Midtown (1-212 247 7800, www.carnegiehall.org). Subway N, Q, R, W to 57th Street-Seventh Avenue. **Box office** 11am-6pm Mon-Sat; noon-6pm Sun. Phone bookings 8am-8pm daily. Tickets vary. **Map** p116 D22 ⑰ Classical music*
Artistic director Clive Gillinson continues to put his stamp on Carnegie Hall. The stars – both soloists and orchestras – still shine

brightly inside this renowned concert hall in the Isaac Stern Auditorium. But it's the spunky upstart Zankel Hall that has generated the most buzz, offering an eclectic mix of classical, contemporary, jazz, pop and world music. Next door, the Weill Recital Hall hosts intimate concerts and chamber music programmes. Keep an eye out for Ensemble Connect, which consists of some of the city's most exciting young musicians and also performs at the Juilliard School, among other venues.

New York City Center

131 W 55th Street, between Sixth & Seventh Avenues, Midtown (1-212 581 1212, www.nycitycenter.org). Subway B, D, E to Seventh Avenue; F to 57th Street; N, Q, R, W to 57th Street-Seventh Avenue. Tickets $25-$150. **Map** *p116 M5* ⑱ *Performance*
Before Lincoln Center changed the city's cultural geography, this was the home of the American Ballet Theatre, the Joffrey Ballet and the New York City Ballet. Built in 1923, the Moor-ish Revival building was a Shriners meeting hall before being converted to a performing arts centre two decades later. The lavish decor is golden, as are the companies that perform in the opulent mainstage theatre, including Dance Theater of Harlem and Alvin Ailey American

In the know
Lofty retreat

If you need respite from the traffic in Midtown East, slip into **Tudor City** on a hill between First and Second Avenues, from 41st to 43rd Streets. The peaceful residential enclave features a charming park where you can rest your feet. Head for the development's east-facing terrace for an impressive view of the United Nations complex.

Dance Theater. The popular Fall for Dance festival, in autumn, features mixed bills for just $15.

Radio City Music Hall

1260 Sixth Avenue, at 50th Street, Midtown (1-212 247 4777, www. radiocity.com). Subway B, D, F, M to 47th-50th Streets-Rockefeller Center. **Box office** *10am-6pm daily. Tickets vary.* **Map** *p116 E23* ⑲ *Live music*
Few rooms scream 'New York City!' more than this gilded hall, which in recent years has drawn The xx, Dave Chappelle and New Order as headliners. The greatest challenge for any performer is to not be upstaged by the awe-inspiring art deco surroundings, although those same surroundings lend historic heft to even the flimsiest showing. The venue is home to high-kicking precision dance company the Rockettes and their seasonal 'spectaculars'.

Midtown East & Murray Hill

Shopping, dining and entertainment options wane east of Fifth Avenue in the 40s and 50s. However, the area has some striking architecture. Completed in 1930 by architect William Van Alen, the art deco **Chrysler Building** pays homage to the automobile industry with vast radiator-cap eagles in lieu of traditional gargoyles and a brickwork relief sculpture of racing cars complete with chrome hubcaps. **Murray Hill** spans 30th to 40th Streets, between Third and Fifth Avenues. Townhouses of the rich and powerful were once clustered around Madison and Park Avenues, but these days the neighbourhood is populated mostly by upwardly mobiles fresh out of university and only a few streets retain their former elegance.

Sights & museums

Grand Central Terminal

From 42nd to 44th Streets, between Vanderbilt & Lexington Avenues (audio tours 1-917 566 0008, www. grandcentralterminal.com). Subway S, 4, 5, 6, 7 to 42nd Street-Grand Central. **Map** *p116 E24.*
Each day, the world's largest rail terminal sees more than 750,000 people shuffle through its Beaux Arts threshold – many of them sightseers. Designed by Warren & Wetmore and Reed & Stern, the gorgeous transport hub opened in 1913 with lashings of Botticino marble and staircases modelled after those of the Paris opera house. After mid-century decline, the terminal underwent extensive restoration and is now a destination in itself, with shops, restaurants and bars, including a ground-level food market with an outpost of Murray's Cheese, a sprawling Apple Store (1-212 284 1800) on the East Balcony, and the Campbell (1-212 297 1781), a watering hole in the former office-cum-pied-à-terre of 1920s financier John Campbell.

The opulent ceiling mural in the main concourse, by French painter Paul Helleu, depicts the October zodiac in the Mediterranean sky, complete with 2,500 LEDs, though the constellations are backwards. Visit the website for information about self-guided audio tours ($9; $7 reductions), or download the $5 smartphone app.

Morgan Library & Museum

225 Madison Avenue, at 36th Street (1-212 685 0008, www.themorgan. org). Subway 6 to 33rd Street. **Open** *10.30am-5pm Tue-Thur; 10.30am-9pm Fri; 10am-6pm Sat; 11am-6pm Sun.* **Admission** *$20; $13 reductions; free under-13s; free 7-9pm Fri.* **Map** *p116 E25.*
This Madison Avenue institution began as the private library of financier Pierpont Morgan, and is his cultural gift to the city. Building on the collection Morgan amassed in his lifetime, the museum houses first-rate works on paper, including drawings by Michelangelo, Rembrandt and Picasso; three Gutenberg Bibles; a copy of *Frankenstein* annotated by Mary Shelley; manuscripts by Dickens, Poe, Twain, Steinbeck and Wilde; sheet music handwritten by Beethoven and Mozart; and an original edition of Dickens's *A Christmas Carol* that's displayed every Yuletide. A massive renovation and expansion orchestrated by Renzo Piano brought more natural light into the building and doubled the available exhibition space. The final phase restored the original 1906 building, designed by McKim, Mead & White. Visitors can now see Morgan's spectacular library (the East Room), with its 30ft-high book-lined walls and murals by Henry Siddons Mowbray (who also painted the ceiling of the restored Rotunda).

United Nations Headquarters

Visitors' entrance: First Avenue, at 46th Street (tours 1-212 963 8687, visit.un.org). Subway S, 4, 5, 6, 7 to 42nd Street-Grand Central. **Open** *Visitor centre 9am-4.45pm Mon-Fri; 10am-4.45pm Sat, Sun. Tours 9.30am-4.45pm Mon-Fri.* **Admission** *$22; $13-$15 reductions (under-5s not admitted).* **Map** *p116 F24.*
The UN recently wrapped up extensive renovations to its complex and Le Corbusier's Secretariat building is gleaming. The iconic skyscraper is off-limits to the public, however, so you can only admire the exterior. Hour-long tours discuss the history and role of the UN, and visit the Security Council Chamber and the General Assembly Hall (when they're not in session). Artworks on view include Norman Rockwell's mosaic

The Golden Rule, and José Vela Zanetti's epic, 64ft-long 1953 mural *Mankind's Struggle for a Lasting Peace*. Note that while tickets may be available on site (cash only), it's advisable to book online. All visitors 18 and older must have government-issued photo ID (see website for security guidelines). The UN is closed for two weeks in September for the General Debate, and during high-level meetings (check the website for alerts).

Restaurants & cafés

Agern $$$

Grand Central Terminal, 89 E 42nd Street, between Park & Lexington Avenues (1-646 568 4018, agernrestaurant.com). Subway S, 4, 5, 6, 7 to 42nd Street-Grand Central. **Open** *7-10am, 11.30am-2.30pm, 5.30-10pm Mon-Fri; 5.30-10pm Sat; 5.30-9pm Sun (see website for updates).* **Map** *p116 E24* **15** *Scandinavian*

Escape the commuter clamour of Grand Central in the Scandinavian stillness of the terminal's formal Nordic dining room, a happily incongruous project from Noma co-founder Claus Meyer. The clean-lined space is as blond as a Swede, matched with black-leather banquettes, brass pendant lights and pops of pea-green chevron tiles. In the kitchen, Gunnar Gíslason, the Icelandic chef behind acclaimed Reykjavík restaurant Dill, takes now-familiar Scandi sensations – a sweet beet, freshly cracked out of a salt-baked hull; a tartare of beef heart, fragrant with dill – and executes them exceptionally well. Before you leave to again brave the commuter hustle, you're handed a cloth sack with a still-warm sourdough loaf – consider it the best train snack ever.

♥ Grand Central Oyster Bar & Restaurant $$

Grand Central Terminal, Lower Level, 42nd Street, at Park Avenue (1-212 490 6650, www.oysterbarny. com). Subway S, 4, 5, 6, 7 to 42nd Street-Grand Central. **Open** *11.30am-9.30pm Mon-Sat.* **Map** *p116 E24* **16** *Seafood*

The legendary Grand Central Oyster Bar has been a fixture since 1913. The sometimes surly countermen at the mile-long bar (the best seats in the house) are part of the charm. We suggest avoiding the more complicated fish concoctions and playing it safe with a reliably awe-inspiring platter of iced, just-shucked oysters (the selection sometimes exceeds 30 varieties, including many from nearby Long Island).

Great Northern Food Hall $-$$

Vanderbilt Hall, Grand Central Terminal, 89 E 42nd Street, between Lexington & Park Avenues (1-646 568 4020, www. greatnorthernfood.com). Subway S, 4, 5, 6, 7 to 42nd Street-Grand Central. **Open** *7am-10pm Mon-Fri; 8am-8pm Sat, Sun.* **Map** *p116 E24* **17** *Scandinavian*

As part of his dining takeover of Grand Central Terminal, which also includes Scandinavian dining room Agern (*see p141*), Noma co-founder Claus Meyer unveiled Great Northern Food Hall, a 5,000sq ft marketplace inside former waiting room Vanderbilt Hall. The hall is divided into eight Nordic-inspired food pavilions plus the Restaurant, an inexpensive sit-down eatery. The Grain Bar serves house-made granola, parfaits and porridges in the morning, segueing to savoury grain dishes and craft beers in the evening. The vegetable-focused Almanak offers salads, soups and snacks. Meyers Bageri produces pastries and breads. Brownsville

Roasters pours a seasonally changing coffee programme, and Open Rye features a rotating selection of *smørrebrød*, Danish open sandwiches, built with house-cured meats and fish. There's also a bar, stocked with small-batch spirits and a large selection of aquavit.

Urbanspace Vanderbilt

45th Street, at Vanderbilt Avenue (1-646 747 0810, urbanspacenyc. com/urbanspace-vanderbilt). Subway S, 4, 5, 6, 7 to 42nd Street-Grand Central. Open 6.30am-9pm Mon-Fri; 9am-5pm Sat, Sun. Map p116 E23 ⑱ *Food court*

This sprawling food court from Urbanspace, the team behind seasonal street-side pop-up food markets like Mad Sq Eats and Broadway Bites, includes such cult delicacies as Roberta's wood-fired pizzas, burgers from sought-after Brooklyn food truck Hard Times Sundaes and handmade doughnuts from Dough.

Bars

❤ Fine & Rare

9 E 37th Street, between Fifth & Madison Avenues (1-212 725 3866, www.fineandrare.nyc). Subway 6 to 33rd Street. Open 11.30am-2am Mon-Fri; 5pm-2am Sat; 5pm-midnight Sun. Map p116 E24 ⑧

Set on a quiet street near the Morgan Library & Museum, this sophisticated spirits den oozes retro glam, with tufted leather banquettes, an oversized fireplace, art deco wallpaper, and vintage teller windows sourced from nearby Grand Central Terminal. Jazz acts croon a playlist that pulls from the 1930s, '40s and '50s. Novel takes on classic cocktails include an old-fashioned with a choice of

a rye or rum base that's smoked with either hickory, applewood, mesquite or cherrywood. The drinks list also highlights pricey, hard-to-find bottles, accessible via library-style rolling ladders.

Shops & services

Dover Street Market New York

160 Lexington Avenue, at 30th Street (1-646 837 7750, newyork. doverstreetmarket.com). Subway 6 to 28th or 33rd Street. Open 11am-7pm Mon-Sat; noon-6pm Sun. Map p116 E25 ⑯ *Fashion/ accessories*

In late 2013, Comme des Garçons designer Rei Kawakubo brought her quirky, upscale interpretation of a London fashion market to the former New York School of Applied Design, complete with an outpost of the cult Paris eaterie, Rose Bakery. One of four offspring of the original location on Mayfair's Dover Street (the others are in Tokyo, Beijing and Singapore), DSMNY is a multilevel store that blurs the line between art and commerce. A transparent elevator whisks shoppers through the seven-floor consumer playground. Three pillars running through six of the levels have been transformed into art installations: a stripey patchwork knitted sheath by Magda Sayeg, London Fieldworks' miniature wooden metropolis, and 3D collages by 'junk sculptor' Leo Sewell. In addition to numerous Comme lines, the store stocks luxury labels like Balenciaga and Azzedine Alaïa, newer names such as Simone Rocha and Jacquemus, streetwear brands including NikeLab and Supreme, and an entire floor spotlighting emerging talent.

Uptown

Upper Manhattan was largely rural until the development of Central Park and the elevated train lines (precursors of the subway system) in the late 19th century. Today, the affluent neighbourhoods flanking Manhattan's largest green space are home to some of the city's most venerable museums and cultural institutions. To the north, Harlem and Washington Heights move to a more urban beat, with eclectic architecture and theatrical street life.

Best parks
Central Park (*p148*), Manhattan's bucolic back yard.

Best restaurants
Barney Greengrass (*p151*) for bagels and lox. Old-school luncheonette Lexington Candy Shop (*p162*). Red Rooster Harlem (*p167*) for global soul food and a lively scene. White Gold Butchers (*p154*) for a meaty midday feast.

Classic bar
Quintessential cocktail lounge Bemelmans Bar (*p163*).

Best cultural venue
Lincoln Center (*p152*), home of the top orchestra, opera and ballet companies.

Must-see museums
American Museum of Natural History's (*p150*) dinosaur skeletons and dioramas. Cool local-centric displays at New-York Historical Society (*p145*). Globe- and era-spanning behemoth Metropolitan Museum of Art (*p160*). Solomon R Guggenheim Museum (*p157*) in its stunning Frank Lloyd Wright building.

Best shops
Chic department store Barneys New York (*p163*). Magpie (*p155*), for handmade goods curated by a former museum-shop buyer. The Row (*p164*), a glam flagship for the luxe label. New York food institution Zabar's (*p155*).

Upper West Side

After **Central Park** was completed, magnificently tall residential buildings rose up along Central Park West to take advantage of the views. The first of these great apartment blocks was the **Dakota** (at 72nd Street), so named because its location was considered remote when it was built in 1884. The fortress-like building is known as the setting for *Rosemary's Baby* and the site of John Lennon's murder in 1980. **Morningside Heights**, between 110th and 125th Streets, from Morningside Park to the Hudson, is dominated by **Columbia University**. **Riverside Park**, a sinuous stretch of riverbank along the Hudson from 59th Street to 155th Street, was originally designed by Central Park's Frederick Law Olmsted, and subsequently extended.

Sights & museums

Cathedral Church of St John the Divine
1047 Amsterdam Avenue, at 112th Street (1-212 316 7540, www. stjohndivine.org). Subway B, C, 1 to 110th Street-Cathedral Parkway. **Open** *7.30am-6pm daily (with limited access Sun).* **Admission** *Suggested donation $10. Tours $14-$20; $12-$18 reductions.* **Map** *p165 C15.*
Construction of this massive house of worship, affectionately nicknamed St John the Unfinished, began in 1892 following a Romanesque-Byzantine design by George Heins and Christopher Grant LaFarge. In 1911, Ralph Adams Cram took over with a Gothic Revival redesign. Work came to a halt in 1941, when the US entered World War II. It resumed in earnest in 1979, but a fire in 2001 that destroyed the church's gift shop and damaged two 17th-century Italian tapestries

further delayed completion. It's still missing a tower and a north transept, among other things, but the nave has been restored and the entire interior reopened and rededicated. No further work is planned… for now. In addition to Sunday services, the cathedral hosts concerts and tours (the Vertical Tour, which takes you to the top of the building, is a revelation). It bills itself as a place for all people – and it certainly means it. Annual events include both winter and summer solstice celebrations, the Blessing of the Animals during the Feast of St Francis, which draws pets and their people from all over the city, and even a Blessing of the Bikes every spring.

Museum of Arts & Design

2 Columbus Circle, at Broadway (1-212 299 7777, www.madmuseum. org). Subway A, B, C, D, 1 to 59th Street-Columbus Circle. **Open** *10am-6pm Tue, Wed, Fri-Sun; 10am-9pm Thur.* **Admission** *$16; $12-$14 reductions; free under-19s. Pay what you wish 6-9pm Thur.* **Map** *p146 D22.*

This institution celebrates creative practice with thematic exhibitions that bring together contemporary objects created in a wide range of media – including clay, glass, wood, metal and cloth – with a strong focus on materials and process. The permanent collection of more than 3,000 objects from 1950 to the present includes porcelain ware by Cindy Sherman, stained glass by Judith Schaechter and ceramics by James Turrell. Before moving into Edward Durell Stone's austere 1964 Columbus Circle landmark in 2008, MAD redesigned the ten-storey building. Four floors of exhibition space include the Tiffany & Co Foundation Jewelry Gallery, and you can also watch resident artists create works in studios on the sixth floor. The ninth-floor bistro has views over the park.

❤ New-York Historical Society

170 Central Park West, at 77th Street (1-212 873 3400, www. nyhistory.org). Subway B, C to 81st Street-Museum of Natural History. **Open** *10am-6pm Tue-Thur, Sat; 10am-8pm Fri; 11am-5pm Sun.* **Admission** *$20; $6-$15 reductions; free under-5s. Pay what you wish 6-8pm Fri.* **Map** *p146 D19.*

Founded in 1804 by a group of prominent New Yorkers that included Mayor DeWitt Clinton, the New-York Historical Society is the city's oldest museum, originally based at City Hall. Over the past

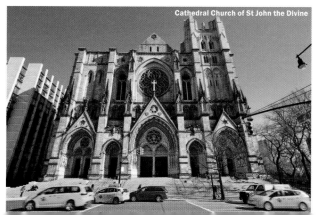

Cathedral Church of St John the Divine

several years, the society has been transforming the interior of its stately 1904 building to make the collection more accessible to a 21st-century audience. The Robert H and Clarice Smith New York Gallery of American History provides an overview of the collection and a broad sweep of New York's place in American history – Revolutionary-era artefacts are juxtaposed with a piece of the ceiling mural from Keith Haring's Pop Shop (the artist's Soho store, which closed after his death in 1990). Touch-screen monitors offer insight into artwork and documents, and large HD screens display a continuous slide show of highlights of the museum's holdings, such as original watercolours from Audubon's *Birds of America*. In the auditorium, an 18-minute film traces the city's development, while downstairs, the DiMenna Children's History Museum engages the next generation. On the recently reopened fourth floor, objects from the permanent collection chronicle various strands of New York history, such as slavery, the Hudson River School artists and 9/11. A striking glass-accented space showcases 100 Tiffany lamps. The new Center for Women's History features artefacts such as tennis gear donated by Billie Jean King and changing exhibitions.

In the know
New-York, New-York

The name of the New-York Historical Society is itself a historical preservation – placing a hyphen between 'New' and 'York' was common in the early 19th century. In fact, according to the Society, the *New York Times*, the paper of record, maintained the convention until 1896.

147

❤ Central Park

In 1858, the newly formed Central Park Commission chose landscape designer Frederick Law Olmsted and architect Calvert Vaux to turn a vast tract of rocky swampland into a rambling oasis of lush greenery. Although it suffered from neglect at various points in the 20th century, the park has been returned to its green glory thanks largely to the not-for-profit Central Park Conservancy. The 1870 Victorian Gothic **Dairy** (mid-park at 65th Street, 1-212 794 6564, www.centralparknyc.org, open 10am-5pm daily) houses one of the conservancy's five visitor centres.

The park has 21 playgrounds, and the southern section abounds with family-friendly diversions, including the **Central Park Zoo** (enter at Fifth Avenue & 64th Street, 1-212 439 6500, www.centralparkzoo.org), known for its penguins and snow leopards. The Tisch Children's Zoo is home to kid-friendly species, such as pot-bellied pigs and goats. The roving characters on the George Delacorte Musical Clock delight little ones every half-hour.

The **Wollman Rink** (between 62nd & 63rd Streets, 1-212 439 6900, www.wollmanskatingrink.com, open late Oct-Mar) doubles as a small children's amusement park, **Victorian Gardens** (1-212 982 2229, www.victoriangardensnyc.com), in the warmer months. Central Park's classic **Carousel** (mid-park at 64th Street, open daily Apr-Oct, call 1-212 439 6900 for out-of-season hours) was built in 1908.

Sheep did indeed graze on the **Sheep Meadow**, the designated quiet zone that begins at 66th Street, until 1934. To the east, between 66th and 72nd Streets, is the **Mall**, an elm-lined promenade that attracts street performers. North of here, overlooking the lake, is the grand **Bethesda Fountain & Terrace**. *Angel of the Waters*, the sculpture in the centre of the fountain, was created by Emma Stebbins, the first woman to be granted a major public art commission in New York City.

Just north is the **Loeb Boathouse** (mid-park, between 74th & 75th Streets, 1-212 517 2233, www.thecentralparkboathouse.com), which houses a restaurant and bar. From here, you can take a rowing boat out on the lake, which is crossed by the elegant Bow Bridge.

To the east, near the 72nd Street and Fifth Avenue entrance to the park is **Conservatory Water**. The small pond is a mecca for model-yacht racers in summer. Kids can't resist climbing on the bronze rendering of Lewis Carroll's Alice, the Mad Hatter and the White Rabbit north of the pond, while the Hans Christian Andersen statue is a gathering point for free Saturday-morning storytelling sessions in summer (early June-Sept 11am-noon, www.hcastorycenter.org).

West of the Bethesda Fountain, near the W 72nd Street entrance, sits **Strawberry Fields**, which memorialises John Lennon, who lived in, and was shot in front of, the nearby Dakota Building. It features a mosaic of the word 'imagine' that was donated by the city of Naples. Tucked just inside the western boundary of the park near 81st Street is the

Swedish Cottage. Designed as a schoolhouse, it was Sweden's entry in the 1876 Centennial Exposition in Philadelphia and now houses a tiny marionette theatre (1-212 988 9093, www. cityparksfoundation.org). The **Delacorte Theater** hosts **Shakespeare in the Park** (*see p59*), a summer run of free open-air plays. Nearby **Belvedere Castle**, a Victorian folly, overlooks the Turtle Pond. Just north is the **Great Lawn** (mid-park, between 79th & 85th Streets), a playing field that doubles as an outdoor concert spot. Behind the **Metropolitan Museum of Art** (*see p160*) is the Obelisk, a 69-foot hieroglyphics-covered granite monument dating from around 1500 BC, which was given to the US by the Khedive of Egypt in 1881.

In the mid 1990s, the **Reservoir** (mid-park, between 85th & 96th Streets) was renamed in honour of the late Jacqueline Kennedy Onassis, who used to jog round it. A turn here gives great views of the skyscrapers rising above the park; in spring, the cherry trees that ring the reservoir path and the bridle path below it make it particularly beautiful. In the northern section, the exquisite **Conservatory Garden** (entrance on Fifth Avenue, at 105th Street) comprises formal gardens inspired by English, French and Italian styles.

♥ American Museum of Natural History

Central Park West, at 79th Street (1-212 769 5100, www.amnh. org). Subway B, C to 81st Street-Museum of Natural History. **Open** *10am-5.45pm daily.* **Admission** *Suggested donation $22; $12.50-$17 reductions.* **Map** *p146 C19.*

The American Museum of Natural History's fourth-floor dino halls are home to the largest and arguably most fabulous collection of dinosaur fossils in the world. Nearly 85% of the bones on display are original, but during the museum's mid 1990s renovation, several specimens were remodelled to incorporate more recent discoveries. The Tyrannosaurus rex, for instance, was once believed to have walked upright, Godzilla-style; it now stalks prey with its head lowered and tail raised parallel to the ground.

The Hall of North American Mammals has undergone an extensive restoration of its formerly faded 1940s dioramas. A life-size model of a blue whale hangs from the cavernous ceiling of the Hall of Ocean Life, while in the Hall of Meteorites the focal point is Ahnighito, the largest iron meteor on display in the world, weighing in at 34 tons. Other halls explore human origins, world ecosystems and environmental preservation.

The spectacular Rose Center for Earth & Space offers insight into recent cosmic discoveries via shows in the Hayden Planetarium and a simulation of the origins of the Universe in the Big Bang Theater. The museum also screens digital nature films in 3D, and the roster of temporary exhibitions is thought-provoking for all ages.

New-York Historical Society *p145*

Restaurants & cafés

❤ Barney Greengrass $-$$
541 Amsterdam Avenue, between 86th & 87th Streets (1-212 724 4707, www.barneygreengrass. com). Subway B, C, 1 to 86th Street. **Open** *Shop 8am-6pm Tue-Sun. Restaurant 8.30am-4pm Tue-Fri; 8.30am-5pm Sat, Sun.* **No cards** *on weekends.* **Map** *p146 C18* ❶
American

Despite decor that Jewish mothers might call 'schmutzy', this legendary deli is a madhouse at breakfast and brunch. Enormous egg platters come with a choice of smoked fish (such as sturgeon or Nova Scotia salmon). Prices are on the high side, but portions are large, and that goes for the sandwiches too. Soup – matzo-ball or cold pink borscht – is a less costly option.

Per Se $$$$
4th Floor, Time Warner Center, 10 Columbus Circle, at 60th Street (1-212 823 9335, www.perseny. com). Subway A, B, C, D, 1 to 59th Street-Columbus Circle. **Open** *5.30-9.30pm Mon-Thur; 11.30am-1pm, 5.30-9.30pm Fri-Sun.* **Map** *p146 D22* ❷ *French*

Expectations are high at Per Se – and that goes both ways. You're expected to wear the right clothes (jackets are required for men) and pretend you aren't eating in a shopping mall. The restaurant, in turn, is expected to deliver one hell of a tasting menu for $325 (including service). And it does. Dish after dish is flawless, beginning with Thomas Keller's signature Oysters and Pearls (a sabayon of pearl tapioca with oysters and caviar). An all-vegetable version is also available, plus a dessert tasting menu.

Shake Shack $
366 Columbus Avenue, at 77th Street (1-646 747 8770, www. shakeshack.com). Subway B, C to 81st Street-Museum of Natural History; 1 to 79th Street. **Open** *11am-11pm daily.* **Map** *p146 C19* ❸ *American*

The spacious offspring of Danny Meyer's wildly popular Madison Square Park concession stand is now one of many locations across the city and beyond. Shake Shack is still a contender for New York's best burger. Patties are made from fresh-ground, all-natural Angus beef, and the franks are served Chicago-

❤ Lincoln Center

Columbus Avenue, between 62nd & 65th Streets, Upper West Side (1-212 875 5456, CenterCharge 1-212 721 6500, www.lincolncenter.org). Subway 1 to 66th Street-Lincoln Center. Box offices 10am-6pm or 8pm Mon-Sat; noon-6pm Sun. Map p146 C21.

Built in the early 1960s, this massive complex is the nexus of Manhattan's performing arts scene. The campus, which is just over 16 acres and home to 11 arts organisations, has undergone a major revamp in recent years, providing new performance facilities as well as more inviting public gathering spaces and restaurants. Venues are spread out across the square of blocks from 62nd to 66th Streets, between Amsterdam and Columbus Avenues, plus **Jazz at Lincoln Center** further south (Broadway, at 60th Street, 1-212 258 9800, www.jazz.org). In addition to box offices at individual Lincoln Center venues, a central box office (open noon-7pm Tue-Sat; noon-5pm Sun) at the **David Rubenstein Atrium** (between W 62nd & W 63rd Streets, Broadway & Columbus Avenues) sells discounted tickets to same-week performances. The space is also a venue for frequent free performances (see www.lincolncenter.org/atrium for further details).

Big stars such as conductor Valery Gergiev and pianist Emanuel Ax are Lincoln Center's musical meat and potatoes. Lately, though, the divide between the flagship Great Performers season, featuring top international soloists and ensembles, and the more audacious (and free), multidisciplinary Lincoln Center Out of Doors summer festival (*see p61*) continues to narrow. For other festivals, *see p57*.

An 18-month renovation turned the cosy home of the Chamber Music Society of Lincoln Center (www.chambermusicsociety. org), **Alice Tully Hall**, into a world-class, 1,096-seat theatre. A contemporary foyer with an elegant (if a bit pricey) café is immediately striking, but, more importantly, the revamp brought dramatic acoustic improvements. A renovation is also planned (though a date hasn't been set) for the comfortable 2,700-seat **David Geffen Hall**, the headquarters of the renowned New York Philharmonic (1-212 875 5656, www.nyphil.org).

The grandest of the Lincoln Center buildings, the **Metropolitan Opera House**, hosts the Metropolitan Opera (1-212 362 6000, www.metopera. org) from September to May. Opera's biggest stars appear here regularly, and music director emeritus James Levine, who stepped down in 2016, turned the orchestra into a true symphonic force. His successor, Yannick Nézet-Séguin, takes up the baton in 2020 due to previous commitments. The Met had already started becoming more inclusive before current impresario Peter Gelb took the reins in 2006. Now, the company is placing a priority on creating novel theatrical experiences with visionary directors (Robert Lepage, Bartlett Sher, David McVicar) and assembling a new company of physically graceful, telegenic stars (Anna Netrebko, Sonya Yoncheva, Peter Mattei).

In spring and summer, the majestic space is home to American Ballet Theatre, which presents full-length traditional story ballets, contemporary classics by Frederick Ashton and Antony Tudor, and new works by the company's stellar artist-in-residence, Alexei Ratmansky. The acoustics are wonderful, but the theatre is immense: get as close to the stage as you can afford.

The neoclassical New York City Ballet headlines at the opulent **David H Koch Theater**, which Philip Johnson designed to resemble a jewellery box. During its spring, autumn and winter seasons, ballets by George Balanchine are performed by a wonderful crop of dancers including the luminous Sara Mearns; there are also works by Jerome Robbins, Peter Martins (the company's ballet master in chief) and resident choreographer Justin Peck.

The majestic and prestigious **Lincoln Center Theater** complex (Telecharge 1-212 239 6200, www.lct.org) has a pair of amphitheatre-style drama venues. Its Broadway house, the 1,080-seat **Vivian Beaumont Theater**, is home to star-studded and elegant major productions. Downstairs is the 299-seat **Mitzi E Newhouse Theater**, an Off Broadway space devoted to new work by the upper layer of American playwrights. Since 2012, **LCT3** has presented the work of emerging playwrights and directors at the **Claire Tow Theater**, built on top of the Beaumont.

Cinephiles frequent the **Walter Reade Theater** and the **Elinor Bunin Munroe Film Center**, programmed by the **Film Society of Lincoln Center** (www.film linc.org).

White Gold Butchers

style on potato buns and topped with Rick's Picks Shack relish. Frozen-custard shakes hit the spot, and there's beer and wine if you want something stronger. **Other locations** throughout the city.

❤ White Gold Butchers $$
375 Amsterdam Avenue, at 78th Street (1-212 362 8731, www.whitegoldbutchers.com). Subway 1 to 79th Street. **Open** *Butcher shop 10am-8pm daily. Restaurant 10am-4.30pm, 5.30-11pm Mon-Thur; 10am-4.30pm, 5.30pm-midnight Fri; 8am-4.30pm, 5.30pm-midnight Sat; 8am-4.30pm, 5.30-11pm Sun.* **Map** *p146 C19* ❹ *American*
Known for her fondness for offal, Michelin-starred chef April Bloomfield helms this Upper West Side meat market-slash-all-day restaurant with long-time partner Ken Friedman and star butchers Erika Nakamura and Jocelyn Guest. The latter two can be found behind the retail counter, divvying up cuts for not only uptown locals but also the other restaurants in the Bloomfield-Friedman portfolio, including the Spotted Pig and the Breslin. The sit-down corner of the restaurant has tufted leather banquettes and a gold-painted steer head mounted on an exposed-brick wall. Full table service is relegated to dinner only, but we prefer the more laid-back lunch set-up, when you order straight from the counter. Standout midday options include house-made hot dogs piled with kimchi or Bloomfield's version of a chopped cheese, a Bronx and Harlem bodega staple that's a cross between a burger and a Philly cheesesteak. Built with a boutique beef blend ribboned with gooey American cheese and topped with pickled jalapeños, pickles and mayo on a poppy-seed kaiser roll, it's pricier than any bodega sandwich you've ever had, but it's substantially better, too.

Shops & services

Levain Bakery
167 W 74th Street, between Columbus & Amsterdam Avenues (1-212 874 6080, www.levainbakery. com). Subway 1 to 79th Street. **Open** *8am-7pm Mon-Sat; 9am-7pm Sun.* **Map** *p146 C20* ❶ *Food & drink*
Levain sells breads, muffins, brioche and other delectable baked goods, but we're crazy about the cookies. A full 6oz each, the

massive mounds stay gooey in the middle. The lush, brownie-like double-chocolate variety, made with extra-dark French cocoa and semi-sweet chocolate chips, is a truly decadent treat. **Other locations** 351 Amsterdam Avenue, between 76th & 77th Streets, Upper West Side (1-646 455 0952); 2167 Frederick Douglass Boulevard (Eighth Avenue), between 116th & 117th Streets, Harlem (1-646 455 0952).

♥ Magpie
488 Amsterdam Avenue, between 83rd & 84th Streets (1-212 579 3003, www.magpienewyork.com). Subway 1 to 86th Street. **Open** *11am-7pm Tue-Sat; 11am-6pm Sun.* **Map** *p146 C19* ❷ *Gifts/homewares*
Sylvia Parker worked as a buyer at the American Folk Art Museum gift shop before opening this eco-friendly boutique. The slender space, which is decorated with bamboo shelving and Hudson River driftwood, is packed with locally made, handcrafted, sustainable and fair-trade items. Finds include hand-embellished cushions and ceramics, recycled-resin jewellery, attractively packaged soaps and candles.

♥ Zabar's
2245 Broadway, at 80th Street (1-212 787 2000, www.zabars.com). Subway 1 to 79th Street. **Open** *8am-7.30pm Mon-Fri; 8am-8pm Sat; 9am-6pm Sun.* **Map** *p146 C19* ❸ *Food & drink*
Zabar's is more than a shop – it's a New York City landmark. It began life in 1934 as a tiny storefront specialising in Jewish 'appetising' delicacies, and has gradually expanded to take over half a block of prime Upper West Side real estate. What never cease to surprise, however, are the reasonable prices – even for high-end foods. Besides the famous smoked fish and rafts of delicacies,

Zabar's has fabulous bread, cheese, olives and coffee, plus kitchen gadgets and homewares.

Entertainment

Beacon Theatre
2124 Broadway, between 74th & 75th Streets, Upper West Side (1-212 465 6500, www.beacontheatre. com). Subway 1, 2, 3 to 72nd Street. **Box office** *11am-7pm Mon-Sat (varies on event days). Tickets vary.* **Map** *p146 C20* ❶ *Live music*
This spacious former vaudeville theatre hosts a variety of popular acts, from comedian John Oliver to jazz-rock legends Steely Dan. While the vastness can be daunting to performers and audience alike, the baroque, gilded interior and uptown location make you feel as though you're having a real night out on the town.

Upper East Side

Although Manhattan's super-rich now live all over town, the Upper East Side exudes old money. Along Fifth, Madison and Park Avenues, stately mansions and townhouses rub shoulders with deluxe apartment buildings guarded by uniformed doormen. Fifth Avenue from 82nd to 105th Streets is known as **Museum Mile** because it's lined with more than half a dozen celebrated institutions.

Sights & museums

Cooper Hewitt, Smithsonian Design Museum

2 E 91st Street, at Fifth Avenue (1-212 849 8400, www.cooperhewitt. org). Subway 4, 5, 6 to 86th Street. **Open** *10am-6pm Mon-Fri, Sun; 10am-9pm Sat.* **Admission** *$18; $9-$12 reductions; free under-19s. Pay what you wish 6-9pm Sat.* **Map** *p146 E18.*

The museum began as a collection created for students of the Cooper Union for the Advancement of Science and Art by the Hewitt sisters – granddaughters of the institution's founder, Peter Cooper – and opened to the public in 1897. Part of the Smithsonian since the 1960s, the Cooper Hewitt is the only museum in the US solely dedicated to historic and contemporary design. In 1976, it took up residence in the former home of steel magnate Andrew Carnegie.

Thanks to a three-year renovation, completed in 2014, historic spaces such as the Teak Room, with its intricately carved wall panelling and cabinets, have been painstakingly restored. The addition of a 6,000sq ft gallery on the third floor – formerly occupied by the National Design Library, now in an adjacent building – provides more room for rotating exhibitions. These include the excellent Selects series, in which a prominent artist, designer, architect or other tastemaker curates their favourite items from the collection.

Each visitor receives a high-tech pen, allowing them to 'collect' objects, explore them and even create their own designs on high-definition screens on tables. The second floor showcases objects from the permanent collection, with textiles, product design, decorative arts, drawings, prints and graphic design, organised by theme. Items from different eras and geographical areas are attractively grouped together, creating interesting juxtapositions and revealing links. The varied holdings include oil sketches by Hudson River School painter Frederic Church (1826-1900) and a 1996 concept design for the Air Jordan XIII sneaker by the shoe's original designer, Tinker Hatfield. The digital Immersion Room lets you fully experience the institution's impressive collection of wallcoverings – the largest in the US.

Frick Collection

1 E 70th Street, at Fifth Avenue (1-212 288 0700, www.frick.org). Subway 6 to 68th Street-Hunter College. **Open** *10am-6pm Tue-Sat; 11am-5pm Sun.* **Admission** *(under-10s not admitted) $22; $12-$17 reductions. Pay what you wish 2-6pm Wed. Free 6-9pm 1st Fri of the mth (except Jan).* **Map** *p146 E20.*

Industrialist, robber baron and collector Henry Clay Frick commissioned this opulent mansion with a view to leaving his legacy to the public. Designed by Thomas Hastings of Carrère & Hastings (the firm behind the New York Public Library) and built in 1914, the building was inspired by 18th-century British and French architecture.

❤ Solomon R Guggenheim Museum

1071 Fifth Avenue, between 88th & 89th Streets (1-212 423 3500, www.guggenheim.org). Subway 4, 5, 6 to 86th Street. **Open** *10am-5.45pm Mon-Wed, Fri, Sun; 10am-7.45pm Sat.* **Admission** *$25; $18 reductions; free under-12s. Pay what you wish 5.45-7.45pm Sat.* **Map** *p146 E18.*

While its winding cantilevered curves have become as integral to New York's architectural landscape as the spire of the Chrysler Building or the arches of the Brooklyn Bridge, the Solomon R Guggenheim Museum caused quite a stir when it debuted in 1959. Many felt its appearance clashed with the rest of staid Fifth Avenue, while Willem de Kooning and Robert Motherwell complained that their art was not best appreciated from the museum's interior ramps. Some critics suggested the building was less a museum than a monument to its architect, Frank Lloyd Wright. These criticisms were of little concern to Wright. When someone complained that the walls wouldn't be high enough to display certain paintings, he retorted that the canvases should be cut in half. The architect died six months before the completion of his only major building in New York City. (There's also a house designed by Wright in the Lighthouse Hill section of Staten Island that isn't open to the public).

In 1992, the addition of a ten-storey tower provided space for additional galleries, a café and an auditorium. Today, the Rotunda is devoted to large-scale changing exhibitions. Solomon R Guggenheim's original founding collection, amassed in the 1930s, includes works by Kandinsky, Chagall, Picasso, Franz Marc and others. The Solomon R Guggenheim Foundation's holdings have since been enriched by subsequent bequests, including the Thannhauser Collection, with paintings by Impressionist and post-Impressionist Masters such as Manet, Cézanne and Gaugin, and the Panza di Biumo Collection of American minimalist and conceptual art from the 1960s and '70s.

In an effort to preserve the feel of a private residence, labelling is minimal, but you can opt for a free audio guide, download the app or pay $2 for a booklet. Works spanning the 14th to the 19th centuries include masterpieces by Rembrandt, Vermeer, Whistler, Gainsborough, Holbein and Titian, and exquisite period furniture, porcelain and other decorative objects. Aficionados of 18th-century French art will find two rooms especially enchanting: the panels of the Boucher Room (1750-52) depict children engaged in adult occupations; the Fragonard Room contains the artist's series *Progress of Love* – four of the paintings were commissioned (and rejected) by Louis XV's mistress Madame du Barry. A gallery in the enclosed garden portico is devoted to decorative arts and sculpture. It's advisable to check before visiting in 2019 and beyond since the museum is planning a major expansion of its exhibition spaces.

Jewish Museum

1109 Fifth Avenue, at 92nd Street (1-212 423 3200, www.thejewishmuseum.org). Subway 4, 5, 6 to 86th Street; 6 to 96th Street. **Open** *11am-5.45pm Mon, Tue, Sat, Sun; 11am-8pm Thur; 11am-5.45pm Fri (11am-4pm Nov-Mar). Closed Jewish holidays.* **Admission** *$15; $7.50-$12 reductions; free under-19s. Free Sat. Pay what you wish 5-8pm Thur.* **Map** *p146 E18.*

The Jewish Museum is housed in a magnificent 1908 French Gothic-style mansion – the former home of the financier, collector and Jewish leader Felix Warburg. Inside, the centrepiece exhibition 'Scenes from the Collection' presents rotating selections of the museum's cache of around 30,000 works of art, artefacts and media installations from antiquity to the present day. The excellent temporary shows, which spotlight Jewish artists or related themes, appeal to a broad audience. You can nosh on bagels, knishes and other delicacies at an outpost of famed Lower East Side purveyor, Russ & Daughters (*see p91*).

Museum of the City of New York

1220 Fifth Avenue, between 103rd & 104th Streets (1-212 534 1672, www.mcny.org). Subway 6 to 103rd Street. **Open** *10am-6pm daily.* **Admission** *Suggested donation $18; $12 reductions; free under-20s.* **Map** *p146 E16.*

This institution provides a great introduction to NYC. The entire first floor is devoted to 'New York at its Core', a permanent exhibition chronicling the city's 400-year history, from its beginnings as a Dutch colony to the urban force it is today. In addition to high-tech interactive displays, which allow you to virtually 'meet' key players from the past, the hundreds of objects include a 17th-century Lenape war club, a ceremonial shovel from the groundbreaking of the first subway, a Studio 54 guest list from the nightclub's heyday, and Milton Glaser's original concept sketch for the 1976 'I Heart New York' campaign. A 28-minute film, *Timescapes*, which also illuminates the growth of Gotham, is shown free with admission every 40 minutes from 10.20am to 5pm. But the museum's jewel is the amazing Stettheimer Dollhouse, created in the 1920s by Carrie Stettheimer, whose artist friends reinterpreted their masterpieces in miniature to hang on the walls. Look closely and you'll spy a tiny version of Marcel Duchamp's *Nude Descending a Staircase*. Temporary shows, on such varied subjects as gay culture and the gilded age, spotlight the metropolis from different angles.

Neue Galerie

1048 Fifth Avenue, at 86th Street (1-212 628 6200, www.neuegalerie. org). Subway 4, 5, 6 to 86th Street. **Open** *11am–6pm Mon, Thur-Sun; 11am-8pm 1st Fri of the mth.* **Admission** *(under-12s not admitted)* $20; $10-$15 reductions. Free 6-8pm 1st Fri of the mth.* **Map** *p146 E18.*

Set within a refined 1914 mansion designed by New York Public Library architects Carrère & Hastings, the elegant Neue Galerie showcases German and Austrian fine art, objects and furnishings from the late 19th and early 20th centuries in several exquisitely restored rooms. The creation of the late art dealer Serge Sabarsky and cosmetics mogul Ronald S Lauder, it has the largest concentration of works by Gustav Klimt and Egon Schiele outside of Vienna, including Klimt's gorgeous *The Woman in Gold* – the portrait of Adele Bloch-Bauer that was returned to the subject's family (and subsequently purchased by the Neue Galerie) after being stolen by the Nazis in World War II. Factor in a stop at the chic Café Sabarsky (*see below*) for coffee and ravishing Viennese pastries, or something more substantial.

Park Avenue Armory

643 Park Avenue, between 66th & 67th Streets (1-212 616 3930, www. armoryonpark.org). Subway 6 to 68th Street-Hunter College. **Open** *during events; see website for details.* **Tours** *$15; $10 reductions.* **Map** *p146 E21.*

Once home to the Seventh Regiment of the National Guard, this impressive 1881 structure contains a series of period rooms dating from the late 19th century, designed by such luminaries as Louis Comfort Tiffany and the Herter Brothers. The vast Wade Thompson Drill Hall has become one of the city's premier alternative spaces for art, concerts and theatre.

Restaurants & cafés

Café Sabarsky $$

Neue Galerie, 1048 Fifth Avenue, at 86th Street (1-212 288 0665, www. neuegalerie.org/cafes/sabarsky). Subway 4, 5, 6 to 86th Street. **Open** *9am-6pm Mon, Wed; 9am-9pm Thur-Sun.* **Map** *p146 E18* ⑤

Austrian/café

Purveyor of indulgent pastries and whipped cream-topped *einspänner* coffee for Neue Galerie patrons by day, this sophisticated, high-ceilinged restaurant, inspired by a classic Viennese *kaffeehaus*, is helmed by chef Kurt Gutenbrunner of modern Austrian restaurant Wallsé. Appetisers are most adventurous – the creaminess of the *spätzle* noodles a perfect base for sweetcorn, tarragon and wild mushrooms – while main course specials, such as wiener schnitzel tartly garnished with lingonberries, are capable yet ultimately feel like the calm before the *Sturm und Drang* of dessert. Try the *klimttorte*, which masterfully alternates layers of hazelnut cake with chocolate. Note: the eatery is closed on Tuesdays.

JG Melon $

1291 Third Ave, at 74th Street (1-212 744 0585). **Open** *11.30am-2.30am Mon-Sat; 11.30am-1am Sun. Subway Q to 72nd Street, 6 to 77th Street.* **No cards.** **Map** *p146 F20* ⑥

American

This classic bar and eatery, with its nostalgic neon sign, green-and-white checked tablecloths and tie-sporting staff, is constantly packed with a preppy local crowd and visitors eager to try the headlining burger. The plump, loosely packed round is made with a hush-hush beef blend from Master Purveyors,

💙 Metropolitan Museum of Art

1000 Fifth Avenue, at 82nd Street (1-212 535 7710, www.metmuseum. org). Subway 4, 5, 6 to 86th Street. **Open** *10am-5.30pm Mon-Thur, Sun; 10am-9pm Fri, Sat.* **Admission** *Suggested donation (incl same-day admission to the Met Breuer & the Met Cloisters) $25; $12-$17 reductions; free under-12s.* **Map** *p146 E19.*

The Met, which opened in 1880, now occupies 13 acres of Central Park. Its original Gothic Revival building was designed by Calvert Vaux and Jacob Wrey Mould, but is now almost hidden by subsequent additions. The encyclopedic globe- and millennia-spanning holdings include fine and decorative art, arms and armour, musical instruments and ancient artefacts. The first floor's north wing contains the collection of ancient Egyptian art and the glass-walled atrium housing the Temple of Dendur, moved en masse from its original Nile-side setting and now overlooking a reflective pool.

In the north-west corner is the American Wing with its grand Engelhard Court, flanked by the salvaged façade of Wall Street's Branch Bank of the United States and a stunning loggia designed by Louis Comfort Tiffany for his Long Island estate. The centrepiece of the wing's Galleries for Paintings, Sculpture and Decorative Arts is Emanuel Gottlieb Leutze's iconic 1851 painting *Washington Crossing the Delaware*.

In the southern wing are the halls housing Greek and Roman art. Turning west brings you to the Arts of Africa, Oceania and the Americas collection; it was donated by Nelson Rockefeller as a memorial to his son Michael, who disappeared while visiting New Guinea in 1961. A wider-ranging bequest, the two-storey Robert Lehman Wing, is at the western end of the floor. This eclectic

collection is housed in a recreation of the Lehman family townhouse and features works by Botticelli, Bellini, Ingres and Rembrandt, among others. At ground level, the Anna Wintour Costume Center is the site of the Met's blockbuster fashion exhibitions.

Upstairs, the central western section is dominated by the European Paintings galleries, which hold an amazing reserve of old masters, including Rembrandt, Rubens, Vermeer, Velázquez and Goya. To the south, the 19th-century European galleries contain some of the Met's most popular works – in particular the two-room Monet holdings and a colony of Van Goghs that includes his oft-reproduced *Irises*.

Walk eastward and you'll reach the galleries of the Art of the Arab Lands, Turkey, Iran, Central Asia and Later South Asia. In the north-east wing of the floor, you'll find the sprawling collection of

Asian art; be sure to check out the ceiling of the Jain Meeting Hall in the South-east Asian gallery. You can rest your feet in the Astor Court, a tranquil recreation of a Ming Dynasty garden, or head up to the Iris & B Gerald Cantor Roof Garden (usually open May-Oct), which offers changing site-specific installations and Central Park views.

In 2016, the museum took over the modernist Madison Avenue building designed by Hungarian architect Marcel Breuer, formerly home to the Whitney Museum of American Art. As per an agreement, the Met rechristened it the **Met Breuer** (945 Madison Avenue, at 75th Street, 1-212 731 1675) and has devoted it to exhibitions spotlighting the institution's stellar collection of 20th- and 21st-century art. For the Cloisters, which houses the Met's medieval art collection, *see p166.*

the same source for the choice cuts found at legendary steakhouses like Peter Luger and Keens. Veiled with melty American cheese, the juicy, griddle-cooked beaut is served on a modest Arnold bun with red onions and crinkled pickle chips.

❤ Lexington Candy Shop $

1226 Lexington Avenue, at 83rd Street (1-212 288 0057, www. lexingtoncandyshop.net). Subway 4, 5, 6 to 86th Street. **Open** *7am-7pm Mon-Fri; 8am-7pm Sat; 8am-6pm Sun.* **Map** *p146 E19* ⑦ *American*

You won't find much candy for sale at this well-preserved retro lunchroom, which opened in 1925. But in addition to the usual diner fare (burgers, egg creams), the extensive menu lists such old-fashioned items as Lime Rickeys and liverwurst sandwiches. If you come for breakfast, order the doorstop slabs of french toast.

Rôtisserie Georgette $$$

14 E 60th Street, between Fifth & Madison Avenues (1-212 390 8060, www.rotisserieg.com). Subway N, Q, R to Fifth Avenue-59th Street. **Open** *noon-2.30pm, 5.45-10pm Mon; noon-2.30pm, 5.45-11pm Tue-Fri; 5.45-11pm Sat; noon-3pm, 5-9.15pm Sun (closed Sun Jul, Aug).* **Map** *p146 E22* ⑧ *French/ American*

Georgette Farkas, who was Daniel Boulud's publicist for nearly two decades, opened this 90-seat rotisserie, furnished with caramel-coloured banquettes and showcasing spit-fired roasts, including beef, lamb, poultry and whole fish. The menu also includes seasonal starters, salads and sides, such as pancetta-studded brussels sprouts and three takes on potatoes (traditional roasted, twice-baked with Gruyère mashed potatoes, or baked with apples and tarragon). The wine list showcases lesser-known French producers.

Bars

Bar Pleiades

The Surrey, 20 E 76th Street, between Fifth & Madison Avenues (1-212 772 2600, www.barpleiades. com). Subway 6 to 77th Street. **Open** *noon-midnight Mon-Thur, Sun; noon-1am Fri, Sat.* **Map** *p146 E20* ①

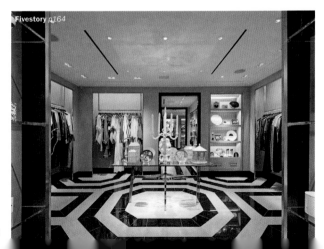

Fivestory p164

Bloomingdale's *p164*

Designed as a nod to Coco Chanel, Daniel Boulud's chic bar in the Surrey hotel is framed in black lacquered panels that recall an elegant make-up compact. The luxe setting and moneyed crowd might seem a little stiff, but the seasonally rotating cocktails are so exquisitely executed you probably won't mind. Light eats are provided by Café Boulud next door.

♥ Bemelmans Bar

The Carlyle, 35 E 76th Street, at Madison Avenue (1-212 744 1600, www.thecarlyle.com). Subway 6 to 77th Street. Open noon-12.30am Mon, Sun; noon-1am Tue-Thur; noon-1.30am Fri, Sat. Map p146 E19 ❷

The Plaza may have Eloise, but the Carlyle has its own children's book connection – the wonderful 1947 murals of Central Park by *Madeline* creator Ludwig Bemelmans in this, the quintessential classy New York bar. A pianist adds to the atmosphere in the early evening and a jazz trio takes up residence later (9pm Mon, Sun; 9.30pm Tue-Sat), when a $15-$35 cover charge kicks in.

Shops & services

Madison Avenue, between 57th and 86th Streets, is packed with international designer names: Alexander McQueen, Chloé, Derek Lam, Isabel Marant, Prada, Lanvin, Ralph Lauren, Sonia Rykiel, Tom Ford, Valentino and many more.

♥ Barneys New York

660 Madison Avenue, at 61st Street, Upper East Side (1-212 826 8900, www.barneys.com). Subway N, Q, R to Fifth Avenue-59th Street; 4, 5, 6 to 59th Street. Open 10am-8pm Mon-Fri; 10am-7pm Sat; 11am-7pm Sun. Map p146 E22 ❹ *Department store*

Barneys has a reputation for spotlighting more independent designer labels than other upmarket department stores, and it also has its own trend-driven collection. The ground floor showcases luxe accessories, and cult beauty and fragrance brands are in the basement. Head to the seventh and eighth floors for contemporary designer and denim lines.

Bloomingdale's

1000 Third Avenue, at 59th Street (1-212 705 2000, www. bloomingdales.com). Subway N, Q, R to Lexington Avenue-59th Street; 4, 5, 6 to 59th Street. **Open** *10am-8.30pm Mon-Sat; 11am-7pm Sun (hrs vary).* **Map** *p146 F22* ❺
Department store

Ranking among the city's top tourist attractions, Bloomie's is a gigantic, glitzy department store stocked with everything from handbags to home furnishings. The glam beauty section includes an outpost of globe-spanning apothecary Space NK, and you can get a mid-shopping sugar fix at the on-site Magnolia Bakery. The hipper, compact Soho outpost concentrates on contemporary fashion and accessories, denim and cosmetics. Bloomingdale's Outlet sells discounted merchandise.

Fivestory

18 E 69th Street, between Fifth & Madison Avenues (1-212 288 1338, www.fivestoryny.com). Subway 6 to 68th Street-Hunter College. **Open** *10am-6pm Mon-Wed, Fri; 10am-7pm Thur; noon-6pm Sat, Sun.* **Map** *p146 E21* ❻ *Fashion*

At just 26 (with a little help from her fashion-industry insider dad), Claire Distenfeld opened this glamorous, grown-up boutique, which sprawls over two and a half floors of – yes – a five-storey townhouse. The hand-selected stock spans big-name and lesser-known American and European labels and eclectic styles, from urban-casual pieces by Alexander Wang to sleek, tailored looks from Brandon Maxwell and full-length gowns by Carolina Herrera. There are separate spaces for shoes and jewellery.

❤ The Row

17 E 71st Street, between Fifth & Madison Avenues (1-212 755 2017, www.therow.com). Subway 6 to 72nd Street. **Open** *10am-6pm Mon-Wed, Fri, Sat; 10am-7pm Thur.* **Map** *p146 E20* ❼ *Fashion*

The flagship of Ashley and Mary-Kate Olsen's luxurious yet understated label occupies a discreet townhouse. Its elegant, pared-down interior provides the perfect foil for the impeccably tailored pieces in sumptuous fabrics and a muted colour palette. Exquisitely crafted classic loafers and heels are showcased in a separate room, and there's also a small men's line. Even if you can't quite stretch to the one-percenter price tags, it's worth checking out the art peppering the space by the likes of Keith Haring, Andy Warhol and Isamu Noguchi.

Entertainment

Café Carlyle

Carlyle, 35 E 76th Street, at Madison Avenue, Upper East Side (1-212 744 1600, www.thecarlyle. com). Subway 6 to 77th Street. Shows vary. **Admission** *$55-$220 ($75 dinner or $25 food/drink minimum).* **Map** *p146 E19* ❷ *Cabaret*

With its airy murals by Marcel Vertes, this elegant boîte in the Carlyle hotel remains the epitome of New York class, attracting such top-level singers as folk legend Judy Collins, Broadway star Chita Rivera and married cabarettists John Pizzarelli and Jessica Molaskey. Lately, the roster has also included pop stars from the '80s and '90s. Woody Allen often plays clarinet with Eddie Davis and his New Orleans Jazz Band on Monday nights.

Harlem & Washington Heights

Extending north from the top of Central Park, Harlem is the cultural capital of black America – the legacy of the Harlem Renaissance. By the 1920s, it had become the country's most populous African-American community, attracting some of black America's greatest artists: writers such as Langston Hughes and musicians like Duke Ellington and Louis Armstrong.

On 125th Street, Harlem's main artery, street preachers and mix-tape hawkers vie for the attentions of the human parade. Although new apartment buildings, boutiques, restaurants and cafés are scattered around the neighbourhood, Harlem has retained much of its 19th- and early 20th-century architecture because redevelopers shunned it for so long.

East of Fifth Avenue is **East Harlem**, better known to its primarily Puerto Rican residents as El Barrio. The traditional southern boundary with the Upper East Side is 96th Street, but this is increasingly blurred as gentrification creeps northward. From 155th Street to Dyckman (200th) Street is **Washington Heights**, which contains a handful of attractions and picturesque riverside **Fort Tryon Park**.

Harlem Haberdashery p168

Metropolitan Museum of Art) $25; $12-$17 reductions; free under-12s. **Map** p165 B10.
Set in a lovely park overlooking the Hudson River, the Cloisters houses the Metropolitan Museum's medieval art and architecture collections. A path winds through parkland to a castle that seems to date from the Middle Ages; in fact, it was built in the 1930s using pieces from five medieval French cloisters, shipped from Europe by the Rockefeller clan. Highlights include the impressive limestone apse of the 12th-century Fuentidueña Chapel, the Unicorn Tapestries and the Annunciation triptych by Robert Campin.

Sights & museums

Met Cloisters
99 Margaret Corbin Drive, Fort Tryon Park (1-212 923 3700, www. metmuseum.org). Subway A to 190th Street, then 10min walk. **Open** Mar-Oct 10am-5.15pm daily. Nov-Feb 10am-4.45pm daily. **Admission** Suggested donation (incl same-day admission to

Studio Museum in Harlem
144 W 125th Street, between Adam Clayton Powell Jr Boulevard (Seventh Avenue) & Malcolm X Boulevard (Lenox Avenue) (1-212 864 4500, www.studiomuseum. org). Subway 2, 3 to 125th Street. **Open** noon-9pm Thur, Fri; 10am-6pm Sat; noon-6pm Sun. **Admission** Suggested donation $7; $3 reductions; free under-12s. Free Sun. **Map** p165 D13.

The first black fine arts museum in the United States when it opened in 1968, the Studio Museum is an important player in the art scene of the African diaspora. Under the leadership of director and chief curator Thelma Golden (formerly of the Whitney), this vibrant institution, housed in a stripped-down, three-level space, presents shows in a variety of media by black artists from around the world. The museum, which supports emerging visual artists of African descent through its coveted artist-in-residence programme, is planning an expansion project, so it's advisable to call or check the website before visiting.

Restaurants & cafés

Charles Pan Fried Chicken Restaurant $
2461 Frederick Douglass Boulevard (Eighth Avenue), at 132nd street (1-212 281 1800). Subway B, D to 155th Street. **Open** *11am-midnight Mon-Thur; 11am-1.30am Fri, Sat; noon-11.30pm Sun.* **Map** *p165 D12* ⑨ *American Southern*
Fried chicken guru Charles Gabriel's no-frills eatery has hopped around Harlem in recent years, but devotees still rave about his speciality's moist flesh and crackly skin. In addition to the poultry, you can feast on barbecued ribs, mac and cheese, collard greens, yams and other Southern favourites.

❤ Red Rooster Harlem $$
310 Malcolm X Boulevard (Lenox Avenue), between 125th & 126th Streets (1-212 792 9001, www.redroosterharlem.com). Subway 2, 3 to 125th Street. **Open** *11.30am-10.30pm Mon-Thur; 11.30am-11.30pm Fri; 10am-11.30pm Sat; 10am-10pm Sun.* **Map** *p165 D13* ⑩ *American/eclectic*

With its hobnobbing bar scrum, potent cocktails and lively jazz, this buzzy eatery serves as a worthy clubhouse for the new Harlem. Superstar chef Marcus Samuelsson is at his most populist here, drawing on a mix of Southern-fried, East African, Scandinavian and French flavours. At the teardrop-shaped bar, Harlem politicos mix with trendy downtowners, swilling cocktails and gorging on rib-sticking food.

Sprawling basement lounge Ginny's Supper Club (1-212 421 3821, www.ginnyssupperclub. com) is modelled after the Harlem speakeasies of the '20s with eclectic cocktails and a steady line-up of live music.

Bars

Alibi Lounge
2376 Adam Clayton Powell Jr Boulevard (Seventh Avenue), at 139th Street (1-917-472-7789, www.alibiharlem.com). Subway B, C, 2, 3 to 135th Street. **Open** *6pm-2am Tue-Thur, Sun; 6pm-4am Fri, Sat.* **Map** *p165 D11* ❸
Founded in 2016 by a former human rights attorney, this classy space aims to provide a hub for Harlem's gay community. It may not be home to ragers, but you can expect a chill time getting to know well-dressed men over champagne-based cocktails with names like 'Elegance is Attitude'.

ROKC
3452 Broadway, between 140th & 141st Streets (no phone, www.rokcnyc.com). Subway 1 to 137th Street-City College. **Open** *5pm-midnight Mon-Thur; 5pm-1am Fri; 2pm-1am Sat; 2pm-midnight Sun.* **Map** *p165 C11* ❹
Tucked between a neighbourhood bodega and a Latin religious-articles shop, ROKC (ramen,

oysters, kitchen and cocktails, FYI) is an unadorned semi-subterranean room, paint cracking on its white walls and a handful of small tables crammed in front of a long wooden bar. But the drinks, courtesy of former Angel's Share cohorts Shigefumi Kabashima and Tetsuo Hasegawa, along with Joji Watanabe (Experimental Cocktail Club), are stunning showpieces. Swapping out a traditional cocktail glass for a lightbulb (yes, a lightbulb) set in a small pot of pebbled ice, the lavender-flecked Flower is floral without tasting like liquid potpourri, thanks to an elegant balance of Japanese barley vodka, elderflower and tart cranberry. The Tomato/Clam registers like a smoky Bloody Mary, with mescal, a hit of wasabi and copious cracks of black pepper inside a big, beautiful seashell. The kitchen doles out the titular ramen (six varieties), East Coast oysters and Asian snacks.

Shops & services

Harlem Haberdashery

245 Malcolm X Boulevard (Lenox Avenue), between 122nd & 123rd Streets (1-646 707 0070, www. harlemhaberdashery.com). Subway 2, 3 to 125th Street. **Open** *noon-8pm Mon-Fri; 1-8pm Sat; varies Sun.* **Map** *p165 D14* ❽ *Fashion*
File this under 'If it's good enough for Jay Z'. Harlem Haberdashery was founded by the folks behind clothing label 5001 Flavors, which dressed the rapper for his 'Empire State of Mind' video. In addition to locally made urban-meets-preppy clothes for men and women, there are high-top Android Homme sneakers, graphic T-shirts and gold-plated flasks. Fun fact: the boutique is housed in a brownstone where Malcolm X once lived.

Trunk Show Designer Consignment

275-277 W 113th Street, between Adam Clayton Powell Jr Boulevard (Seventh Avenue) & Frederick Douglass Boulevard (Eighth Avenue) (1-212 662 0009, www. trunkshowconsignment.com). Subway B, C to 110th Street-Cathedral Parkway. **Open** *1-8pm Tue-Fri; 12.30-7.30pm Sat; 12.30-6pm Sun.* **Map** *p165 D15* ❾ *Fashion*
Modelling agent Heather Jones graduated from hosting oversubscribed pop-up trunk shows to co-opening this small Harlem storefront. Men's and women's threads and accessories range from edgier brands (Margiela, Rick Owens, Vetements) to Madison Avenue labels (Gucci, Chanel, Céline, Saint Laurent), with in-season items marked down between 20% and 70%. The shop sometimes keeps erratic hours, so it's wise to call before making a special trip.

Entertainment

Apollo Theater

253 W 125th Street, between Adam Clayton Powell Jr Boulevard (Seventh Avenue) & Frederick Douglass Boulevard (Eighth Avenue), Harlem (1-212 531 5300, www.apollotheater.org). Subway A, B, C, D, 1 to 125th Street. **Box office** *10am-6pm Mon-Fri; noon-5pm Sat. Tickets vary.* **Map** *p165 D13* ❸ *Live music*
This 1914 former burlesque theatre has been a hub for African-American artists for decades, and launched the careers of Ella Fitzgerald and D'Angelo, among many others. The now-legendary Amateur Night showcase has been running since 1934. The venue, known for jazz, R&B and soul, mixes veteran talents such as Dianne Reeves with younger artists like Janelle Monae and Esperanza Spalding.

Brooklyn & the Outer Boroughs

Unified in 1898, NYC's five boroughs are more integrated than ever. The turn of the millennium saw an upsurge in migration of the city's young, creative population to the outer boroughs – particularly Brooklyn and Queens. As a result, these areas have developed significant cultural, dining and shopping scenes which, combined with a handful of major attractions, make them well worth the subway ride from Manhattan.

Best sights
Brooklyn Bridge (*p172*), the city's most scenic pedestrian crossing. Bronx Zoo (*p181*), America's largest urban zoo.

Best restaurants
Aska (*p173*), for Michelin-starred Scandinavian tasting menus. Organically delicious ice-cream at Blue Marble Ice Cream (*p174*). Lilia (*p174*), a modern Italian eatery acclaimed for pasta. Olmsted (*p175*), locavore restaurant with on-site mini farm. Old-school steakhouse Peter Luger (*p175*). Roberta's (*p175*), hip destination for pizza and seasonal cuisine.

Best bars
Early 1900s fixture Bohemian Hall & Beer Garden (*p184*). Victorian-style cocktail parlour Clover Club (*p176*). Four Horsemen (*p176*), unstuffy wine bar co-owned by a rock star. Neighbourhood institution Sunny's Bar (*p177*).

Must-see museums
Brooklyn Museum (*p171*), the second borough's answer to the Met. MoMA PS1 (*p182*) for adventurous shows and summer parties. Queens Museum (*p183*) for the extraordinary Panorama of the City of New York.

Best shops
Erie Basin (*p177*) for exquisite, hand-selected jewellery. Hip guys' emporium Modern Anthology (*p178*). Massive indie music store Rough Trade (*p178*). Wooden Sleepers for vintage flannel shirts and workwear (*p178*).

Best cultural venues
Riverside classical venue Bargemusic (*p179*). Brooklyn Academy of Music (*p180*), a venerable institution with fresh programming.

Best nightlife
The extraordinary House of Yes (*p45*). Warehouse-style megaclub Output (*p180*).

Brooklyn

Settled by the Dutch in the early 17th century, Brooklyn was America's third largest municipality before it became part of New York City. Not only is the second borough a destination in its own right, offering some of the city's best restaurants and nightlife, but 'Brooklyn' has become shorthand for a particular brand of indie cool, recognised the world over. Attractions and cultural draws are concentrated in **Brooklyn Heights**, **Dumbo** and **Prospect Heights**, but **Williamsburg**, **Bushwick** and **Red Hook** are great dining, drinking and shopping territory.

Brooklyn Heights is home to leafy, brownstone-lined streets and the **Brooklyn Heights Promenade**, offering spectacular waterfront views of lower Manhattan, New York Harbor and the **Brooklyn Bridge**, a marvel of 19th-century engineering. Nearby, post-industrial Dumbo is the gateway to **Brooklyn Bridge Park** (riverside, from the Manhattan Bridge to Atlantic Avenue), with lawns, freshwater gardens and a Manhattan skyline panorama. The centrepiece is **Jane's Carousel** (www.janescarousel.com), a vintage merry-go-round restored by local artist Jane Walentas, housed in a Jean Nouvel-designed Plexiglas pavilion.

Central Park may be bigger and far more famous, but **Prospect Park** (www.prospectpark.org) has a more rustic quality. The massive Civil War memorial arch at Grand Army Plaza (intersection of Flatbush Avenue, Eastern Parkway & Prospect Park West, Prospect Heights) sits near the main entrance, around the corner from the **Brooklyn Museum**.

Sights & museums

Brooklyn Botanic Garden

*990 Washington Avenue, at Eastern Parkway, Prospect Heights (1-718 623 7200, www.bbg.org). Subway B, Q to Prospect Park; S to Botanic Garden; 2, 3 to Eastern Parkway-Brooklyn Museum; 2, 3, 4, 5 to Franklin Avenue. **Open** Mar-Oct 8am-6pm Tue-Fri; 10am-6pm Sat, Sun. Nov 8am-4.30pm Tue-Fri; 10am-4.30pm Sat, Sun. Dec-Feb 10am-4.30pm Tue-Sun. **Admission** $15; $8 reductions; free under-12s. See website for free admission days.*

This 52-acre haven of luscious greenery was founded in 1910. In spring, when Sakura Matsuri, the annual Cherry Blossom Festival, takes place, prize buds and Japanese culture are in full bloom. Linger in serene spots like the Japanese Hill-and-Pond Garden, one of the first Japanese-inspired gardens in the US, and the Shakespeare Garden, brimming with plants mentioned in the Bard's works. Start your stroll at the eco-friendly visitor centre, which has a green roof filled with 45,000 plants.

❤ Brooklyn Museum

*200 Eastern Parkway, at Washington Avenue, Prospect Heights (1-718 638 5000, www.brooklynmuseum.org). Subway 2, 3 to Eastern Parkway-Brooklyn Museum. **Open** 11am-6pm Wed, Fri-Sun; 11am-10pm Thur; 11am-11pm 1st Sat of mth (except Sept). **Admission** Suggested donation $16; $10 reductions; free under-20s. Some special exhibitions $20. Free 5-11pm 1st Sat of mth (except Sept).*

Among the many assets of Brooklyn's premier institution are the third-floor Egyptian galleries; highlights include the Mummy Chamber, an installation of 170 objects, including human and animal mummies. Also on this level, works by Cézanne, Monet and Degas, part of an impressive European art collection, are displayed in the museum's skylighted Beaux-Arts Court. The Elizabeth A Sackler Center for Feminist Art on the fourth floor is dominated by Judy Chicago's monumental mixed-media installation, *The Dinner Party*. The fifth floor is mainly devoted to American works, including Albert Bierstadt's immense *A Storm in the Rocky Mountains, Mt Rosalie*, and the Visible Storage-Study Center, where paintings, furniture and other objects are intriguingly juxtaposed. It's always worth checking the varied schedule of temporary shows, and the institution is also home to the Norm, a restaurant helmed by Michelin-starred chef Saul Bolton.

Brooklyn Museum

🖤 Brooklyn Bridge

Subway A, C to High Street; J to Chambers Street; 4, 5, 6 to Brooklyn Bridge-City Hall.

Every day, thousands of people walk or bike across the wide, wood-planked promenade of the Brooklyn Bridge, taking in views of New York Harbor, the Statue of Liberty and the skyscrapers of lower Manhattan (not to mention the motorists on the car level below). But it was once an even more vital link in New York's infrastructure.

Designed by John Roebling, the bridge was built in response to the harsh winter of 1867, when the East River froze over, severing connection between Manhattan and what was then the nation's third most populous city. When it opened in 1883, the 5,989-foot-long structure was not only the world's longest bridge, but also the first in the world to use steel suspension cables.

Construction began on the Brooklyn side. To lay the foundation on bedrock 44 feet below, workers in airtight containers chipped away at the riverbed. More than 100 were paralysed with the bends, caused by the change in air pressure when they surfaced.

When the Manhattan side was built, chief engineer Washington Roebling – John Roebling's son – got the bends too. He wasn't the only family casualty: John died in 1869 after his foot was crushed by a docking ferry. Washington spent the next decade watching the bridge's progress through a telescope and relaying directions through his wife, Emily. (A plaque on the Brooklyn tower honours her.) Fearing more deaths on the Manhattan tower, he stopped construction before it reached the 100-foot-deep bedrock. To this day, the tower rests on sand and hardpan.

Brooklyn Bridge

City Reliquary

*370 Metropolitan Avenue, at Havemeyer Street, Williamsburg (1-718 782 4842, www.cityreliquary. org). Subway G to Metropolitan Avenue; L to Lorimer Street. **Open** noon-6pm Thur-Sun. **Admission** $7; $5 reductions; free under-13s.*
This not-for-profit mini-museum of New York history is crammed with fascinating Gotham ephemera. The collection includes memorabilia from both NYC World's Fairs, a shrine to the Brooklyn Dodgers' Jackie Robinson, hundreds of Lady Liberty figurines and such anachronistic objects as subway tokens and seltzer bottles. Other idiosyncratic relics include a vintage barber-shop diorama furnished with a chair from Barber Hall of Famer Antonio Nobile's Bay Ridge, Brooklyn, shop, and a transplanted Chinatown newsstand.

Green-Wood Cemetery

*Fifth Avenue, at 25th Street, Sunset Park (1-718 210 3080, www.green-wood.com). Subway R to 25th Street. **Open** varies by season; usually 8am-6pm daily. **Admission** free.*
Filled with Victorian mausoleums, cherubs and gargoyles, hills and ponds, this lush 478-acre landscape is the resting place of some half-million New Yorkers, among them Jean-Michel Basquiat, Leonard Bernstein, Boss Tweed and Horace Greeley.

New York Transit Museum

*Corner of Boerum Place & Schermerhorn Street, Brooklyn Heights (1-718 694 1600, www.mta. info/mta/museum). Subway A, C, G to Hoyt-Schermerhorn; 2, 3, 4, 5 to Borough Hall. **Open** 10am-4pm Tue-Fri; 11am-5pm Sat, Sun. **Admission** $10; $5 reductions; free under-2s; free seniors Wed.*
Located in a historic 1936 IND subway station, this is the largest museum in the United States

devoted to urban public transport history. Exhibits explore the social and practical impact of public transport on the development of greater New York; among the highlights is an engrossing walk-through display charting the construction of the city's subway system in the early 1900s, when fearless 'sandhogs' were engaged in dangerous tunnelling. A line-up of turnstiles shows their evolution from the 1894 'ticket chopper' to the current Automatic Fare Card model. But the best part is down another level to a real platform where you can board an exceptional collection of vintage subway and El ('Elevated') cars, some complete with vintage ads. **Other location** New York Transit Museum Gallery Annex & Store, Grand Central Terminal, adjacent to stationmaster's office, main concourse (1-212 878 0106).

Restaurants & cafés

♥ Aska $$$

*47 South 5th Street, between Kent & Wythe Avenues, Williamsburg (1-929 337 6792, askanyc.com). Subway J, M, Z to Marcy Avenue. **Open** 6pm-midnight Tue-Sat.*
Nordic

Inventiveness – rendering uncommon ingredients familiar (and common ingredients unfamiliar) – is what reaped Swedish wunderkind chef Fredrik Berselius much critical acclaim at the original Aska, the Michelin-starred Scandinavian kitchen that operated out of Kinfolk Studios until 2014. While the art-space confines lent a Brooklyn scrappiness to its predecessor, the new digs have a moody cool, styled with animal-skin rugs, neat stacks of highbrow cookbooks and wooden tables covered in edgy black cloth. The dining room is reservation- and tasting-menu-only ($250 for the full 19-course tasting menu or $175 for a ten-course spread). A more casual, light-strung garden out back and a cellar bar downstairs are open to walk-ins looking for cocktails and an à la carte Nordic snack. Berselius's propensity for deeply flavoured stocks, impeccable plating and hand-foraged ingredients didn't change a smidge in the two years he was without a restaurant kitchen, evident in such morsels as a barely cooked scallop served in its shell with grilled coral and a tableside spooning of brown butter popped with scallop broth and pickled elderberries, or a pig's blood pancake you're instructed to wrap around cherry compote and pickled rose.

♥ Blue Marble Ice Cream $

186 Underhill Avenue, between St Johns & Sterling Places, Prospect Heights (1-718 399 6926, www. bluemarbleicecream.com). Subway 2, 3 to Grand Army Plaza. **Open** *7am-10pm Mon-Thur; 7am-midnight Fri; 8am-midnight Sat; 8am-10pm Sun. Ice-cream*
With around 30 rotating seasonal flavours, including tangy strawberry made with ripe pesticide-free fruit, rose-infused Bread & Roses with vanilla

shortbread pieces, and creamy sea salt caramel, Blue Marble is beloved by locals of all ages. Produced in NYC's only certified-organic ice-cream plant, in Sunset Park's Industry City, it's a cut above standard scoops. The shop also serves superior La Colombe coffee. **Other location** Industry City, ground floor, 220 36th Street, between Second & Third Avenues, Sunset Park, Brooklyn (1-718 858 5551).

♥ Lilia $$

567 Union Avenue, at North 10th Street, Williamsburg (1-718 576 3095, www.lilianewyork.com). Subway L to Bedford Avenue. **Open** *5.30-11pm Mon-Fri; 5-11pm Sat, Sun. Italian*
The solo debut from acclaimed A Voce vet Missy Robbins, this airy skylit dining room has an entire menu of destination dishes – the biggest problem you'll have here, other than scoring a free table, is picking a favourite. Maybe it's Robbins's ricotta gnocchi, delicate cheese dumplings covered in a thatch of vibrant, verdant broccoli-basil pesto studded with pistachios. Dreamboat *agnolotti*, tenderly filled with soft sheep's-milk cheese and stained sunset-yellow from

---

**In the know
The L word**

If you're planning to visit between spring 2019 and summer 2020, bear in mind that the L subway line is scheduled to close for essential repairs to the Canarsie Tunnel under the East River, following damage wreaked by Superstorm Sandy. The MTA is working on alternative transport options, but the existing NYC Ferry (www.ferry.nyc) offers a route linking Williamsburg with Wall Street and 34th Street in Manhattan and other Brooklyn stops along the East River.

Olmsted

saffron-laced butter, is also a top contender. But, despite Robbins's obvious proficiency with pasta, her signature dish may very well be, of all things, a casual starter of fritters. Rather than usher out yet another plate of voguish *cacio e pepe*, Robbins rejuvenates the ancient recipe as snacky, savoury doughnuts: crispy, fresh-from-the-fryer hulls dusted in parmesan and pepper give way to a cheese-oozing core that recall Italian-festival street food (in a great way).

❤ Olmsted $$

659 Vanderbilt Avenue, at Park Place, Prospect Heights (1-718 552 2610, www.olmstednyc.com). B, Q to Seventh Avenue; 2, 3 to Grand Army Plaza. **Open** *5-10.30pm daily. American creative*
It would be eye roll-inducing if it weren't so goddamned great: a Brooklyn restaurant so zoom-focused on fresh produce that it's outfitted with a working mini-farm in the back, with a live bird squawks in a corner coop as twentysomethings Instagram their crawfish crackers. But it's what chef Greg Baxtrom does, and all that farm-to-table fuss sets Olmsted apart from like-minded eateries. He cranks out smart, seasonal dishes that are approachable, affordable and downright craveable, such as a tender carrot crêpe filled with plump littleneck clams.

❤ Peter Luger $$$

178 Broadway, at Driggs Avenue, Williamsburg (1-718 387 7400, www.peterluger.com). Subway J, M, Z to Marcy Avenue. **Open** *11.45am-9.45pm Mon-Thur; 11.45am-10.45pm Fri, Sat; 12.45-9.45pm Sun.* **No cards.** *Steakhouse*
At Luger's old-school steakhouse, the menu is limited, but the porterhouse is justly famed. Choose from various sizes, from a small single steak to 'steak for four'. Although a slew of Luger copycats have prospered over the years, none has captured the elusive charm of this stucco-walled, beer hall-style eatery, with worn wooden floors and tables, and waiters in white shirts and bow ties.

❤ Roberta's $$

261 Moore Street, between Bogart & White Streets, Bushwick (1-718 417 1118, www.robertaspizza. com). Subway L to Morgan Avenue. **Open** *11am-midnight Mon-Fri; 10am-midnight Sat, Sun. Italian*
This sprawling hangout is the unofficial meeting place for Brooklyn's sustainable-food movement. Opened in 2008, Roberta's has its own on-site garden that provides some of the ingredients for its locally sourced dishes. The pizzas – like the three-cheese Famous Original, topped with mozzarella, caciocavallo and parmesan – are among Brooklyn's

Brooklyn Heights Promenade

finest. Blanca, a sleek spot in the back, showcases chef Carlo Mirarchi's acclaimed evening-only tasting menu (6pm and 9pm Wed-Fri, 5pm and 8pm Sat, $195).

Vinegar Hill House $$

*72 Hudson Avenue, between Front & Water Streets, Dumbo (1-718 522 1018, www.vinegarhillhouse. com). Subway A, C to High Street; F to York Street. **Open** 6-11pm Mon-Thur; 6-11.30pm Fri; 10.30am-3.30pm, 6-11.30pm Sat; 10.30am-3.30pm, 5.30-11pm Sun.*
American creative

A visit to Vinegar Hill House feels like a magical adventure to another time and place. The cosy, tavern-like eaterie is virtually hidden in a residential street in the forgotten neighbourhood of Vinegar Hill (now essentially part of Dumbo). The frequently changing menu focuses on eclectic seasonal dishes, many cooked in the restaurant's wood-fired oven. In the warmer months, linger over brunch or dinner in the secluded back garden.

Bars

♥ Clover Club

*210 Smith Street, between Baltic & Butler Streets, Cobble Hill (1-718 855 7939, www.cloverclubny. com). Subway F, G to Bergen Street. **Open** 4pm-2am Mon-Thur; 4pm-4am Fri; 10.30am-4am Sat; 10.30am-1am Sun.*

Classic cocktails are the signature tipples at Julie Reiner's Victorian-styled cocktail parlour. Royales, fizzes, punches and cobblers all get their due at the 19th-century mahogany bar. Highbrow snacks (fried oysters, steak tartare) accompany drinks like the eponymous Clover Club (with gin, raspberry syrup, egg whites, dry vermouth and lemon juice).

♥ The Four Horsemen

*295 Grand Street, between Havemeyer & Roebling Streets, Williamsburg (1-718 599 4900, www.fourhorsemenbk.com). Subway G to Metropolitan Avenue; J, M, Z to Marcy Avenue; L to Bedford Avenue. **Open** 5.30pm-1am Mon-Fri; 1pm-1am Sat, Sun.*

You could throw a number of superlatives at the Four Horsemen, and they would comfortably stick. For one, it has the best acoustics of any bar in Brooklyn: cedar-slatted ceilings and burlap-covered walls were designed to reduce the auditory assault of clinking glasses and chatter. It's equipped with the borough's hippest co-proprietor, as well: LCD Soundsystem frontman James Murphy. And it's home to some of New York's most ambitious wine-bar eats, such as sea scallops with pickled sunchokes (Jerusalem artichokes) and nori oil, or plum-glazed ribs sprinkled with togarashi. But the Four Horsemen could coast on its wine prowess alone. The minimalist bar has done ample work to help embed natural wine – that cloudier, funkier, mouthful-of-barn cousin to your more conventional bottle – into Brooklyn nightlife, with its dozen by-the-glass varieties and comprehensive selection of more than 250 bottles, each of which the savvy staff details without a drop of dogma or dismissal.

Maison Premiere
298 Bedford Avenue, between Grand & South 1st Streets, Williamsburg (1-347 335 0446, www.maisonpremiere.com). Subway L to Bedford Avenue. **Open** *4pm-2am Mon-Wed; 4pm-4am Thur, Fri; 11am-4am Sat; 11am-2am Sun.*
Most of NYC's New Orleans-inspired watering holes choose debauched Bourbon Street as their muse, but this gorgeous salon embraces the romance found in the Crescent City's historic haunts. Belly up to the oval, marble-topped bar and get familiar with the twin pleasures of oysters and absinthe: two French Quarter staples with plenty of appeal in Brooklyn. The mythical anise-flavoured liqueur appears in 26 international varieties, in addition to a trim list of cerebral cocktails.

♥ Sunny's Bar
253 Conover Street, between Beard & Reed Streets, Red Hook (1-718 625 8211, www.sunnysredhook. com). Subway F, G to Smith-9th Streets, then B61 bus. **Open** *4pm-midnight Mon; 4pm-2am Tue; 4pm-4am Wed-Fri; 11am-4am Sat; 11am-midnight Sun.* **No cards**.
This treasured time-warp watering hole has been passed down in the same family since 1890. After the death of octogenarian owner Sunny Balzano in 2016, its future seemed shaky, but thanks to the bar's many fans, his widow was able to raise the necessary funds to ensure its survival. The eclectic, convivial crowd brings together hard-drinking regulars, local artists

and hip millennials soaking up the dimly lit, Old World vibe, with its hodge podge of folk art, knick-knacks from the 1940s and perfect location just off New York Harbor. A local music hub, Sunny's holds bluegrass jamborees every Saturday at 9pm (bring an instrument and join in!), and other nights feature everything from sultry jazz singers to blues bands.

Shops & services

Blackbarn Shop
20 John Street, at Pearl Street, Dumbo (1-718 260 6565, www. blackbarnshop.com). Subway A, C to High Street; F to York Street. **Open** *11am-6pm Wed-Sat; noon-5pm Sun; by appointment Mon, Tue.* Homewares
This unique home store shares a cavernous former-industrial space with co-owner Mark Zeff's interior design firm. Mark and his wife Kristen source a combination of vintage and contemporary furnishings and art from around the world, such as dramatic Balinese ceremonial cowry-shell necklaces, handwoven wool blankets from Portugal, Moroccan tea glasses and pottery, and extraordinary artworks such as dioramas by Christopher Tennant incorporating vintage taxidermy birds, shells and other natural materials.

♥ Erie Basin
388 Van Brunt Street, at Dikeman Street, Red Hook (1-718 554 6147, www.eriebasin.com). Subway F, G to Smith-9th Streets, then B61 bus. **Open** *noon-6pm Wed-Sat.* Accessories
For a one-of-a-kind keepsake, check out Russell Whitmore's finely honed collection of jewellery dating from the 18th century to the 1970s. The striking stock spans everything from unusual fin de siècle earrings,

lockets and brooches to art deco cocktail rings. Vintage engagement and wedding rings are a speciality. Whitmore often incorporates antique gems in his EB line of fine jewellery, which is also available in the shop, alongside a selection of furniture and decorative objects. The hours sometimes vary seasonally, so it's best to call before making a special trip.

♥ Modern Anthology
68 Jay Street, between Front & Water Streets, Dumbo (1-718 522 3020, www.modernanthology. com). Subway A, C to High Street; F to York Street. **Open** *11am-7pm Mon-Sat; noon-6pm Sun. Fashion/ homewares*

Design gurus Becka Citron and John Marsala, who helped create the *Man Caves* TV series, are behind this one-stop lifestyle shop that brings together vintage and contemporary homewares, clothing, accessories and grooming products. Understatedly stylish dudes can update their wardrobes with shirts, sweaters and jeans by American labels Todd Snyder, Save Khaki and Raleigh Denim, among other brands. Hip furnishings include sturdy leather seating, industrial pieces, tongue-in-cheek prints and retro barware. **Other location** 123 Smith Street, between Dean & Pacific Streets, Boerum Hill, Brooklyn (1-929 250 2880).

♥ Rough Trade
64 North 9th Street, between Kent & Wythe Avenues, Williamsburg (1-718 388 4111, www.roughtrade. com). Record store

In late 2013, UK indie retailer Rough Trade opened its first Stateside outpost in a 15,000-square-foot Williamsburg warehouse, complete with in-house café. In addition to tens of thousands of all-new titles – roughly half of them vinyl and half CDs – the megastore sells music books, magazines and equipment,

curates rotating art installations, and hosts gigs both ticketed and free by the likes of Television, Beth Ditto, Lower Dens and Beach Fossils (for schedule and tickets, see www.roughtradenyc.com).

Swords-Smith
98 South 4th Street, between Bedford Avenue & Berry Street, Williamsburg (1-347 599 2969, www.swords-smith.com). Subway L to Bedford Avenue; J, M, Z to Marcy Avenue. **Open** *noon-8pm Mon-Fri; 11am-8pm Sat; noon-7pm Sun. Fashion*

Fashion vets Briana Swords (a former womenswear designer for Levi Strauss) and R Smith (a graphic designer whose credits include *Vogue*) are behind this boutique for men and women. The duo offers carefully selected clothing and accessories from more than 80 independent designers in the skylight, minimalist space. Stock is sourced from around the world, including the strong silhouettes and unusual prints of Henrik Vibskov (from Copenhagen) and New York-based Samantha Pleet and Rodebjer. Also look out for unisex pieces by LA's 69, made-in-NYC men's basics by Fanmail, and Buenos Aires designer Martiniano's artisan-crafted shoes.

♥ Wooden Sleepers
395 Van Brunt Street, between Coffey & Van Dyke Streets, Red Hook (1-718 643 0802, www. wooden-sleepers.com). Subway F, G to Smith-9th Streets, then B61 bus. **Open** *11am-7pm Wed-Sun; by appointment Mon, Tue. Fashion*

After running a successful online shop and flea-market booths, Brian Davis found a permanent home for his curated collection of vintage menswear in this appropriately nostalgic storefront in a freestanding clapboard house. Spanning the 1930s to the '90s, the stock is displayed on industrial

Bargemusic

garment racks and weathered wooden shelves, interspersed with old fishing books, canteens and collegiate memorabilia. The classic American workwear, military and outdoor gear include perfectly aged leather bomber jackets, flannel shirts and athletic team T-shirts.

Entertainment

Barclays Center

620 Atlantic Avenue, at Flatbush Avenue, Prospect Heights, Brooklyn (1-917 618 6100, www. barclayscenter.com). Subway B, D, N, Q, R, 2, 3, 4, 5 to Atlantic Avenue-Barclays Center. Box office noon-6pm Mon-Fri; noon-4pm Sat (varies on event days). Tickets vary. Live music

The city's newest arena, home of the rechristened Brooklyn Nets basketball team, opened in 2012 with a series of concerts by native son and Nets investor Jay Z. It quickly proved to be a success. Staff are efficient and amiable, the acoustics are excellent, and there's a top-notch view from nearly every one of the 19,000 seats. But, most importantly, the venue has attracted an unexpectedly cool list of acts, with artists as diverse as the Weeknd, Drake and Luke Bryan gracing its stage.

♥ Bargemusic

Fulton Ferry Landing, between Old Fulton & Water Streets, Dumbo, Brooklyn (1-800 838 3006, www. bargemusic.org). Subway A, C to High Street; F to York Street; 2, 3 to Clark Street. Tickets $40; $20-$35 reductions. Classical music

This former coffee bean barge presents several chamber concerts a week, set against a panoramic view of lower Manhattan. It's a magical experience (and the programming has grown more ambitious in recent years), but be sure to dress warmly in winter. In less chilly months, admire the view from the upper deck during the interval.

🖤 Brooklyn Academy of Music

Peter Jay Sharp Building *30 Lafayette Avenue, between Ashland Place & St Felix Street, Fort Greene, Brooklyn.*
Harvey Theater, *651 Fulton Street, at Rockwell Place, Fort Greene, Brooklyn.*
Richard B Fisher Building, *321 Ashland Place, between Ashland Place & Lafayette Avenue, Fort Greene, Brooklyn.*
All *1-718 636 4100, www.bam.org. Subway B, D, N, Q, R, 2, 3, 4, 5 to Atlantic Avenue-Barclays Center; C to Lafayette Avenue; G to Fulton Street.* **Box office** *Sept-June noon-6pm Mon-Sat; July, Aug noon-6pm Mon-Thur; noon-2pm Fri. Phone bookings Sept-June 10am-6pm Mon-Fri; noon-6pm Sat; noon-4pm Sun (show days); July, Aug 10am-6pm Mon-Thur, 10am-2pm Fri. Tickets vary.* *Performance*
America's oldest performing arts academy continues to present some of the freshest programming in the city. Every year from September through December, the Next Wave Festival showcases avant-garde music, dance and theatre. The nearby BAM Harvey Theater offers a smaller and more atmospheric setting for multimedia creations by composers and performers such as Tan Dun, Meredith Monk and So Percussion. The newest facility, BAM Fisher, has an intimate performance space and studios.

🖤 Output

74 Wythe Avenue, at North 12th Street, Williamsburg (no phone, www.outputclub.com). Subway L to Bedford Avenue. **Open** *10pm-4am Mon-Thur, Sun; 10pm-6am Fri, Sat.* **Admission** *varies.* *Club*
With the opening of Output in 2013, New York nightlife's centre of gravity continued its eastward push into Brooklyn. Akin in ethos to such underground music headquarters as Berlin's Berghain/Panorama

Bar complex or London's Fabric, the club boasts a warehouse-party vibe and a killer sound system. The place is deceptively massive, with a two-floored main room, the smaller Panther Room next door complete with a grand staircase and fireplace, and two rooftop smoking patios. Top-shelf DJs (both international hotshots and local heroes) of every dance-music genre play to packed crowds, spinning the kind of left-field house, techno and bass music you rarely hear in commercially oriented spots. Be sure to head to the rooftop bar – the view of the Manhattan skyline is a stunner.

St Ann's Warehouse

45 Water Street, at Old Dock Street, Dumbo (1-718 254 8779, www. stannswarehouse.org). Subway F to York Street; 2, 3 to Clark Street. **Box office** *noon-6pm Mon-Fri (call for extended hours). Tickets $35-$75.* *Theatre*
A haven for adventurous theatregoers, St Ann's offers an eclectic lineup of plays and music; recent shows have included high-level work by the Wooster Group and National Theatre of Scotland. In 2015, it moved to its impressive new home in the converted 19th-century Tobacco Warehouse on Dumbo's waterfront.

The Outer Boroughs

While **Queens** is the point of arrival for those flying into JFK or LaGuardia airports, the borough hasn't traditionally been on most tourists' must-see list. Now, however, cultural institutions in **Long Island City** and **Astoria** are drawing out-of-towners and Manhattanites across the Ed Koch Queensboro Bridge. Queens is one of the country's most diverse urban areas and **Flushing** has the city's second largest Chinatown.

Memories of urban strife in the 1970s still colour perceptions of

Bronx. While some areas have an edgy feel, it has a handful of attractions and notable art deco architecture on major boulevard the **Grand Concourse**.

To visitors, **Staten Island** is best known for its free ferry (1-718 727 2508, www.nyc.gov/dot), which runs from the Financial District's Whitehall Terminal (4 South Street, at Whitehall Street). A vital public-transport link to Manhattan for locals, it just happens to pass by Lady Liberty.

Sights & museums

♥ Bronx Zoo
2300 Southern Boulevard, Bronx (1-718 220 5100, www.bronxzoo. com). Subway 2, 5 to E Tremont-W Farms Square, then walk to the zoo's Asia entrance; or Metro-North (Harlem Line local) from Grand Central Terminal to Fordham, then take the Bx9 bus to 183rd Street & Southern Boulevard. **Open** *Apr-Oct 10am-5pm Mon-Fri; 10am-5.30pm Sat, Sun. Nov-Mar 10am-4.30pm daily.* **Admission** *$20; $13-$18 reductions; pay what you wish Wed. Some rides & exhibitions cost extra.* The Bronx Zoo shuns cages in favour of indoor and outdoor environments that mimic natural habitats. More than 8,000 animals, representing more than 600 species, live here. Home to monkeys, leopards and tapirs, the lush, steamy Jungle World is a recreation of an Asian rainforest inside a 37,000sq ft building, while lions, giraffes, zebras and other animals roam the African Plains. Step aboard the Wild Asia Monorail (open May-Oct, admission $6), which tours more than 40 acres of exhibits inhabited by gaur, tigers, elephants and more. The popular Congo Gorilla Forest has turned 6.5 acres into a dramatic central African rainforest habitat. A glass-enclosed tunnel winds through the area, allowing visitors to get close to the dozens of primate families in residence, including the largest troop of western lowland gorillas in North America. Tiger Mountain is populated by Siberian and Malayan tigers, while the Himalayan Highlands features snow leopards and red pandas. There's a dedicated children's zoo ($6), and kids will also adore Madagascar!, featuring exotic animals from the lush island nation off the eastern coast of Africa, including five species of lemurs, tortoises and hissing cockroaches.

Bronx Zoo

MoMA PS1

❤ MoMA PS1

22-25 Jackson Avenue, at 46th Avenue, Long Island City, Queens (1-718 784 2084, www.momaps1. org). Subway E, M to Court Square-23rd Street; G, 7 to Court Square; G to 21st Street. **Open** *noon-6pm Mon, Thur-Sun.* **Admission** *Suggested donation $10; $5 reductions; free under-16s.*

MoMA PS1 mounts cutting-edge shows in a distinctive Romanesque Revival building (formerly a public school, hence the name). The contemporary art centre became an affiliate of MoMA in 1999, and the two institutions sometimes stage collaborative exhibitions, such as the quinquennial Greater New York. The DJed summer Warm Up parties are a fixture of the dance-music scene and on-site eaterie M Wells Dinette is a foodie destination.

Museum of the Moving Image

36-01 35th Avenue, at 36th Street, Astoria, Queens (1-718 777 6888, www.movingimage.us). Subway R, M to Steinway Street; N, W to 36th Avenue. **Open** *10.30am-5pm Wed, Thur; 10.30am-8pm Fri; 10.30am-6pm Sat, Sun.* **Admission** *$15; $7-$11 reductions; free under-3s. Free 4-8pm Fri.*

Following a major expansion in 2011, the Museum of the Moving Image became one of the foremost museums in the world dedicated to TV, film and video. The institution's collection, galleries and state-of-the-art screening facilities are housed on the campus of Kaufman Astoria Studios. On the second and third floors, the core exhibition, Behind the Screen, contains approximately 1,400 artefacts – including the super creepy stunt doll used in *The Exorcist*, with full head-rotating capabilities, and the (surprisingly small) model of the Tyrell Corporation building from *Blade Runner*, alongside interactive displays. A new gallery devoted to Muppets creator Jim Henson should be open by publication of this guide.

New York Botanical Garden

Bronx River Parkway, at Fordham Road, Bronx (1-718 817 8700, www. nybg.org). Subway B, D, 4 to Bedford Park Boulevard, then 20min walk or Bx26 bus to the garden's Mosholu Gate; or Metro-North (Harlem Line local) from Grand Central Terminal to Botanical Garden. **Open** *Jan, Feb 10am-5pm Tue-Sun. Mar-Dec 10am-6pm Tue-Sun.* **Admission** *$23-$28; $10-$25 reductions. Grounds only free Wed, 9-10am Sat.*

The serene 250 acres comprise 50 gardens and plant collections, including the Peggy Rockefeller Rose Garden, the Everett Children's Adventure Garden and the last 50 original acres of a forest that once covered the whole city area. In spring, clusters of lilac, cherry, magnolia and crab apple trees burst into bloom; in autumn you'll see vivid foliage in the oak and maple groves. The Azalea Garden features around 3,000 vivid azaleas and rhododendrons. The grand Enid A Haupt Conservatory, built in 1902, contains A World of Plants, a series of environmental galleries that takes you on an eco-tour through tropical rainforests, deserts and a palm tree oasis.

Noguchi Museum

9-01 33rd Road, at Vernon Boulevard, Astoria, Queens (1-718 204 7088, www.noguchi.org). Subway N, W to Broadway, then 15min walk or Q104 bus to 11th Street; 7 to Vernon Boulevard-Jackson Avenue, then Q103 bus to 10th Street. **Open** *10am-5pm Wed-Fri; 11am-6pm Sat, Sun. May-Sept 10am-8pm 1st Fri of the mth.* **Admission** *$10; $5 reductions; free under-12s. Free 1st Fri of the mth. No pushchairs/strollers.*

When Japanese-American sculptor and designer Isamu Noguchi (1904-88) opened his Queens museum in 1985, he became the first living artist in the US to establish such an institution. The Noguchi Museum occupies a former photo-engraving plant across the street from the studio he had occupied since the 1960s (its location allowed him to be close to stone and metal suppliers along Vernon Boulevard). Noguchi designed the entire building to be a meditative oasis amid its gritty, industrial setting. Eleven galleries, spread over two floors, are filled with his sculptures, as well as drawn, painted and collaged studies, architectural

models, and stage and furniture designs. The serene garden features a minimalist fountain and such works as his megalithic 1978 Core (*Cored Sculpture*) carved from volcanic basalt.

♥ Queens Museum

New York City Building, Flushing Meadows Corona Park, Queens (1-718 592 9700, www. queensmuseum.org). Subway 7 to Mets-Willets Point, then 15min walk. **Open** *11am-5pm Wed-Sun.* **Admission** *Suggested donation $8; $4 reductions; free under-19s.*

Facing the Unisphere, the 140ft stainless-steel globe created for the 1964 World's Fair, in Flushing Meadows Corona Park, the Queens Museum occupies the former New York City Building, which was built to house the Gotham-themed pavilion for the earlier World's Fair in 1939.The highlight is the extraordinary Panorama of the City of New York, a 9,335sq ft scale model of the five boroughs first exhibited here in 1964. Dreamed up by urban planner Robert Moses, it features Lilliputian landmarks such as the Empire State Building (15 inches tall) and the statue of Liberty (less than two inches), plus thousands of other structures, all rendered in remarkable detail. As well as changing historical, cultural and art exhibitions, the museum is home to the World's Fair Storage and Gallery, which displays more than 900 artefacts.

Yankee Stadium

River Avenue, at 161st Street, Bronx (1-718 293 4300, www.yankees. com). Subway B, D, 4 to 161st Street-Yankee Stadium. **Open** *Tours vary; see website for details.*

In 2009, the Yankees vacated the fabled 'House that Ruth Built' and moved into their new $1.3-billion stadium across the street. Monument Park, an open-air museum behind centre field that celebrates the exploits of past Yankee heroes, can be visited as part of a tour ($25, $23 reductions, $20 booked online, free under-3s; 1-646 977 8687), along with the New York Yankees Museum, the dugout, and – when the Yankees are on the road – the clubhouse.

Restaurants & cafés

M Wells Steakhouse $$

43-15 Crescent Street, between 43rd Avenue & 44th Road, Long Island City, Queens (1-718 786 9060, www. magasinwells.com). Subway N, W, 7 to Queensboro Plaza. **Open** 5-10.30pm Wed-Sat. *Steakhouse/eclectic*

At Hugue Dufour and Sarah Obraitis's cool spin on a classic steakhouse, hipsters mingle with families in a former auto-body shop for smoky steaks cooked over a wood fire, shellfish and creative takes on classics such as a charred iceberg salad with creamy blue cheese. Long Island trout are fished from a large tank on the edge of the dining room and poached to order. The quirky power couple also offers creative cuisine at M Wells Dinette, inside MoMA PS1, where schoolroom-themed decor pays homage to the building's roots.

Spicy & Tasty $

39-07 Prince Street, between Roosevelt & 39th Avenues, Flushing, Queens (1-718 359 1601, www.spicyandtasty.com). Subway 7 to Flushing-Main Street. **Open** 11am-10.30pm daily. **No cards.** *Chinese*

Any serious trip to Flushing for spicy Szechuan food should begin here. Revered by in-the-know regulars, this brightly lit eatery serves plates of peppercorn-laden pork and lamb swimming in a chilli sauce that's sure to set even the most seasoned palate aflame. Stock up on cold-bar options, like zesty sesame noodles, crunchy chopped cucumbers and smooth, delicate tofu – you'll need the relief. Service is speedy and mercifully attentive to water requests.

Bars

♥ Bohemian Hall & Beer Garden

29-19 24th Avenue, between 29th & 31st Streets, Astoria, Queens (1-718 274 4925, www.bohemianhall. com). Subway N, W to Astoria Boulevard. **Open** 5pm-1am Mon-Thur; 3pm-3am Fri; noon-3am Sat; noon-midnight Sun.

This authentic Czech beer garden, established in the early 20th century, features plenty of mingle-friendly picnic tables, where you can sample cheap, robust platters of sausage, goulash and other specialities alongside 14 mainly European drafts. Though the huge, linden-canopied garden is open year-round (in winter, the area is tented and heated), summer is prime time to visit.

Dutch Kills

27-24 Jackson Avenue, at Dutch Kills Street, Long Island City, Queens (1-718 383 2724, www. dutchkillsbar.com). Subway E, M, R to Queens Plaza. **Open** 5pm-2am Mon-Thur, Sun; 5pm-3am Fri, Sat.

What separates Dutch Kills from NYC's other mixology temples modelled after vintage saloons is the abundance of elbow room. Settle into one of the deep, dark-wood booths in the front, or head for the back to perch at the bar. Cocktails are mostly classic, with prices slightly lower than in similar establishments in Manhattan.

New York Essentials

Accommodation

New York's hotel business is booming – the official tourism board reports that more than 60 new properties have opened during the past two years. And despite an average room rate of more than $300 a night in the autumn high season, hotels are nearly full most of the year, according to data and analytics specialist STR. There is now more choice than ever in popular areas like Greenwich Village, Soho and the Lower East Side. But a significant percentage of new development is in the outer boroughs, especially Brooklyn.

Information and prices

In response to the competition, hotels increasingly offer perks such as guest bikes, free Wi-Fi and local calls, and enhanced in-room technology such as tablets. The best time to get a bargain is during the frigid months of January and February, when rates are at their lowest, according to STR's data, but deals can also be had in high summer, especially August, when high temperatures and humidity drive locals who can afford it to nearby resort areas like the Hamptons. You may also find reduced prices on individual hotel websites or reservation sites such as Booking.com. Peak season is September and October, when high-profile events such as Fashion Week draw hordes of visitors and the autumn cultural calendar is in full swing.

Building regulations, accommodation taxes and a law prohibiting rentals of less than 30 days in buildings with three or more units makes hosting B&Bs challenging in New York City, but long-established agency **City Sonnet** (1-212 614 3034, www.citysonnet.com) can arrange stays in Manhattan or Long Island City, Queens, starting at around $145 a night. For longer periods, the agency offers stylish, individually decorated one- and two-bedroom lofts, starting at $2,800 a month. Rates include all fees. Alternatively, you can rent a Brooklyn loft space for 30 days or more at **Habitat 101** (1-718 349-2200, www.habitat101brooklyn.com), a converted factory in hip Greenpoint with locally crafted furniture and artwork, from $3,000 for a studio.

We've listed our favourite places to stay in the city in each price category, but you can find additional listings at www.timeout.com/newyork. Note that rates can vary wildly according to the season or room category and most NYC accommodation is non-smoking.

Luxury

The Beekman

123 Nassau Street, between Ann & Beekman Streets, Financial District (1-212 233 2300, www.thompsonhotels. com). Subway A, C, J, Z, 2, 3, 4, 5 to Fulton Street; R, W to City Hall, 4, 5, 6 to Brooklyn Bridge-City Hall. **Rooms** *287.* **Map** *p69 E32.*

During a stay at the Beekman Hotel, you'll keep returning to one thing: its breathtaking nine-storey Victorian atrium, capped by a pyramidal skylight. Not only are most of the rooms located off the galleries surrounding it, but the image of that dramatic centrepiece will linger in your mind. Originally built in 1881, the early skyscraper was in a state of neglect when it was acquired by Thompson Hotels and restored. The airy, high-ceilinged guest quarters mix period detail with a contemporary sensibility: wooden floors, custom-designed oak beds with leather headboards and luxurious Sferra linens, eclectic vintage pieces, and sleek marble-tiled bathrooms. Flanking the atrium bar, the hotel's two restaurants, chef Tom Colicchio's Fowler & Wells and period-perfect French bistro Augustine, draw a chic crowd that keeps the common areas buzzing.

Gramercy Park Hotel
2 Lexington Avenue, at 21st Street, Gramercy Park (1-212 920 3300, 1-866 784 1300, www.gramercyparkhotel. com). Subway 6 to 23rd Street.
Rooms *190.* **Map** *p76 E26.*
Other NYC hotels have guest-only rooftops or gardens, but only one boasts access to the city's most storied private outdoor space: Gramercy Park. The hotel's interior resembles a baronial manor occupied by a rock star, with rustic wooden beams and a roaring fire in the lobby; a $65 million art collection, including works by Richard Prince, Damien Hirst and Andy Warhol; and studded velvet headboards and mahogany drink cabinets in the bedrooms. Get a taste of the Eternal City in Maialino, Danny Meyer's tribute to Roman trattorias, and end the evening with a nightcap at the exclusive Rose Bar.

Greenwich Hotel
377 Greenwich Street, between Franklin & North Moore Streets, Tribeca (1-212 941 8900, www.thegreenwichhotel. com). Subway 1 to Franklin Street.
Rooms *88.* **Map** *p76 D31.*
The design inspiration at this Tribeca retreat, co-owned by Robert De Niro, is as international as the jet-set clientele. Individually decorated rooms combine custom-made English leather seating, Tibetan rugs and gorgeous Moroccan or Carrara-marble-tiled bathrooms,

most outfitted with capacious tubs that fill up in a minute flat (bath salts from Nolita spa Red Flower are provided). In the tranquil subterranean spa, the pool is beneath the frame of a 250-year-old Kyoto farmhouse. For dinner, there's no need to rub shoulders with the masses at the busy house restaurant, Locanda Verde – have your meal delivered to the cloistered courtyard.

New York EDITION
5 Madison Avenue, at 24th Street, Flatiron District (1-212 413 4200, www.editionhotels.com).
Subway R, W, 6 to 23rd Street.
Rooms *273.* **Map** *p76 E26.*
Fancy spending the night in one of the city's most iconic buildings, overlooking Madison Square Park? The Metropolitan Life clock tower is now home to a hotel from Ian Schrager-Marriott brand EDITION. Inside the 1909 skyscraper, the clean-lined rooms are light and luxurious, done up with blond-wood floors and creamy linen seating, offset by walnut headboards. You'll find products with an exclusive scent by cult perfumer Le Labo in the minimalist stone-accented bathrooms. The Clocktower restaurant – helmed by Michelin-starred London chef Jason Atherton – pays homage to the building's period with clubby mahogany panelling, a billiards room and 24-carat-gold bar.

In the know
Price categories

Our price categories are based on hotels' standard prices (not including seasonal offers or discounts) for one night in a double room with en suite shower/bath.

Luxury	$500+
Expensive	$300-$500
Moderate	$150-$300
Budget	up to $150

The Ludlow

The Plaza

768 Fifth Avenue, at Central Park South, Midtown (1-212 759 3000, 1-888 850 0909, www.theplazany.com). Subway N, R, W to Fifth Avenue-59th Street. **Rooms** *282.* **Map** *p116 E22.*

The closest thing to a palace in New York, this 1907 French Renaissance-style landmark reopened in 2008 after a two-year, $400-million renovation. Although 152 rooms were converted into private condo units, guests can still check into one of 282 elegantly appointed quarters with Louis XIV-inspired furnishings and white-glove butler service. The opulent vibe extends to the bathrooms, which feature mosaic baths, 24-carat gold-plated sink fittings and even chandeliers – perhaps to make the foreign royals feel at home. Embracing the 21st century, the hotel has equipped every room with an iPad. The legendary Oak Room and Oak Bar, both designated landmarks, are now open only for private events, but you can still take afternoon tea in the restored Palm Court. There's also a luxurious Guerlain spa and an upscale food hall conceived by celebrity chef Todd English, which includes both old and new cult NYC purveyors, such as William Greenberg Desserts and No. 7 Sub.

The Surrey

20 E 76th Street, between Fifth & Madison Avenues, Upper East Side (1-212 288 3700, 1-888 419 0052, www. thesurreyhotel.com). Subway 6 to 77th Street. **Rooms** *189.* **Map** *p146 E20.*

Occupying an elegant 1920s building given a $60 million overhaul, the Surrey updates the grand hotel model. The coolly elegant limestone and marble lobby showcases museum-quality contemporary art, and guestrooms are dressed in a refined palette of cream, grey and beige, with the addition of luxurious white marble bathrooms. But the centrepiece is undoubtedly the incredibly comfortable DUX by Duxiana bed, swathed in sumptuous Sferra linens. The hotel is flanked by top chef Daniel Boulud's Café Boulud and his chic cocktail destination, Bar Pleiades (*see p162*). There's also a luxurious spa.

Expensive
Chambers Hotel
15 W 56 Street, between Fifth & Sixth Avenues, Midtown (1-212 974 5656, www. chambershotel.com). Subway E, M to Fifth Avenue-53rd Street. Rooms 77. Map p116 E22.

Room design at this small boutique hotel takes its cue from upscale New York loft apartments, combining designer furniture with raw concrete ceilings, exposed pipes, floor-to-ceiling windows and polished walnut floorboards or Tibetan wool carpeting. Guest quarters also feature some of the 500-piece art collection. Everything is designed to make you feel at home, from the soft terrycloth slippers in bright colours to the architect's desks stocked with a roll of paper and coloured pencils should creative inspiration hit. There's no need to leave the hotel for meals, since David Chang's Má Pêche and an outpost of his Milk Bar are on site.

The Ludlow
180 Ludlow Street, between Houston & Stanton Streets, Lower East Side (1-212 432 1818, www.ludlowhotel.com). Subway F to Lower East Side-Second Avenue. Rooms 175. Map p76 G29.

With a prime spot on the buzzing Lower East Side, this purpose-built red-brick boutique property has an artfully aged interior, but the design is eclectic. An oak-panelled lobby leads to a sprawling living room with a salvaged limestone fireplace and a bar that spills out on to an ivy-clad patio. Rooms mix classic and contemporary elements: big factory-style windows, rustic ceiling beams, Indo-Portuguese four-poster beds and petrified-wood nightstands. Bathrooms are fitted with brass rain showers or soaking tubs and Maison Margiela robes. The hotel restaurant, Dirty French, is helmed by the team behind Carbone (*see p104*).

NoMad Hotel
1170 Broadway, at 28th Street, Flatiron District (1-212 796 1500, www.thenomadhotel.com). Subway R, W to 28th Street. Rooms 168. Map p116 E26.

Like nearby hipster hub the Ace Hotel, the NoMad is a self-contained microcosm encompassing destination dining – courtesy of Daniel Humm and Will Guidara, of the Michelin-three-starred Eleven Madison Park (*see p123*) – and a buzzing bar. Jacques Garcia, designer of Paris celeb hangout Hôtel Costes, transformed the interior of a 1903 New York office building into this convincing facsimile of a grand hotel. The chic rooms, furnished with vintage Heriz rugs and distressed-leather armchairs, are more personal – Garcia based the design on his old Paris apartment. Many feature old-fashioned claw-foot tubs for a scented soak in Côté Bastide bath salts.

Standard, High Line
848 Washington Street, at 13th Street, Meatpacking District (1-212 645 4646, www.standardhotels.com). Subway A, C, E to 14th Street; L to Eighth Avenue. Rooms 338. Map p76 C29.

The lauded West Coast mini-chain arrived in New York in 2009. Straddling the High Line, the retro 18-storey structure has been configured to give each room an exhilarating view, either of the river or a midtown cityscape. Quarters are compact (from 230sq ft) but the combination of floor-to-ceiling windows, curving tambour wood panelling and 'peekaboo' bathrooms (with Japanese-style tubs or huge showerheads) give a sense of space. Eating and drinking options include a chop house, a beer garden and a swanky top-floor bar. Nightspot Le Bain has a massive jacuzzi and 180-degree vistas. **Other location** 25 Cooper Square, between 5th & 6th Streets, East Village (1-212 475 5700).

Wythe Hotel
80 Wythe Avenue, at North 11th Street, Williamsburg, Brooklyn (1-718 460 8000, www.wythehotel.com). Subway L to Bedford Avenue. Rooms 72.

A 1901 cooperage near the waterfront topped with a three-storey glass-and-aluminium addition, the Wythe embodies Brooklyn industrial-artisan chic. Andrew Tarlow, the man behind local eateries Diner and Marlow & Sons, is a partner, so it's not surprising that the ground-floor restaurant, Reynard, was an instant hit. In many of the rooms, floor-to-ceiling windows offer a Manhattan skyline panorama. Heated concrete floors, exposed brick, reclaimed-timber beds and witty wallpaper create a rustic-industrial vibe, offset by fully plugged-in technology: a cable by the bed turns your iPhone into a surround-sound music system.

Moderate
Ace Hotel New York
20 W 29th Street, at Broadway, Flatiron District (1-212 679 2222, 1-212 991 0551, www.acehotel.com). Subway R, W to 28th Street. **Rooms** *285.* **Map** *p116 E26.*
Founded in Seattle by a pair of DJs, this cool chainlet has expanded beyond the States to London and Panama. In its New York digs, the musical influence is clear: select rooms in the 1904 building have functioning turntables, stacks of vinyl and gleaming Martin guitars. And while you'll pay a hefty amount for the sprawling loft spaces, there are options for those on a smaller budget, outfitted with vintage furniture and original art. In the buzzing lobby, the bar is set within a panelled library salvaged from a Madison Avenue apartment, and DJs or other performers add to the atmosphere almost every night. On-site dining options includes chef April Bloomfield's popular Breslin Bar & Dining Room and the John Dory Oyster Bar. There's even an outpost of Opening Ceremony (*see p82*) if you haven't a thing to wear.

Boro Hotel
38-28 27th Street, at 39th Avenue, Long Island City, Queens (1-718 433 1375, www.borohotel.com). Subway N, W to 39th Avenue. **Rooms** *108.*
There's one thing you can't get in a Manhattan hotel room: the spectacular skyline views that are only possible from the other side of the water. But

the interior of this boutique hotel will also catch your eye. Exposed concrete ceilings and cinderblocks, nods to the area's industrial roots, are softened with white oak flooring. Guest rooms with floor-to-ceiling windows are sparsely furnished with cool contemporary pieces like custom-made leather chairs, Jasper Morrison for Vitra cork stools and, in some quarters, deep freestanding soaking tubs. Many rooms include balconies, and you can also take in the view from public terraces on the tenth and 12th floors. The library-lounge has books curated by NYC institution Strand Book Store.

citizenM New York
218 W 50th Street, between Broadway & Eighth Avenue, Theater District (1-212 461 3638, www.citizenm.com). Subway C, E to 50th Street; N, R, W to 49th Street; 1 to 50th Street. **Rooms** *230.* **Map** *p116 D23.*
The fast-growing citizenM brand aims to democratise the luxury-hotel experience. With rates starting at around $200 a night, guests can kick back on a $10,000 Vitra armchair in the eclectic lobby and admire the 26ft-tall installation *Walking in Times Square* by Julian Opie. Catering to a time-zone-crossing, tech-savvy clientele (the M stands for 'mobile'), the Amsterdam-based company has devised a new model informed by its founders' travel frustrations, cutting high-overhead amenities like room service in the process. The 24-hour canteenM dispenses cocktails (until 2am), coffee, all-day breakfast and other dishes. The compact rooms focus on the essentials: an extra-large king-size bed and a powerful rain shower (in a cool cubicle with coloured ceiling lights). You can control the hue, and everything else in

In the know
Taxing times

When budgeting for accommodation, don't forget to factor in 14.75 per cent tax, plus an extra $3.50 per night for most rooms.

the room – from the blinds to the digital wall art – using a Samsung tablet.

Duane Street Hotel

130 Duane Street, at Church Street, Tribeca (1-212 964 4600, www. duanestreethotel.com). Subway A, C, 1, 2, 3 to Chambers Street. **Rooms** *43.* **Map** *p76 E31.*

Opened on a quiet Tribeca street in 2007, this boutique property takes its cues from its well-heeled residential neighbourhood, offering loft-inspired rooms with high ceilings, oversized triple-glazed windows, hardwood floors and a chic, monochrome colour scheme. Free Wi-Fi, L'Occitane products in the slate-tiled bathrooms, plus bike loan and complimentary passes to the nearby swanky Equinox gym cement the value-for-money package – a rare commodity in this part of town.

James New York

27 Grand Street, at Thompson Street, Soho (1-212 465 2000, 1-888 526 3778, www.jameshotels.com). Subway A, C, E to Canal Street. **Rooms** *114.* **Map** *p76 E30.*

Hotel art displays are usually limited to eye-catching lobby installations or forgettable in-room prints. Not so at the James, where the corridor of each guest floor is dedicated to the work of an individual artist, selected by a house curator. Although compact, bedrooms make the most of the available space with high ceilings and wall-spanning windows. Natural materials warm up the clean contemporary lines, and full-size bathroom products are courtesy of Intelligent Nutrients. A two-level 'urban garden' (open May-Oct) houses an outdoor bar and eatery. The rooftop bar, Jimmy, opens on to the (tiny) seasonal pool. **Other location** 22 E 29th Street, at Madison Avenue, Flatiron District (1-212 532 4100).

Budget
Bowery House

220 Bowery, between Prince & Spring Streets, Nolita (1-212 837 2373, www.

theboweryhouse.com). Subway J, Z to Bowery. **Rooms** *126.* **Map** *p76 F29.*

Two young real-estate developers transformed a 1927 Bowery flophouse into this stylish take on a hostel. Corridors with original wainscotting lead to cubicles (singles are a cosy 35sq ft) with latticework ceilings to allow air circulation, although some of the 'cabins', as they're called, have windows. Quarters with double or queen-size beds are also available. It might not be the best bet for light sleepers, but the place is hopping with pretty young things attracted to the hip aesthetic and the location. Cabins are decorated with vintage prints and historical photographs, and Egyptian cotton robes are provided in the double-occupancy options. The (gender-segregated) communal bathrooms have rain showerheads and products from local spa Red Flower. When you want more breathing room, hang out in the guest lounge, outfitted with chesterfield sofas and a huge LCD TV, or on the large roof terrace.

Carlton Arms Hotel

160 E 25th Street, at Third Avenue, Gramercy Park (1-212 679 0680, www. carltonarms.com). Subway 6 to 23rd Street. **Rooms** *54.* **Map** *p116 F26.*

The Carlton Arms Art Project started in the late 1970s, when a small group of creative types brought fresh paint and new ideas to a run-down shelter. Today, the site is a bohemian backpackers' paradise and a live-in gallery – every room, bathroom and hallway is festooned with outré artwork, including a couple of early stairwells by Banksy. Eye-popping themed quarters include the Money Room and a tribute to the traditional English cottage. New works are introduced regularly and artists return to restore their creations. About a third of the rooms have private bathrooms; the rest are shared.

Harlem Flophouse

242 W 123rd Street, between Adam Clayton Powell Jr Boulevard (Seventh Avenue) & Frederick Douglass Boulevard (Eighth Avenue), Harlem (1-347 632 1960, www.harlemflophouse.com).

Subway A, B, C, D to 125th Street.
Rooms 5. **Map** p165 *D14*.
The dark-wood interior, moody lighting and lilting jazz make musician René Calvo's uptown inn feel more like a 1920s speakeasy than a 21st-century lodging. The airy guest quarters, which are named after jazz greats and prominent Harlem figures, have restored tin ceilings and working sinks in antique cabinets, and are furnished with a quirky mix of junk-store finds and period knick-knacks. Four of the rooms are on the top two floors and each pair shares a bathroom. The ground-floor Ellington room has private facilities and a garden.

The Jane

113 Jane Street, at West Street, West Village (1-212 924 6700, www. thejanenyc.com). Subway A, C, E to 14th Street; L to Eighth Avenue. **Rooms** 171. **Map** p76 *C29*.
Opened in 1908 as the American Seaman's Friend Society Sailors Home and Institute, the six-storey landmark was a residential hotel until hoteliers Eric Goode and Sean MacPherson took it over. The Jane's wood-panelled, 50sq ft rooms were inspired by vintage train sleeper compartments: there's a single or bunk bed with built-in storage and brass hooks for hanging up your clothes – but also iPod docks and wall-mounted TVs. Alternatively, opt for a more spacious, wainscoted Captain's Cabin with private facilities – many have terraces or Hudson River views. If entering the hotel feels like stepping on to a film set, there's good reason. Inspiration came from various celluloid sources, including *Barton Fink's* Hotel Earle for the lobby.

Pod 39

145 E 39th Street, between Lexington & Third Avenues, Murray Hill (1-212 865 5700, www.thepodhotel.com). Subway S, 4, 5, 6, 7 to 42nd Street-Grand Central. **Rooms** 366. **Map** p116 *F24*.
The Pod's contemporary budget-hotel concept has spread to four locations across the city, including a brand-new Brooklyn outpost. Pod 39 occupies a 1918 residential hotel for single men – you can hang out by the fire or play ping-pong in the redesigned gents' sitting room. As the name suggests, rooms are snug, but not oppressively so. A range of configurations includes single or queen-size beds, or stainless-steel bunk beds equipped with individual TVs and bedside shelves inspired by airplane storage. But you should probably know your roommate well since the utilitarian, subway-tiled bathrooms are partitioned off with sliding frosted-glass doors. April Bloomfield's on-site eaterie Salvation Taco supplies the margaritas and snacks at the sprawling seasonal rooftop bar.
Other locations Pod 51, 230 E 51st Street, between Second & Third Avenues (1-212 355 0300); Pod Times Square, 400 West 42nd Street, at Ninth Avenue; Pod Brooklyn, 247 Metropolitan Avenue, at Driggs Avenue, Williamsburg, Brooklyn.

Yotel New York

570 Tenth Avenue, at 42nd Street, New York, Hell's Kitchen (1-646 449 7700, www.yotel.com). Subway A, C, E to 42nd Street-Port Authority. **Rooms** 713. **Map** p116 *C24*.
The British team behind this futuristic hotel is known for airport-based capsule accommodation that gives travellers just enough space to get horizontal between flights. Yotel New York has ditched the 75sq ft cubbies in favour of 'premium cabins' more than twice the size. Adaptable furnishings (such as motorised beds that fold up futon-style) maximise space, and the bathroom has streamlined luxuries such as a heated towel rail and monsoon shower. If you want to unload excess baggage, the 20ft tall robot (or Yobot, in the hotel's playful lingo) will stash it for you in a lobby locker. In contrast with the compact quarters, the sprawling public spaces include a massive wraparound terrace bar.

Getting Around

ARRIVING & LEAVING

By air
John F Kennedy International Airport *1-718 244 4444, www.panynj. gov/airports/jfk.html.*
The **subway** (*see p194*) is the cheapest option. The **AirTrain** (www.airtrainjfk. com, $5, plus $1 for a MetroCard if required) links to the A train at Howard Beach or the E, J and Z trains at Sutphin Boulevard-Archer Avenue ($2.75-$3).

NYC Airporter buses 1-718 777 5111, www.nycairporter.com; one way $18, round trip $34) connect JFK and Manhattan, with stops near Grand Central Terminal, Penn Station and Port Authority Bus Terminal. Buses run every 30mins from 6am to 11.30pm daily.

SuperShuttle (1-800 258 3826, www. supershuttle.com) vans offer shared door-to-door services between NYC and the major airports, but can be time-consuming if there are multiple drop-offs.

A **yellow cab** to or from Manhattan will charge a flat $52.80 fare, plus toll (usually around $10), a $4.50 rush-hour supplement weekdays between 4pm and 8pm, and tip (15 per cent is the norm). If you're travelling to or from the outer boroughs the fare will be on the meter (*see p195*).

LaGuardia Airport *1-718 533 3400, www.panynj.gov/airports/laguardia. html.*
Seasoned New Yorkers take the **M60 Select Bus Service** ($2.75), which terminates at W 106th Street at Broadway in Morningside Heights. The ride takes 40-60mins, depending on traffic, and buses run 24hrs daily. The route crosses Manhattan at 125th Street in Harlem. Get off at Lexington Avenue for the 4, 5 and 6 trains; at Malcolm X Boulevard (Lenox Avenue) for the 2 and 3; or at St Nicholas Avenue for the A, B, C and D trains.

Less time-consuming options include **NYC Airporter** buses (one way $15, round trip $28). **Taxis** and **car** services charge about $30-$40, plus toll and tip.

Newark Liberty International Airport *1-973 961 6000, www.panynj. gov/airports/newark-liberty.html.*
The best bet is the $13, half-hour trip via New Jersey Transit to or from Penn Station. The airport's monorail, **AirTrain Newark** (www.airtrainnewark. com), is linked to the NJ Transit and Amtrak train systems.

Bus services operated by **Coach USA** (1-877 894 9155, www.coachusa. com) run to Manhattan, stopping at three midtown locations: Grand Central Terminal, Bryant Park and Port Authority Bus Terminal (one way $16, round trip $28); buses leave every 15-30mins. A **car** or **taxi** will run at $50-$75, plus toll and tip.

By bus
Most out-of-town buses come and go from the Port Authority Bus Terminal. **Greyhound** (1-800 231 2222, www. greyhound.com) runs long-distance travel to US destinations. The company's **BoltBus** (1-877 265 8287, www.boltbus.com), booked online, serves several East Coast cities. **New Jersey Transit** (1-973 275 5555, www. njtransit.com) runs services to most of New Jersey and parts of New York State. Finally, **Peter Pan** (1-800 343 9999, www.peterpanbus.com) runs extensive services to cities across the North-east.

Port Authority Bus Terminal
625 Eighth Avenue, between 40th & 42nd Streets, Garment District (1-212 564 8484, www.panynj.gov/ bus-terminals/port-authority-bus-terminal.html). Subway A, C, E to 42nd Street- Port Authority. Map p116 24D.

By rail

America's national rail service is run by **Amtrak** (1-800 872 7245, www.amtrak. com). Nationwide routes are slow and infrequent (yet full of character), but there are some good fast services linking the eastern seaboard cities. (For commuter rail services, *see p195*)

Grand Central Terminal *42nd to 44th Streets, between Vanderbilt & Lexington Avenues, Midtown East. Subway S, 4, 5, 6, 7 to 42nd Street-Grand Central.* **Map** *p116 E24.*
Grand Central is home to Metro-North, which runs trains to more than 100 stations in New York State and Connecticut.

Penn Station *31st to 33rd Streets, between Seventh & Eighth Avenues, Garment District. Subway A, C, E, 1, 2, 3 to 34th Street-Penn Station.* **Map** *p116 D25.*
Amtrak, Long Island Rail Road and New Jersey Transit trains depart from this terminal.

PUBLIC TRANSPORT

Changes to schedules can occur at short notice, especially at weekends – check the MTA's website before travelling and pay attention to the posters on subway station walls and announcements on trains and subway platforms.

Metropolitan Transportation Authority (MTA) *511 local, 1-877 690 5116 outside New York State, 1-212 878 7000 international, www.mta.info.*
The MTA runs the subway and bus lines, as well as services to points outside Manhattan.

Fares & tickets

Although you can pay with exact change (no dollar bills) on buses, to enter the subway system you'll need either a single-ride ticket ($3, available from station vending machines only) or a **MetroCard**. You can buy MetroCards from booths or vending machines in the stations, from the New York Transit Museum in Brooklyn (*see p173*) or Grand Central Terminal (*see left*).

The standard base fare across the subway and bus network on a MetroCard is $2.75. Up to three children 44 inches tall and under can ride for free on subways and local buses when accompanied by a fare-paying adult. Free transfers between the subway and buses are available only with a MetroCard (for bus-to-bus transfers on cash fares, *see left*). Up to four people can use a pay-per-ride MetroCard, sold in denominations from $5.50 to $80. (There is an additional $1 for a new MetroCard.) If you put $5.50 or more on the card, you'll receive a five per cent bonus, reducing the cost of each ride. However, if you're planning to use the subway or buses often, an Unlimited Ride MetroCard is great value. These cards are offered in two denominations, available at station vending machines but not at booths: a seven-day pass ($32) and a 30-day pass ($121). Both are good for unlimited rides within those periods, but you can't share a card with your travelling companions.

Subway

Cleaner and safer than it has been for decades, the city's subway system is one of the world's largest and cheapest. For fares and MetroCards, *see left*. Trains run around the clock.

Stations are most often named after the street on which they're located. Entrances are marked with a green and white globe (open 24 hours) or a red and white globe (limited hours). Many stations have separate entrances for the uptown and downtown platforms – look before you pay. Trains are identified by letters or numbers, colour-coded according to the line on which they run. Local trains stop at every station on the line; express trains stop at major stations only. Bear in mind that on some lines the local and express services change at weekends and late at night – for example the local W service is replaced by the usually express N.

We've provided weekday transport information in our listings and on the maps, so be sure to check www.mta.info for weekend guidance.

You can ask MTA staff in service booths for a free copy of the subway map, or refer to enlarged maps displayed in each subway station.

City buses

White and blue MTA buses are usually the best way to travel crosstown and a pleasant way to travel up- or downtown, as long as you're not in a hurry. They have a digital destination sign on the front, along with a route number preceded by a letter (M for Manhattan, B for Brooklyn, Bx for the Bronx, Q for Queens and S for Staten Island). Maps are posted on most buses and at all subway stops; they're also available from the Official NYC Information Center (see p202). All local buses are equipped with wheelchair lifts.

The fare is payable with a MetroCard (see p194) or exact change ($2.75 in coins only; no pennies or dollar bills). MetroCards allow for an automatic transfer from bus to bus, and between bus and subway. If you pay cash, and you're travelling uptown or downtown and want to go crosstown (or vice versa), ask the driver for a transfer when you get on – you'll be given a ticket for use on the second leg of your journey, valid for two hours. Select Bus Service (SBS) on some busy routes offer faster travel at the same fare with self-service ticket machines at bus stops. Insert your MetroCard or coins and a receipt will be issued. You can then board the bus via any door and there's no need to show the receipt unless asked to do so by an inspector. The MTA's express buses head to the outer boroughs for a $6.50 fare.

Rail

Commuter rail services include **Metro-North Railroad** (511 local, 1-212 532 4900 outside New York State, www. mta.info/mnr), which runs from Grand Central Terminal to towns north of Manhattan. **Long Island Rail Road** (511 local, 1-718 217 5477 outside New York State, www. mta.info/lirr) links Penn Station, Brooklyn and Queens to towns throughout Long Island. **New Jersey Transit** (1-973 275 5555, www. njtransit.com) reaches most of New Jersey, some points in New York State and Philadelphia from Penn Station. **PATH Trains** (1-800 234 7284, www. panynj.gov/path) run from six stations in Manhattan to various New Jersey destinations, including Hoboken, Jersey City and Newark.

Boat

Operated by cruise company Hornblower, the **NYC Ferry service** (www.ferry.nyc) launched in spring 2017, offering routes between Manhattan (East 34th Street in midtown or Wall Street in the Financial District) and popular outer borough destinations including Dumbo, Williamsburg and Red Hook in Brooklyn, and Long Island City, Astoria and Rockaway Beach in Queens. A one-way fare costs $2.75 and the fleet is equipped with free Wi-Fi and a boutique news stand that sells coffee and booze. However, each boat has a capacity for just 149 people, which has led to long queues at landing stations.

Taxis

If the centre light atop the taxi is lit, the cab is available and should stop if you flag it down. Get in and then tell the driver where you're going. (New Yorkers generally give cross-streets rather than addresses.) By law, taxis cannot refuse to take you anywhere inside the five boroughs or to New York airports. Green Boro Taxis serving the outer boroughs can be hailed on the street in the Bronx, Queens (excluding airports), Brooklyn, Staten Island and Manhattan north of West 110th and East 96th Streets. Use only yellow or green medallion (licensed) cabs.

Taxis will carry up to four passengers for the same price: $2.50 plus 50¢ per fifth of a mile or per minute idling, plus 80¢ in taxes and surcharges, and an extra $1 during rush hour (4-8pm Mon-Fri). The average fare for a three-mile ride is about $15, but this varies depending on the time and traffic.

If you have a problem, take down the medallion and driver's numbers, posted on the partition. Always ask for a receipt – there's a meter number on it. To complain or to trace lost property, call 311 or visit www.nyc.gov/taxi. Tip 15-20 per cent, as in a restaurant. All taxis now accept major credit cards.

Car services

Car services are regulated by the Taxi & Limousine Commission. Unlike cabs, drivers can make only pre-arranged pickups. Don't try to hail one, and be wary of those that offer you a ride. Companies such as **Carmel** (1-212 666 6666, www.carmellimo.com) and **Dial 7** (1-212 777 7777, www.dial7.com) will pick you up anywhere in the city for a set fare. Popular ride-matching services booked via mobile app, **Uber** (www.uber.com) and **Lyft** (www.lyft.com), typically offer lower prices.

DRIVING

Car hire

You need a credit card to rent a car in the US, and usually must be at least 25 years old. Car hire is cheaper in the city's outskirts and further afield than in Manhattan. NYC companies add around 20 per cent in taxes. If you just want a car for a few hours, **Zipcar** (US: 1-866 494 7227, www.zipcar.com; UK: 0333 240 9000, www.zipcar.co.uk) is cost effective.
Alamo *US: 1-844 354 6962, www. alamo.com. UK: 0800 028 2390, www. alamo.co.uk.*
Budget *US: 1-800 218 7992, www. budget.com. UK: 0808 284 4444, www. budget.co.uk.*
Enterprise *US: 1-855 266 9289, www. enterprise.com. UK: 0800 800 227, www.enterprise.co.uk.*
Hertz *US: 1-800 654 3131, www.hertz. com. UK: 0843 309 3099, www.hertz. co.uk.*

Parking

Make sure you read parking signs and never park within 15 feet of a fire hydrant (to avoid a $115 ticket and/or having your car towed). Parking is off-limits on most streets for at least a few hours daily. The Department of Transportation provides information on daily changes to regulations (dial 311). If precautions fail, call 1-212 971 0771 for Manhattan towing and impoundment information; go to www.nyc.gov for phone numbers in other boroughs.

CYCLING

While biking on NYC's streets is only recommended for experienced cyclists, the **Citi Bike** system (www.citibikenyc. com, 1-855 245 3311) gives you temporary access to bikes at hundreds of stations in Manhattan, Brooklyn and Queens. Visitors can purchase a 24-hour ($12) or three-day ($24) pass at a station kiosk with a credit or debit card. You'll then receive a 'ride code' that will allow you to undock and ride for 30 minutes at a stretch. A longer trip will incur an extra fee.

The Manhattan Waterfront Greenway, a 32-mile route that circumnavigates the island of Manhattan, is a fantastic asset: you can ride, uninterrupted, along the Hudson River from Battery Park to Upper Manhattan's Fort Tryon Park, as well as long stretches of the East River. You can download the NYC Bike Map from www.nyc.gov/planning.

Bike and Roll (451 Columbus Avenue, between 81st & 82nd Street, Upper West Side, 1-212 260 0400, bikenewyorkcity. com) offers cycle hire and tours from its location near Central Park. Rates (including helmet) start at $28 for two hours ($16 for kids' bikes).

WALKING

One of the best ways to take in NYC is on foot. Most of the streets are laid out in a grid pattern and are relatively easy to navigate.

Resources A-Z

ACCIDENT & EMERGENCY

In an emergency only, dial **911** for ambulance, police or fire department, or call the operator (dial 0). For hospitals, *see below*; for helplines, *see p199*; for the police, *see p201*.

You will be billed for any emergency treatment. Call your travel insurance company before seeking treatment to find out which hospitals accept your insurance. The following hospitals have emergency rooms:

New York Presbyterian/ Lower Manhattan Hospital *170 William Street, between Beeckman & Spruce Streets, Financial District (1-212 312 5000). Subway 1 to Chambers Street; 2, 3 to Fulton Street; 4, 5, 6 to Brooklyn Bridge-City Hall.* **Map** *p69 F32.*

Mount Sinai Hospital *Madison Avenue, at 100th Street, Upper East Side (1-212 241 6500). Subway 6 to 103rd Street.* **Map** *p146 E16*

New York-Presbyterian Hospital/ Weill Cornell Medical Center *525 E 68th Street, at York Avenue, Upper East Side (1-212 746 5454). Subway 6 to 68th Street.* **Map** *p146 F21*

Mount Sinai West *1000 Tenth Avenue, at 59th Street, Upper West Side (1-212 523 4000). Subway A, B, C, D, 1 to 59th Street-Columbus Circle.* **Map** *p146 C22.*

AGE RESTRICTIONS

Buying/drinking alcohol 21.
Driving 16.
Sex 17.
Smoking 18.

CUSTOMS

US Customs allows foreigners to bring in $100 worth of gifts without paying duty. One carton of 200 cigarettes (or 100 cigars) and one litre of liquor (spirits) are allowed. Plants, meat and fresh produce of any kind cannot be brought into the country. You will have to fill out a form if you are carrying more than $10,000 in currency. You will be handed a white form on your inbound flight to fill in, confirming that you haven't exceeded any of these allowances.

Bring prescription drugs in a clearly marked container, and bring your doctor's statement or a prescription. Check in with the US Customs and Border Protection Service (www.cbp. gov) before you arrive if you're unsure.

DISABLED

Under New York City law, facilities constructed after 1987 must provide complete access for the disabled – restrooms, entrances and exits included.

Travel Advice

For up-to-date information on travel to a specific country – including the latest on safety and security, health issues, local laws and customs – contact your home country government's department of foreign affairs. Most have websites with useful advice for would-be travellers

Australia
www.smartraveller.gov.au

Canada
www.voyage.gc.ca

New Zealand
www.safetravel.govt.nz

Republic of Ireland
www.dfa.ie

UK
www.fco.gov.uk/travel

USA
www.state.gov/travel

In 1990, the Americans with Disabilities Act made the same requirement federal law. Many older buildings have added disabled-access features. There has been widespread compliance with the law, but call ahead to check facilities.

All Broadway theatres are equipped with devices for the hearing-impaired; call **Sound Associates** (1-888 772 7686, www.soundassociates.com) for more information. For the visually impaired, **HAI** (1-212 273 6182, www.hainyc.org) offers live audio descriptions of selected theatre performances.

DRUGS

Possession of marijuana can result in anything from a $100 fine and a warning (for a first offence, 25g or less) to felony charges and prison time (for greater amounts and/or repeat offenders). Penalties are greater for the sale and cultivation of marijuana.

Possession of 'controlled substances' (cocaine, ecstasy, heroin, etc) is not taken lightly, and charges come with stiff penalties – especially if you are convicted of possession with intent to sell. Convictions carry anything from a mandatory one- to three-year prison sentence to a maximum of 25 years.

ELECTRICITY

The US uses a 110-120V, 60-cycle alternating current rather than the 220-240V, 50-cycle AC used in Europe. The transformers that power or recharge newer electronic devices such as laptops are designed to handle either current, and may need nothing more than an adaptor for the wall outlet. Other appliances may also require a power converter. Adaptors and converters can be purchased at airport shops, pharmacies, department stores and at branches of electronics chain Radio Shack (www.radioshack.com).

Climate

Average temperatures and monthly rainfall in New York

	Temp High (°C/°F)	Temp Low (°C/°F)	Rainfall (mm/in)
January	6/ 43	-3/27	85 /3.3
February	7/44	-3/27	57 / 2.25
March	9/48	1/34	90 / 3.5
April	16/61	6/43	96 / 3.75
May	20/68	12/54	114 / 4.5
June	27/81	17/63	98 / 3.75
July	29/84	20/68	101 / 4.0
August	28/82	20/68	87 / 3.5
September	24/75	16/61	104 / 4.0
October	18/64	10/50	94 / 3.75
November	12/54	5/41	69 / 2.7
December	13/55	4/39	85 / 3.3

EMBASSIES & CONSULATES

Check the phone book for a list of consulates and embassies. *See also p197* **Travel Advice**.
Australia *1-212 351 6500*.
Canada *1-212 596 1628*.
Ireland *1-212 319 2555*.
New Zealand *1-212 832 4038*.
UK *1-212 745 0200*.

HEALTH

Public health care is virtually nonexistent in the US, and private health care is very expensive. Make sure you have comprehensive medical insurance before you travel. For HIV testing and HIV/AIDS counselling, *see below* **Helplines**. For a list of hospitals, *see p197*.

Dentists
New York County Dental Society *1-212 573 8500, www.nycdentalsociety.org*. ***Open*** *8.30am-5.30pm Mon-Fri*.
Can provide local referrals. An emergency contact line at the number listed above runs outside office hours; alternatively, use the search facility on the society's website.

Pharmacies
The fact that there's a Duane Reade pharmacy on almost every corner of Manhattan is lamented among chain-deriding locals; however, it is convenient if you need an aspirin pronto. Several branches of Duane Reade and its parent company Walgreens, including the one at 145 Fourth Avenue, at 14th Street, Union Square 1-212 677 0214, www.walgreens. com), are open 24 hours. Competitor Rite Aid (with one of several 24-hour branches at 301 W 50th Street, at Eighth Avenue, 1-212 247 8384, www.riteaid. com) is also widespread.

HELPLINES

All numbers below are open 24 hours unless otherwise stated.

National STD & AIDS Hotline *1-800 232 4636*. ***Open*** *8am-8pm Mon-Fri*.
NYPD Sex Crimes Report Line *1-212 267 7273*.
Samaritans *1-212 673 3000*.
Counselling for suicide prevention.
SAMHSA (Substance Abuse and Mental Health Services Administration) National Helpline *1-800 662 4357*

ID

Always make sure you carry picture ID: even people well over 18 or 21 may be carded when buying tobacco or alcohol, ordering drinks in bars, or entering clubs.

LEFT LUGGAGE

There are luggage-storage facilities at arrivals halls in **JFK Airport** (Terminal 1: 7am-11pm, $4-$16 per bag per day; call 1-718 751 2947); (Terminal 4: 24hrs, $4-$16 per bag per day; call 1-718 751 4020). At **Penn Station**, Amtrak offers checked baggage services for a small fee for some of its ticketed passengers. Due to heightened security, luggage storage is not available at the Port Authority Bus Terminal, Grand Central Terminal, LaGuardia or Newark airports.

One midtown alternative is to leave bags with the private firm, located between Penn Station and Port Authority, listed below.
Schwartz Luggage Storage *357 W 37th Street, at Ninth Avenue, Garment District (1-212 290 2626, www.schwartztravel. com)*. ***Open*** *8am-11pm daily. Rates $2.50 per bag per hour or $8-$10 per bag per day. No cards. Map p116 C24*.
Other location *4th Floor, 34 W 46th Street, between Fifth & Sixth Avenues, Midtown (same phone)*.

LGBT

Lesbian, Gay, Bisexual & Transgender Community Center *208 W 13th Street, between Seventh & Eighth Avenues, West Village (1-212 620 7310, www.gaycenter. org)*. *Subway A, C, E, 1, 2, 3 to 14th Street;*

L to Eighth Avenue. **Open** *9am-10pm Mon-Sat; 9am-9pm Sun.* **Map** *p76 D29.* Founded in 1983, the Center provides information and a support network for residents and visitors. It's used as a venue by more than 400 groups, and public programming includes everything from book signings and film screenings to comedy nights and theatrical performances. It's also home to the city's only LGBT bookstore, the Bureau of General Services – Queer Division, plus a cyber centre and outpost of ethically conscious Think Coffee. The National Archive of Lesbian, Gay, Bisexual and Transgender History and the Pat Parker/Vito Russo Library are also based here. Don't miss the erotic Keith Haring mural, *Once Upon A Time,* that adorns a former bathroom.

LOST PROPERTY

For lost credit cards or travellers' cheques, *see below.*
Grand Central Terminal *Lower level, near Track 100. 1-212 532 4900.* **Open** *7am-6pm Mon-Fri. You can call 24 hrs a day to file a claim if you've left something on a Metro-North train.*
JFK Airport *1-718 244 4225, or contact your airline.*
LaGuardia Airport *1-718 533 3988, or contact your airline.*
Newark Liberty International Airport *1-973 961 6243, or contact your airline.*
Penn Station: *Amtrak 1-212 630 6596.* **Open** *6am-5pm daily.*
Penn Station: *Long Island Rail Road 1-718 217 5477.* **Open** *7.20am-7.20pm Mon-Fri.*
Penn Station: *New Jersey Transit 1-973 275 5555.* **Open** *6am-11pm Mon-Fri; 7am-11pm Sat, Sun.*
Subway & Buses *New York City Metropolitan Transit Authority, 34th Street-Penn Station, near the A-train platform, Garment District (call 511).* **Open** *8am-3.30pm Mon, Tue, Fri; 11am-6.30pm Wed, Thur.*
Taxis *311, www.nyc.gov/taxi.*

MONEY

All paper money is the same size, so make sure you fork over the right bill. It comes in denominations of $1, $2, $5, $10, $20, $50 and $100 (and higher, but you'll never see those bills).

Coins include copper pennies (1¢) and silver-coloured nickels (5¢), dimes (10¢) and quarters (25¢).

ATMs
The city is full of ATMs – in bank branches, delis and many small shops. Most of them accept Visa, MasterCard and major bank cards, but some charge a fee for transactions. It's also wise to check with your bank about its fees for foreign transactions. Most ATM cards double as debit cards, if they bear the Maestro or Cirrus logo.

Banks & bureaux de change
Banks are generally open from 9am to 6pm Monday to Friday, though some stay open longer and/or on Saturdays. You need photo ID, such as a passport, to cash travellers' cheques. Many banks will not exchange foreign currency and some bureaux de change, limited to tourist-trap areas, close at around 6pm or 7pm.
Travelex *(www.travelex.com)* offers a complete range of foreign-exchange services, with locations in visitor-heavy areas and airports.

Credit cards & travellers' cheques
Credit cards are essential for renting cars and booking hotels, and handy for buying tickets over the phone and the internet. The five major cards accepted in the US are **American Express**, **Diners Club**, **Discover**, **MasterCard** and **Visa**.

If your cards or travellers' cheques are lost or stolen, call the following numbers:
American Express *1-800 528 4800 1-800 221 7282 travellers' cheques.*
Diners Club *1-800 234 6377.*
Discover *1-800 347 2683.*
Mastercard *1-800 627 8372.*
Visa *1-800 847 2911, 1-800 227 6811 travellers' cheques.*

Tax

Sales tax is 8.875 per cent in New York City, and is applicable to restaurant bills, services and the purchase of just about anything, except most store-bought foods, clothing and shoes under $110.

In the US, sales tax is almost never included in the price of the item, but added on to the final bill at the till. There is no tax refund option for foreign visitors.

OPENING HOURS

Banks *9am-6pm Mon-Fri; generally also Sat mornings.*
Businesses *9am or 10am to 5pm or 6pm Mon-Fri.*
Post offices *9am-5pm Mon-Fri (a few open as early as 7.30am and close as late as 8.30pm); some are open Sat until 3pm or 4pm.* The James A Farley Post Office *(see below)* is open 24 hours daily for automated services.
Pubs & bars *4pm-2am Mon-Thur, Sun; noon-4am Fri, Sat (but hours vary widely).*
Shops *9am, 10am or 11am to 7pm or 8pm Mon-Sat (some open at noon and/or close at 9pm).* Many are also open on Sun, usually from 11am or noon to 6pm.

POLICE

In an emergency only, dial **911**. For the location of your nearest police precinct or information about police services, call 1-646 610 5000 or visit www.nyc.gov.

POSTAL SERVICES

It costs 49¢ to send a 1oz letter within the US. Each additional ounce costs 21¢. Postcards mailed within the US cost 34¢. The Global Forever Stamp ($1.15) can be used to send a postcard or 1oz letter anywhere in the world. Faster Priority Mail and Priority Express Mail options are available for both domestic and international destinations. Call 1-800 275 8777 or see www.usps.com for more information.
James A Farley Post Office *421 Eighth Avenue, between 31st & 33rd Streets,* *Garment District (1-212 330 3296, 1-800 275 8777 24hr information, www. usps.com). Subway A, C, E to 34th Street-Penn Station.* **Open** *24 hrs daily. Counter service 7am-10pm Mon-Fri; 9am-9pm Sat; 11am-7pm Sun.* **Map** *p116 D25.*

PUBLIC HOLIDAYS

New Year's Day *1 Jan*
Martin Luther King, Jr Day *3rd Mon in Jan*
Presidents Day *3rd Mon in Feb*
Memorial Day *last Mon in May*
Independence *Day 4 July*
Labor Day *1st Mon in Sept*
Columbus Day *2nd Mon in Oct*
Veterans Day *11 Nov*
Thanksgiving Day *4th Thur in Nov*
Christmas Day *25 Dec*

SAFETY & SECURITY

New York's crime rate, particularly for violent crime, is at its lowest since the 1990s. Most crime occurs late at night and in low-income neighbourhoods. Still, a bit of common sense won't hurt. Don't flaunt your money and valuables, keep phones and other electronic gadgets out of sight, and try not to look obviously lost. Avoid deserted and poorly lit streets, walk facing oncoming traffic so no one can drive up alongside you undetected, and close to or on the street. Muggers prefer to hang back in doorways and shadows. If you are threatened, hand over your valuables at once, then dial 911.

Be extra alert to pickpockets and street hustlers – especially in crowded areas like Times Square.

SMOKING

The 1995 NYC Smoke-Free Air Act makes it illegal to smoke in virtually all indoor public places, including the subway. As of May 2011, smoking is also prohibited in NYC parks, pedestrian plazas (such as the ones in Times Square and Herald Square) and on beaches. Violators could face a $50 fine.

TELEPHONES

Dialling & codes

As a rule, you must dial 1 + the area code before a number, even if the place you are calling is in the same area code. The area codes for Manhattan are **212** and **646**; Brooklyn, Queens, Staten Island and the Bronx are **718** and **347**; **917** is reserved mostly for mobile phones and pagers. Numbers preceded by **800**, **877** and **888** are free of charge when dialled from within the US.

In an **emergency**, dial 911. All calls are free (including those from pay and mobile phones).

For the **operator**, dial 0. If you're not used to US phones, then note that the ringing tone is long; the engaged tone, or 'busy signal', consists of much shorter, higher pitched beeps.

Collect calls are also known as reverse-charge calls. To make one, dial 0 followed by the number, or dial AT&T's 1-800 225 5288.

For **directory assistance**, dial 411 or 1 + area code + 555 1212. For a directory of toll-free numbers, dial 1-800 555 1212.

For **international calls**, dial 011 + country code (Australia 61; New Zealand 64; UK 44), then the number (omitting any initial zero).

Mobile phones

Most US mobile phones will work in NYC, but since the US doesn't have a standard national network, visitors should check with their provider that their phone will work here, and whether they need to unlock a roaming option. Visitors from other countries will need a tri-band handset and a roaming agreement. AT&T (www.att.com) sells non-contract prepaid GoPhones for under $40 per month, while T-Mobile (prepaid-phones.t-mobile.com) offers a Tourist Plan SIM card for three weeks or under for $30.

Public phones

New York City's old-school payphones are being replaced by **LinkNYC** (www.

link.nyc) connection points, offering free US calls as well as Wi-Fi and access to maps and city services on a built-in tablet. If you need to make long-distance calls, use a phone card, available from many convenience stores.

TIME

New York is on Eastern Standard Time, which is five hours behind Greenwich Mean Time. Clocks are set forward one hour in early March for Daylight Saving Time (Eastern Daylight Time) and back one hour at the beginning of November. Going from east to west, Eastern Time is one hour ahead of Central Time, two hours ahead of Mountain Time and three hours ahead of Pacific Time.

TIPPING

In restaurants, it's customary to tip at least 15 per cent, and since NYC tax is 8.875 per cent, a quick way to calculate the tip is to double the tax. In many restaurants, when you are with a group of six or more, the tip will be included in the bill. For tipping on taxi fares, *see p195*.

TOURIST INFORMATION

Official NYC Information Center
*Macy's Herald Square, 151 W 34th Street, between Broadway & Seventh Avenue, Garment District (1-212 484 1222, www.nycgo.com). Subway A, C, E, 1, 2, 3 to 34th Street-Penn Station; B, D, F, M, N, Q, R to 34th Street-Herald Square. **Open** 10am-10pm Mon-Sat; 11am-9pm Sun. **Map** p116 D25.*
Located on the mezzanine of Macy's, the city's official (private, non-profit) visitors' information centre offers advice, maps, leaflets and coupons, and sells tour tickets and discount passes. For other locations around the city, go to www.nycgo.com/articles/official-nyc-information-centers. **Other locations** throughout the city.

VISAS & IMMIGRATION

Visas

The **Visa Waiver Program** (VWP; www.cbp.gov/esta) allows citizens of 38 countries, including Australia, Ireland, New Zealand and the UK to visit the US for up to 90 days (for business or pleasure) without a visa. Visitors must have a machine-readable passport (e-passport) valid for the full 90-day period, a return ticket, and authorisation to travel through the ESTA (Electronic System for Travel Authorization) scheme. You must fill in the ESTA form at least 24 hours before travelling (72 hours is recommended) and pay a $14 fee; the form can be found at https://esta.cbp.dhs.gov/esta).

If you do not qualify for entry under the VWP, you will need a visa; leave plenty of time to check before travelling.

Immigration

Your airline will give all visitors an immigration form to be presented to an official when you land. Fill it in clearly and be prepared to give an address at which you are staying (a hotel is fine).

Visitors to the US are photographed and electronically fingerprinted on arrival.

WEIGHTS & MEASURES

Despite attempts to bring in metric measurements, you'll find imperial used in almost all contexts in New York and throughout the US. People think in ounces, inches, gallons and miles.

Index

Credits

Crimson credits
Editor Lisa Ritchie
Assistant editor Ros Sales
Proofreader Anna Norman
Fact checker Lisa Brown
Layouts Emilie Crabb, Patrick Dawson
Cartography John Scott

Series Editor Sophie Blacksell Jones
Production Manager Kate Michell
Design Mytton Williams

Chairman David Lester
Managing Director Andy Riddle

Advertising Media Sales House
Marketing Lyndsey Mayhew
Sales Joel James

Acknowledgments
The editor would like to thank all
contributors to previous editions of *Time
Out New York* whose work forms the basis
of this guide.

Photography credits
Front cover ferrantraite/iStock.com
Back cover andersphoto/Shutterstock.com
Interior Photography credits, see *p203*.

Publishing information
New York Shortlist 10th edition
© TIME OUT ENGLAND LIMITED 2017
December 2017

ISBN 978 1 78059 258 9
CIP DATA: A catalogue record for this book is
available from the British Library

Published by Crimson Publishing
21D Charles Street, Bath, BA1 1HX (01225
584 950, www.crimsonpublishing.co.uk) on
behalf of Time Out England.

Distributed by Grantham Book Services
Distributed in the US and Canada by
Publishers Group West (1-510-809-3700)

Printed by Grafostil